VICTORIAN
ARCHITECTURE

VICTORIAN ARCHITECTURE

James Stevens Curl

DAVID & CHARLES
Newton Abbot London

For Pam with gratitude

(*Frontispiece*) Fig 49 The Strand
Music Hall, London, by Enoch
Bassett Keeling. The design
exhibits all the angular spikiness
so characteristic of Keeling's
early work. (Building News,
1864)

British Library Cataloguing in Publication Data
Curl, James Stevens, *1937–*
    Victorian architecture.
    1. Great Britain. Buildings. Architectural features,
    history.
    I. Title
    720'.941

    ISBN 0-7153-9144-5

Typeset by Typesetters (Birmingham) Ltd
Smethwick, West Midlands
and printed in Great Britain
by Butler & Tanner Limited, Frome and London
for David & Charles plc
Brunel House   Newton Abbot   Devon

CONTENTS

ACKNOWLEDGEMENTS

Since I wrote *Victorian Architecture: Its Practical Aspects* (published in 1972) much has changed. The rate of wholesale destruction of Victorian fabric has slowed, but problems of neglect, inner-city decay, decisions by Secretaries of State for the Environment, mindless vandalism and the march of time have all taken their toll of the rich legacy our Victorian forefathers left us. The apparently iron certitudes of much of the Victorian Age, the amazing ability to get things done quickly (as in the extraordinary speed with which the Crystal Palace was conceived, designed and built), and the sense of individual responsibility and integrity that is evident in so much of Victorian Britain (although there were many examples of chicanery and outright fraud), seem to have vanished. The belief that 'progress' would inevitably solve the problems of disease, urbanisation, poverty, hygiene and moral decay has proved illusory. In architecture and planning the almost universal admiration for the 'Modern Movement' prevalent after the Second World War in Britain has at last started to fail as the poverty of its vocabulary, the free-for-all of its syntax, and the bogusness of its pseudo-scientific pretensions become clear to all but the most obtuse of observers. It is as though all the riches of a great language had been abandoned for monosyllabic grunts, approved of by those who were too idle to learn, to develop or to practise an architecture that had evolved over many centuries. The same attitudes have been apparent in education, where free expression has been encouraged at the expense of acquiring the means for such expression.

In contrast, the Victorian period offered a wealth of building types, opportunities, materials, structures and styles, and Victorian architects designed and built fabric that was marvellously richly textured, full of variety, often very interesting and usually well adapted to its use. What remains of the fabric is frequently remarkable, beautifully detailed and constructed and sound today, where it has survived the vagaries of fashion or crass alterations in recent times. Victorian architecture is sometimes Beautiful, often Picturesque (especially from 1870), and not infrequently Sublime (until 1870); it is sometimes noble and moving, often richly coloured and textured, and never entirely lacking in evidence of study of precedent, language and grammar. It is often learned, occasionally absurd (even grotesque), ugly, beautiful, grand, mean, vulgar, pretentious, lively, amazing, overwhelming, exquisite, charming and delightful: it is many things besides, but it is rarely dull, and it is never as dehumanised or as alien as the creations of 1945 to the present so often have been. Yet the destroyers were among the most vociferous in hating and ridiculing the Victorian achievement, but the friendly Victorian street of terrace-houses with its corner pubs and shops was never universally loathed as has been the case with the vast housing schemes of the 1950s, '60s and '70s. I submit that the Victorian Age has much to teach us in this respect, and this book is intended as a mere introduction to the great wealth of architectural languages and styles, materials, building types and structures the Victorians gave us.

I acknowledge my debt to the many sources quoted in the References and Select Bibliography and in the list of illustrations. Fascinating glimpses of Victorians' attitudes to their own architecture can be found in Thornbury and Walford's *Old and New London,* Charles Knight's *London* (revised by Walford), and in the architectural magazines of the period, notably *The Builder, The Building News, The Architect* and *The Studio.* I am grateful to the staff of The RIBA British Architectural Library, the Royal Archives at Windsor Castle and the RIBA Drawings Collection. Mr Ralph Hyde and the staff of the Guildhall Library, City of London, have been very helpful. I thank Mr Victor Belcher, Mr Peter Bezodis, Mr Howard Colvin, Mr John Greenacombe, Miss Hermione Hobhouse, Miss Janet Perry, Mr Timothy Richards and Mr John Sambrook for valuable information. Miss Iona Cruickshank, Mr Mark Geraghty and Mr Rodney Roach helped with the illustrations. The late Mr A. H. Buck was most kind, as was Dame Penelope Jessel, while the late Mr A. W. Pullan gave permission to use material relating to Sir Edmund Du Cane. Mr Robert Blow and Mr Ian Leith of the Architectural Section of the Royal Commission on the Historical Monuments of England were helpful beyond all duty, while Miss Kitty Cruft of the National Monuments Record of Scotland (the Royal Commission on the Ancient and Historical Monuments of Scotland) and Mr Chris Denvir of the Greater London Photograph Library rendered courteous assistance. I am also grateful to Mr Mark Haworth-Booth, Curator of Photographs at the Victoria and Albert Museum Picture Library, to Mr Anthony F. Kersting of London, to Mr J. A. Wierzbicki, Marketing Services Manager of the Public Transport Commission of New South Wales, and to Mrs S. L. Evans of the Royal Commission on Ancient and Historical Monuments in Wales for help with illustrations. Mr Roger Towe gave valuable assistance with the Bibliography. I also thank the Editor of *Country Life* and IPC Magazines plc, Taylor & Francis Ltd, and Phillimore & Co Ltd for permission to use material previously published by them and acknowledged in the footnotes. Sir John

Cotterell, Bt, of Garnons, gave permission to reproduce the photograph of Kinmel, for which I am grateful. My family and friends accompanied me on many of the journeys necessary to collect material and their companionship was greatly appreciated. Mrs Pamela Walker typed most of the book from my untidy manuscripts and helped to present the material: she has my very grateful thanks for all her sterling work. J. J. Neal of Leicester completed the task of typing the Select Bibliography.

Sources for figures are from Eastlake's *Gothic Revival* of 1872 or from the author's collection unless otherwise acknowledged.

Sources for photographs are given in abbreviated form as follows after the captions:
1 The Author (JSC)
2 Greater London Photograph Library (GLPL)
3 A. F. Kersting (AFK)
4 Royal Commission on the Historical Monuments of England (RCHME)
5 Royal Commission on the Ancient and Historical Monuments of Scotland (RCAHMS)
6 Royal Commission on Ancient and Historical Monuments in Wales (RCAHMW)
7 By courtesy of the Trustees of the Victoria and Albert Museum (V&A)

James Stevens Curl
Burley-on-the-Hill
Oakham, Rutland
1987–9

1 THE VICTORIAN AGE

Introduction; Victorian Urbanisation; Reform and Change: Facts, Surveys and the Evangelical Conscience; The High-Church Influence; The Beautiful, the Picturesque and the Sublime

We are living in a phase of evolution which is known as the twentieth century and stands for a certain achieved growth of the human mind. But the enormous majority of the human race do not belong to that phase at all . . . Victorians, Tudorians, ghosts surviving from the Middle Ages, and multitudes whose minds properly belong to palaeolithic times, far outnumber the people who truly appertain to the twentieth century
Robert Briffault (1876–1948), Rational Evolution

No architecture is so haughty as that which is simple
John Ruskin (1819–1900), *The Stones of Venice* Vol 2, Ch 6,
Section 73

Introduction
Notions of the Victorian Age in the popular mind tend to be simplistic, distorted and inaccurate. Speeches of politicians, utterances on radio and television and the offerings of journalists are peppered with references to the Victorian period, to Victorian buildings and to Victorian values that indicate widespread misconceptions, prejudice, ignorance and an almost incredible degree of warped perception. All too often the adjective 'Victorian' is used pejoratively to denounce prison and hospital buildings that have become overcrowded, ham-fistedly altered, or not maintained, so that the Victorians are blamed today for the shortcomings of far more recent times.

The Victorian Age began when Princess Alexandrina Victoria of Kent (born 24 May 1819) succeeded to the Throne on the death of her uncle, King William IV, on 20 June 1837: it was to end in one sense with the Queen's death at Osborne House on 22 January 1901.[1] She had reigned for 63 years, 7 months and 2 days, some four years longer than George III. In another sense the Victorian Age with its certainties and doubts, its order and frenetic change, its values and its questionings, was to survive the Queen, but it ended in the catastrophe of the First World War of 1914–18.

There are those who still refer to the Victorian Age as the period when the Industrial Revolution, the railways, slums, the urban poor and dark, disagreeable urban fabric somehow came into being, spoiling beyond redemption a mythical dream of a pre-industrial Britain. Such a view is overly simple. The Industrial Revolution had begun some eighty years before Victoria ascended the throne, while the Stockton and Darlington railway of 1825 and the Liverpool and Manchester railway of 1830 were operative in the reigns of King George IV and King William IV respectively. The first Reform Bill of 1832, schemes of metropolitan improvements, and the first awakenings of the Evangelical Conscience that was to lead to a new concern for the underdog, were all pre-Victorian phenomena. Processes which came to maturity in the reign of Victoria were started long before.

Victorian Urbanisation

The most startling achievement of the Victorian period was the successful urbanisation of Britain, the first society of modern times to become predominantly one of town-dwellers. At the beginning of the nineteenth century twenty per cent of the people dwelt in towns with a population of ten thousand or more: fifty years later some thirty-eight per cent lived in towns of that size, and by then the numbers living in rural parts were fractionally less than those in urban areas. While there had been certain places in Europe, notably the Netherlands, where urban organisation was of considerable antiquity, and a sizeable proportion of the population lived in towns, Victorian Britain was the first truly urbanised *modern* society, and by 1890 London had developed into the largest city in the world (population 4,212,000).[2]

What is perhaps even more remarkable is the change from high to low birth- and death-rates in urban areas towards the end of the Victorian Age, during which the population of Great Britain increased by one hundred per cent. By the end of Victoria's reign over seventy-five per cent of the thirty-six million people lived in towns. These figures reflect not only the great advances in lowering birth- and death-rates, but also the huge successes of the towns, which increased so rapidly in population largely through migration from the rural areas. The phenomenon of urbanisation during the Victorian Age indicated that the towns and cities were magnets for the rural population: urban areas offered new opportunities for personal advancement such as could never be countenanced in the country.[3]

Victorian Britain was remarkably energetic, inventive and aware. Technological resources of an unprecedented magnitude were available, and major works such as the construction of the railways, the sewers, the docks and the water-supply networks were made possible by such resources and by the accumulation of capital. During the Victorian period, gross national product increased four times, and from the 1850s to the year of the Queen's death income per head more than doubled. Investment, opportunity, invention, exploitation of invention, and massive building works do not occur on a basis of subsistence farming or when there is no spare cash. Certainly there were slumps, crashes, disasters, failures and catastrophes, while the story of speculative investment in housing is littered with bankruptcies, yet by the time King Edward VII came to the throne the Victorian legacy was one of unparalleled achievement and unimaginable wealth by the standards of a century earlier. Even more remarkable was the civilising of the urban masses by means of education, sanitary reform, the provision of housing and the stabilisation of society.

The Victorian Age and the great expansion of activity in so many fields (not least in mobility) brought problems on a vast scale. Change and solution, palliative and reform were effected rather often in response to disasters such as epidemics, yet there were many perceptive minds at work, observing the problems and proposing the solutions even before Victoria came to the throne. The short reign of King William IV experienced major problems with the ferocious outbreaks of Asiatic cholera that forced reforms, including the establishment of the first large cemeteries[4] and attempts to provide drinking water and sewers. Constitutional crises over the Great Reform Bill were resolved, the Metropolitan Police Force was formed, and major works of improvement to London's fabric were carried out, to the enrichment of the capital. Most important of all, society and institutions were stabilised for the young Queen's succession. There can be little doubt that the reign of William IV saw the resolution of several pressing problems that could have led to disaster, especially after the unpopularity of King George IV, while the sober and kindly influence of Queen Adelaide in a sense captured the mood of the times that can be summed up as the period when the Evangelical Conscience grew in importance and assumed the moral leadership of much of society.[5]

In the 1830s many towns were growing rapidly, and problems grew with them. No observant intelligent being could fail to notice that there were too many people in towns who had no access to space, light, clean air, pure water, privacy and adequate drainage. A rigidly stratified society tended to leave one layer scarcely aware of living conditions in the layer above or below, but strict segregation could be dented by disaster, such as the epidemics of cholera, typhus and typhoid. These epidemics were not confined to the poorer districts, for cholera was no respecter of class boundaries. It began to be realised that hotbeds of disease could export contagion to other districts. The 1830s were a time of political reform, but this was only one of many factors in the first attempts to grapple with the problems of potty-training man for his urban habitat.

Reform and Change: Facts, Surveys and the Evangelical Conscience
Two of the most significant forces for reform and change contributed to the successful resolution of so many of the problems of overcrowded towns and cities.

The first of these was the collection of documentary evidence, hard facts, statistics and records that enabled a comprehensive picture to be drawn. Unlike previous centuries, the Victorian Age was well-documented and the records offer an enormous quarry from which historians may fashion their studies. Centralised deposits relating to demography were established in the 1830s, and the investigations of the Poor Law Board under Edwin Chadwick into the condition of towns following the epidemics of 1837 and 1838 were unprecedented in scope and scale. The Poor Law Board's *Report on the Sanitary Conditions of the Labouring Population and on the Means of its Improvement,* dated 9 July 1842, was based on information from all over the country. By its thoroughness and impeccably researched facts, it drew attention to a state of affairs that was profoundly shocking. The litany describing foul air, poor drains, filthy water, piecemeal planning, dreadful housing and the condition of the poor was endless and terrible. In 1843 a Royal Commission on the Health of Towns was established: this corroborated what Chadwick and his colleagues had reported and added further evidence that was an indictment of public administration, of drains and water supplies, of standards of overcrowding and hygiene, and of buildings that housed the poor. The Commission revealed that laissez-faire did not work for the less fortunate members of society, and that the system created inhuman conditions that were a threat to the health of society as a whole.

The second force for reform and change was that remarkable phenomenon of the early nineteenth century, the Evangelical Conscience. Spiritual torpor was endemic in many parts of eighteenth-century England (although it was not as general as is commonly supposed), and the Augustan sensibilities of the Georgians were apt to be disturbed by the unseemly 'enthusiasm' of the followers of Wesley.[6] The Evangelicals believed in teaching by example, by temperance, by moderation, by good works and by observing the 'Sabbath'. Clerical piety was insisted upon, and there can be no doubt of the colossal impact the Evangelicals had on the tone of nineteenth-century society long before Victoria came to the throne.

The main impetus of the Evangelicals seems to have come from Cambridge and the Milners, but the appointment of John Venn (1759–1813) as Rector of Clapham (where his father Henry [1725–97] had been curate) in 1792 established that parish as a centre of Evangelical influence through the Thorntons, Wilberforce, Grant, Zachary Macaulay, and Lord Teignmouth. The Clapham Sect (as it became known) reached into the Establishment, politics, Church, and the City of London, and was bound by faith, by philanthropic zeal, by its campaigns against drunkenness and vice, and by its desire to bring literacy and the Bible into every home. The Clapham Sect contained members of wealth and prominence and it exerted an influence far beyond what its numbers might indicate: in the Clapham Sect was the beginning of the Evangelical movement that led to the formation of the conscience of the Victorian age.[7]

The High-Church Influence
There was a further religious factor which must be taken into account in any discussion of the ethos of the Victorian period. The Evangelical movement within the Church of England lacked a certain coherence in upholding the historical ecclesiastical principles of seventeenth-century divines and, like many of the dissenting sects, was over-dependent on the personalities of charismatic preachers rather than on tradition, on the legitimacy of Apostolic Succession, and on the catholicity of ritual. In the Evangelical tradition, the major emphasis is on the relationship between the Bible and direct experience: the Anglo-Catholic tradition lays major emphasis on ecclesiology. The Anglo-Catholics or Ritualists within the Church of England have always insisted upon the 'Catholic' character of the Anglican Church, and have regarded the Church of England as being in full continuity with the pre-Reformation Church *in* England, with no historical or Apostolic break. The so-called Oxford Movement of the early years of the reign of King William IV set out to revive an almost lost belief in that historic continuity of the institutions and liturgy of the Church of England.

Secularism, utilitarianism, the Evangelical movement, and religious expediency were advancing fast when, in 1833, ten Anglican Bishoprics in Ireland were suppressed, and John Keble (1792–1866) commenced his campaign against 'National Apostasy.' In that year the first of the *Tracts for the Times* was published: these tracts contained arguments that dealt with the historic bases of ecclesiastical doctrine, principle and practices within the national Church. *Tract 90* of John Henry Newman (1801–90) was totally unacceptable to the 'Low-Church' or Evangelical party, and so great were the animosities within the Church that there were several secessions to the Roman Catholic Church.[8]

Further secessions occurred in 1850 as a result of the Gorham case, when many High Churchmen went over to Rome, while numerous Evangelicals, disturbed by what seemed to be a secular interference in ecclesiastical matters, also left the Church, and became Dissenters.

The High-Church party acquired two formidable pressure groups in the Cambridge Camden Society (founded in 1839) and the Oxford Society for Promoting the Study of Gothic Architecture. Of the two, the Cambridge Society, which became the Ecclesiological Society, was the more important, for it published *The Ecclesiologist* from 1841, a journal that was the chief arbiter of taste in considerations of architectural correctness in churches. It will be recalled that A. W. N. Pugin's *Contrasts* had appeared in 1836. This polemical book compared architecture of Pugin's own day with that of the Middle Ages, and found the modern work wanting. In his published works, Pugin, a convert to Roman Catholicism, introduced the idea of Pointed Architecture as the only 'Christian' style, and thereby set various cats among the pigeons of theory, prejudice and taste. Gothic architecture had enjoyed a certain fashionable notoriety in the eighteenth century at Strawberry Hill, Fonthill and elsewhere, but it began to become more than fashionable when it was given the Royal imprimatur at Windsor Castle and Carlton House. After the Palace of Westminster was destroyed in a fire in 1834, the terms of the architectural competition stipulated that the designs for the new building should be either Gothic or Elizabethan in style, reflecting a growing taste for what was seen to be an indigenous 'English' architecture. Charles Barry won the competition with a scheme that, although 'Third-Pointed' or 'Perpendicular' Gothic in its detail, owed much to Classical principles in its planning. Barry and Pugin, with the Palace of Westminster, created a major building of the Gothic Revival that set the seal on the respectability of Gothic at a time when major building activities were demanded throughout the land.

If the Evangelicals had been the most significant group behind the changes in national consciousness in the first half of the nineteenth century, the High-Church party assumed an important rôle in the second, and certainly from the time of the appearance of *The Ecclesiologist* in 1841. In that year many churches, in town and country, were shamefully neglected. The Ecclesiologists asked why private houses were kept clean and comfortable, when the House of God often had broken or boarded windows, damp walls, rotting roofs and ancient decorative features hidden or mutilated.[9] They also explained the arrangement and purposes of the fabric of medieval churches to a surprised (and suspicious) Protestant nation. Suggestions for the restoration and furnishing of naves and chancels were made, and cautious moves towards rubrical reform were taken. The Oxford Society for Promoting the Study of Gothic Architecture from the very beginning cautioned against over-zealous works that might 'restore' a building within an inch of its life: even so, many insensitive schemes virtually scraped any genuine fabric away and left buildings looking like dull and mechanical copies (some not even copies but conjectures of what might have been appropriate, and often was not). There can be no doubt that the architectural societies of Oxford and Cambridge popularised the Gothic cause: graduates who 'left their college rooms for curates' quarters in remote parishes, or to settle down as doctors and attorneys in many a country town, carried away with them a pleasant recollection'[10] of field days and explorations, meetings, papers and lively discussions about medieval architecture.

Symbolism, ceremony, sacred imagery and decorative adjuncts (with which Ecclesiology and the High-Church party increasingly became concerned) were frowned upon by the Evangelicals to whom simplicity, severity and sermonising were more important than 'idolatrous gewgaws.'[11] Even chancels, with their Popish rood-screens, sedilia, piscina and credence table, were regarded as relics of the Dark Ages,[12] while crosses were never seen in rigidly Evangelical surroundings. The very name of the altar was a 'scandal and a stumbling-block' to the right-minded.[13] The Evangelicals, in short, saw the Ecclesiologists and the revival of medieval art and architecture as damaging to Protestantism and indeed to the needs of the community, for they argued that two or three plain brick boxes with plaster ceilings could be put up for the price of one stone church with its groined or open timber roof, chancel, stained glass and all the paraphernalia of the Gothic Revival. The ideal Evangelical church building was free of any 'semblance of religious superstition', and innocent of those 'artistic attractions'[14] which might prove to be snares and delusions leading to Rome itself. Ideal Protestant churches were cheap, and did not offer any appeal to aesthetic sensibilities. The transformation of ordinary church services in the Anglican Communion from a conventional and scarcely reverend meeting into a picturesque rite, with a corresponding revival of rubrical usage, sacred music, art and architecture, was a remarkable achievement: the High-Church party won much in the space of a generation, and had a profound effect on architecture and on the building trades. Demand was created for encaustic tiles, stained-glass windows, elaborate metal-work, quality church furnishings, vestments, and all the details necessary for a full and scholarly revival of Gothic architecture: the impact on the training of craftsmen, artists, architects, and on the construction industries was enormous. Architectural design, freed from the tyrannies of symmetry demanded by Neoclassicism, could blossom in the altogether more free climate of Gothic: architects could experiment with asymmetrical silhouettes, with façades pierced with openings only where they were needed, and with the breaking up of huge masses to provide cunningly detailed buildings with a prominent vertical emphasis.

Parochial clergy with Tractarian High-Church leanings achieved great success in bringing Christianity, literacy and morality to the poorer quarters of London and many other towns and cities. The splendid churches and parochial buildings of the Gothic Revival must have seemed like oases of civilisation and hope in the fabric of the Victorian city. Charles Kingsley, in *Alton Locke,* describes a new church being built in a poor suburb of a city:

> . . . month after month I watched it growing; I had seen one window after another fitted with tracery, one buttress after another finished off with its carved pinnacle; then I had watched the skeleton of the roof gradually clothed in tiling; and then the glazing of the windows . . . Were they going to finish that handsome tower? No; it was left with its wooden cap, I supposed, for further funds. But the nave, and the *deep chancel*[15] behind it, were all finished, and surmounted by a cross . . .
>
> And then there was a grand procession of surplices and lawn sleeves . . . the bell rang to morning and evening prayers – for there were daily services there, and saints' day services, and Lent services, and three services on a Sunday, and six or seven on Good Friday and Easter Day. The little musical bell above the chancel-arch seemed always ringing . . .
>
> And then a Gothic school-house rose at the churchyard end . . . and women came daily for alms; and when the frosts came on, every morning I saw a crowd, and soup carried away in pitchers, and clothes and blankets given away . . .
>
> . . . it was a pleasant sight, as every new church is to the healthy-minded man, . . . a fresh centre of civilization, mercy, comfort for weary hearts, relief from frost and hunger; a fresh centre of instruction, humanizing, disciplining . . . to hundreds of little savage spirits; altogether a pleasant sight . . .[16]

Thus the Gothic style was an ever-present reminder of the potency of the Christian Revival, be it Anglo-Catholic, Evangelical, or Roman Catholic. Even the Dissenters began to ape the grander Gothic churches, often with ludicrous results, for Gothic church architecture by its very nature had roots in the rich panoply of medieval religion, far removed from plain Sabbatarianism, Evangelical ideals, or a tradition of sermonising to packed static congregations.

However, the Gothic Revival, although of prime importance in church architecture, in the movements away from symmetry and in the changes of trend within the building industry, was not all-embracing. True, there were Gothic-Revival colleges, like Keble, Lancing and Rugby, Gothic-Revival hotels like St Pancras Station Hotel in London, Gothic-Revival houses like those of North Oxford and Leicester's Stoneygate, and even Gothic-Revival public-house details like those of the Citadel in Belfast. Nevertheless, the majority of Victorian commercial buildings, like banks, offices, warehouses and even factories, remained firmly Classical in inspiration.

The Beautiful, the Picturesque and the Sublime

Eighteenth-century rationalists had attempted to categorise aspects in their surroundings under the headings Beautiful, Picturesque, and Sublime. Ever since the Florentine Renaissance, architecture aspired to an expression of the ideal state with systems of proportion based on anthropometric perfection: this was the Beautiful. The Picturesque relied not on the precision of proportion and measurement, but on more emotional responses to associations evocative of persons or events. The Picturesque (from *Pittoresco,* meaning 'in the manner of the painters') was also associated with contrived compositions, particularly those of Claude Lorraine, Salvator Rosa, and the Poussins, and was essentially an anti-urban aesthetic concerned with individuality: it was linked with notions of pleasing the eye, with singularity, and with impinging upon the sensibilities with the force of a landscape painting. To Sir Uvedale Price (1747–1829) the Picturesque comprised all the qualities of nature and art that could be appreciated in studies of painting since the time of Titian, and he argued (in his *Essay on the Picturesque* of 1794) in favour of 'natural' beauty, deploring contemporary fashions (such as those established by 'Capability' Brown [1716–83]) for laying out grounds because they were at variance with all the principles of landscape painting. Price's arguments were admirably set out by his friend and neighbour, Richard Payne Knight (1750–1824), in his didactic poem *The Landscape*, of 1794. Price and Knight had a considerable influence on the design of gardening and landscapes in later years, and unquestionably helped to create a climate in which the asymmetrical, serene, reposeful and informal aspects of much architectural and landscape design developed in the nineteenth and early twentieth centuries.

It is one of the oddities of so much Anglo-Saxon scholarship that the works of the anti-urbanists have been given so much credence. William Morris, John Ruskin, Thomas Carlyle, Matthew Arnold, Ebenezer Howard, and many others were influential in the creation of an anti-urban climate of opinion, and have attracted the attention of students sympathetic to their hatred of the nineteenth-century city. The cosy images of English suburbia created from the 1870s were not accidents: they were the direct result of an anti-urban climate of opinion that has been one of the more enduring aspects of Romanticism. This is even odder when we consider the reality that a future for a traditional predominantly rural England had been ended partly by the repeal[17] of the Corn Laws in 1846. Just as the Union of Great Britain[18] and Ireland had made Catholic Emancipation inevitable (the Roman Catholic Relief Act[19] was passed in 1829), and the suppression of Anglican Bishoprics in Ireland under its Church Temporalities (Ireland) Act[20] of 1833 had given impetus to the Tractarian movement and subsequent upheavals, events in Ireland once more had far-reaching effects on national affairs. Potato blight arrived in September 1845 and caused such mayhem in areas where subsistence farming was the norm that Parliament was obliged to repeal the Corn Laws in 1846. Duties on imported corn were virtually abolished, and so the protection given to British farmers by the Laws was removed. Duties on the importation of corn were suspended under a single-section Act in 1847[21] as a result of the problems caused by the Irish famine. The 'Hungry Forties' was a term not confined to Ireland, for the entire United Kingdom suffered.

The repeal of the Corn Laws and the abolition of duties on imported corn turned the balance between town and country; from that time on England would import food and live by exporting manufactured goods. No longer was England to be self-sufficient: it was to be an urbanised industrial nation living by trade. In other words, a political decision was made that altered the character of the nation, and Ireland was the catalyst that promoted the change. The repeal of the Corn Laws was seen as a victory for the unlanded classes over the old aristocratic High-Tory interests in land: the consequences were as significant as those created by the Great Reform Bill of 1832, for power was shifting away from the landed classes to the industrialists and entrepreneurs, and, by association, eventually to organised industrial labour.

Once the majority of the population lived in cities a romantic nostalgic longing for a lost rural paradise was fostered by representatives of middle-class opinion who denigrated the enormous achievements of thrusting, intelligent, energetic entrepreneurs, and attempted to build a Utopian, dreamlike, and questionable ideal of a rural paradise that had never existed. In doing so they helped to engender a type of snobbery, an arrogant and patronising attitude, and a dangerous set of delusions that have survived to this day concerning the creation of wealth and the means by which 'socially desirable' aims can be achieved. In fact, the anti-urbanists and critics of the Victorian era were frightened of the one thing that gave the Victorian city its great quality: they hated and were frightened of the Sublime.

During the eighteenth century the term 'Sublime' contrasted with the idea of the 'Beautiful'. Burke, in his *Philosophical Enquiry into the Origin of our Ideas of the Sublime and Beautiful,* published in 1757, associated the Sublime with Terror. Wild, grand, and terrifying aspects of nature were celebrated by many artists during the eighteenth century as indicative of the Sublime, but the nineteenth-century towns and cities also contained obvious aspects of the Sublime that clearly worried romantics like Morris and Howard. Splendour, darkness, vastness, blackness, flaming chimneys, roaring steam-propelled trains hurtling through tunnels or over huge ravines on viaducts grander than anything the Romans had built (as at Welwyn [*Plate 1*] or the great bridges over the eastern rivers on the line between London and Edinburgh); gigantic docks, warehouses and ports, near basins crammed with great ships (*Plate 2*); and cobbled streets illumined by the yellow glare of gaslight, alive with all the damp, malodorous, noisy, vital activity of humanity on the move, the make and in a state of perpetual motion and change, constituted the essence of the Sublime. It was no wonder that the faint-hearted commentators from comfortable homes were frightened out of their wits: the nineteenth-century urban environment was Sublime. It was dangerous, noisy, dirty, visually stupendous, completely new, mighty, energetic, terrible, magnificent, busy, lively, bustling, and exciting. It was also a magnet to which the rural poor flocked. It was successful, it created wealth, it gave opportunities not dreamed of in some frightful rural slum, and it could kill. Mills (not dark, but flashing with light and noise), warehouses, gasworks, gaols, railway stations, canals, cuttings, communal centres, gin-palaces, music-halls, theatres, and row upon row of crisp, clean houses (far superior to the rural hovel) provided the essentially Sublime vision of the nineteenth-century urban milieu: here was an aesthetic experience far removed from the pretty cottage covered with roses (never mind the mean and filthy interior), and beyond the understanding of middle-class theorists who were scared to death by the sheer energy of it all.

Some of the problems of the new urbanisation could be found in the fact that it was lively, dangerous, tempting and expansionist: it threatened the countryside, it was aggressively colonialist, and it could not be stopped. It was not pretty, nor was it in any way part of the cult of the beautiful, although there were later attempts at Bedford Park and elsewhere to bring a new aesthetic derived from the Picturesque, from the new eclecticism of the Domestic Revival and 'Queen-Anne' styles, and from an appreciation of rural vernacular architecture. Much of the

21

Victorian urban fabric was not concerned with the nicely measured perspectives of the rules of taste as laid down by the Palladians and others: it was perforce out of scale, megalomaniac and menacing: it held within its vast compass the raucous laughter of drunken women, the sober discourse of the serious, the tub-thumping hell-fire sermons of the Evangelical demagogue, the rich wonder of a scented ritualist service, the noise and excitement of modern travel, the vulgarity and abundance of exhibitions and shows, the vast energies and possibilities of choice in markets, manufactures and industries, and the shock of the new that was yet connected with the old through allusion, metaphor and motif.

'Ugly Victorian buildings' is a phrase that drops from the lips of the ignorant, for the assumption that because a building is Victorian it must be ugly is still widespread. Yet the *cognoscenti* of the 1840s did not regard the fabric being erected as ugly at all: in fact they took care to ensure that new tunnel entrances, viaducts, factories, railway stations and other structures were well designed and fit for their purpose. An express train, pulled by a great steam locomotive, roaring out of a stone-dressed Neoclassical tunnel entrance in a cloud of steam and smoke on the permanent ways was Sublimely terrible, full of energy, speed, power, noise, and a new sense of purpose and dynamism.

Ideas of exciting pain, danger, terror, emotion, feeling or astonishment could be associated with the Sublime. Power, strength, violence, noise, smoke, energy, light, all suggest Sublime terror. Vacuity, darkness, solitude and silence were just as important in considerations of the Sublime, as Edmund Burke reminds us, while hugeness, greatness, height, ruggedness, enormous chimneys and infinity all suggest the Sublime. Uniformity, uninterrupted progression (like a vast scheme for a factory façade), and repetitive architectural motifs (such as arcades, colonnades, and windows) also indicate the Sublime. Any structure that is vast, and which suggests that it was made with immense forces, great numbers of labourers, and gigantic endeavour suggests the awefulness of the Sublime. Magnificence, blazing lights, dungeonesque darkness, blackness, gloomths and seething depths, blast-furnaces, fogs and smoke were part of the immensity of the Sublime. Noble severity, a new toughness (suggested by certain eighteenth-century architects), and a grasping of architectural nettles to design building types for which there was no precedent (like railway stations, factories driven by steam power, and vast commercial premises) were part of the Victorian urban experience.

Plate 1 The Railway Viaduct at Digswell, near Welwyn by Lewis Cubitt of 1849–50, a Sublime repetition of forty-nine brick arches. (*JSC*)

23

Joseph Mallord William Turner (1775–1851) suggested the Sublime in his extraordinary visions of shipwrecks, express trains and steamships, and Joseph Wright of Derby (1734–97) painted Sublime mills blazing with light in the valleys of industrial Derbyshire. In 1826 the Prussian architect Karl Friedrich Schinkel visited England and was enthusiastic about the industrial buildings of the north – the immense factories, chimneys and viaducts – and he likened the chimneys to obelisks. To Schinkel the thousands of smoking obelisks were grand and Egyptian: he understood the excitement of the Sublime. In the record of his visit he noted the hugeness of new buildings in Manchester, the tremendous vaults of the London docks, and the expression of power in the iron cranes and railways.[22]

The grandeur of the Victorian urban fabric before 1870 was largely the creation of a taste encouraged by the aristocracy and by those who sought the approval of that aristocracy which had the security of background to demand of its architects the same bravura in factory, viaduct, tunnel entrance and commercial palazzo. After the repeal of the Corn Laws and the shift of power away from the great landowners, taste unquestionably changed, reflecting the aspirations of the middle classes rather than those of the landed aristocracy. There was a reaction against the great palatial Classical stucco-faced domestic architecture of Nash at Regent's Park, of Basevi at Bayswater and South Kensington, and, by association, the magnificent Italianate terraces of first-rate town houses of Victorian Kensington. After 1870 or thereabouts the rush to suburbia became a stampede, for there the Sublime was nowhere to be found: the cult of the Picturesque was embraced, the aesthetic movement of art for art's sake (the very antithesis of Pugin's ideas), and the rediscovery of vernacular architecture, the development of the so-called 'Queen-Anne' style, and the Domestic Revival had all gathered momentum. The marvellous fabric of urban and industrial structures, and of all contained within the Sublime as a concept, began to be seen as merely 'ugly', and eyes accustomed to more homely imagery were averted from scenes that had once excited a Wright, a Turner and a Schinkel.[23] Driving energy and power, once expressed in architecture as they had been in industrial machinery, were no longer respectable. Work and trade were seen to be somehow vulgar: middle-class aspirations led to the mystique of professionalism in a way that would have been very odd to a Brunel, a Stephenson or an Arkwright.

Even a cursory glance at the built fabric of the time reveals railway termini, tunnels, cuttings, viaducts, prisons, hospitals, barracks, tenements, warehouses, docks, bridges, cranes, wharfs, jetties, mills, factories, chimneys, foundries, offices, town halls, court-houses, churches and public buildings that were impressive and thrilling works of architecture. Many early-Victorian buildings could be described as being exemplars of the architecture of rhetoric and perhaps can only be understood as such. Perhaps that is why, for the last century or so, much of the built fabric of the early-Victorian period has been disliked, even feared. The nation (or rather the Establishment) has rejected rhetoric, for it is embarrassed by it: it is too showy, too emotional, too upsetting and altogether too grand. Calamities, emergencies, war and national disasters invoke a self-conscious and limited rhetoric, but at other times the consensus of the compromise prevails. Stupendous, Sublime, gigantic, confident public architecture tells us much about early-Victorian Britain: here was *architecture parlante* indeed, even more stunning than anything of which the eighteenth-century French designers had dreamed. The Piranesian intensity of the catacombs at Kensal Green Cemetery, of the retaining walls beside the tracks leading to Liverpool Street Station in London, of the tunnel entrances north of King's Cross on the railway-line to York, of the marvellous viaduct at Welwyn in Hertfordshire (*Plate 1*), of the repetitive arches of the London and Greenwich Railway (reminiscent of the Claudian aqueduct that strides over the Roman *campagna*), of the blank walls of Leicester Gaol, and of the Greek-Revival Doric arch that once led to Euston and the north were all strong stuff: too strong for the more intimate, reticent, 'aesthetic' tastes of society after the 1870s.

Paradoxically, it was the railways that first made the exodus to the countryside possible, for without them the middle classes could not have escaped to their versions of reduced Arcady. Yet the railways had not only been catalysts for Sublime structures (disliked and feared by those who sought suburbia), but had been the agencies for great changes, especially in the poorer parts of cities, where the over-crowded dwellings of the poor that lay in the way of the railways were swept away, but no provision was made for rehousing displaced populations. The deep gorges of railway cuttings, pursuing their ways to the termini, were often Sublime, striking terror into the hearts of those who beheld them. Such cavernous Piranesian cuttings, lined by battered brick or stone retaining walls, were often frontiers, separating one urban area from another, but they were also the gates to cities and the ravines through which commuters could escape by the lines along which they were deposited in new clusters set in the countryside.

When the Tramways Act of 1870 gave municipal authorities powers to buy out private tramways compulsorily after twenty-one years of operation, a further linear spread of the urbanising and suburbanising process was encouraged. Mechanical means of transport, quick, efficient and cheap, helped to create the Victorian city, and to make possible those Arcadian suburbs and rib-like streets of terrace-houses linked to town centres by spines of railways and tramways. Under the roads and out of sight were the huge networks of drains, sewers and water-mains that helped to reduce mortality and to bring new standards of hygiene on a scale unknown even in the time of the Roman Empire.

The Victorian Age saw the linking of towns and cities by the railways, which made much of the growth possible. At first the railways encouraged the concentration of people in urban areas, then in the settlements linked or created by the railways. A Victorian town or city was, nevertheless, urban in character, although some of the new, bosky suburbs (like Bedford Park) were tending to become suburban in appearance. From the 1870s, as has been noted earlier, this tendency to suburbanisation increased, although the linear nature of public transport confined it physically. With the coming of the motor-car and the motor-bus the urban fabric began to spread in a non-linear way, and spread thinly in all directions too, so that huge areas of land became neither urban nor rural, but suburban in character. It was with the availability of the motor-car to ever-increasing numbers of people that Victorian urban patterns ended. Just as the massive investment in railways helped to create the urban milieu of the Victorian age, so the coming of universal car ownership marked the demise of the Victorian urban fabric in the twentieth century.

2 THE QUESTION OF STYLE I

Introduction; Pugin; The Ecclesiologists; John Ruskin;
E.-E. Viollet-le-Duc

Tous les genres sont bons, hors le genre ennuyeux (All styles are
good, except the boring kind)
Voltaire, L'Enfant Prodigue: Preface

The waste of time, of energy, and printer's ink, involved by endless
discussions on the respective merits of Mediaeval and Renaissance
architecture during twenty years, can only be realised by those
who have studied the current art literature of that period.
Charles L. Eastlake, *A History of the Gothic Revival* (1872) 333

Introduction

A frequent charge against the Victorians is that their architecture is not
beautiful, and that it is less refined than that of the Georgians. It is not
generally realised that this was a matter of deliberate choice, for the
Victorians were reacting against what they saw as dull, monotonous
and boring architecture: not for them were the uniform heights, the
thin pilasters, and the reticence of Georgian brickwork. A glance at
Pugin's *Contrasts* of 1836 is enough to show that by then much late
Georgian architecture was held in contempt, especially that of the
period known as Regency. Much of the hatred was directed towards
the supposedly moral failings of stucco-faced façades, while the
handling of Classical details by architects such as Nash came in for
severe censure. The Victorians loathed Regency and Georgian architecture, not just for what it was, but because it was the product of what,
to the Victorians, was an age of religious torpor and moral failure: the
Age of the Prince Regent was morally repellent, therefore the
architecture of that age was suspect. Such notions may seem absurd,
but they have persisted well into our own time, especially in the
polemical works of the supporters of the so-called Modern Movement.

The Victorians wanted to replace Georgian London by a Victorian
London, as is made clear by this quotation from *The Builder* of 1868:

Commercial public works, of a magnitude unrivalled since the
days of imperial Rome . . . are educating our workmen, from the

lowest to the highest, to a style of craftsmanship entirely unknown in this country at the commencement of the present century. Private wealth, under the stimulus already given to good taste, is replacing the dead walls and unmeaning windows of the Georgian style of street building, the poorest and least picturesque that was ever common in any civilised nation, by not altogether unsuccessful efforts to create a *Victorian* London.[1]

For the Victorians the problems of creating a Victorian London (or a Victorian Belfast, Leeds, Liverpool, or Manchester, for that matter) were compounded by the multiplicity of styles available to their architects. If the Georgians had enjoyed a tyranny under the Palladians, they also had a growing problem of choice once the Picturesque became accepted as a standard of taste and the stimulus for many English landscapes deliberately created 'in the manner of the painters', as at Stourhead in Wiltshire.

The Picturesque could consist of, or contain, physical attributes that would have an effect on the sensibilities: even objects that were rough, irregular or intricate could produce a 'curious' reaction. Hence, even items once seen as ugly could be enjoyed as Picturesque.

Payne Knight's *Analytical Inquiry into the Principles of Taste* of 1805 argued that Picturesque beauty comprises effects of refracted light revealed by painting and separated from other kinds of beauty, and objects rendered significant through associations with paintings (a definition expanded by Archibald Alison [1757–1839]). The aesthetics of associationism encouraged the concept of architecture as physical memory. Payne Knight noted that, 'as all the pleasures of the intellect arise from the association of ideas, the more the materials of association are multiplied, the more will the sphere of those pleasures be enlarged. To a mind richly stored, almost every object of nature or art . . . either excites fresh trains and combinations of ideas . . . so that recollection enhances enjoyment, and enjoyment heightens recollection . . .'[2] In the second half of the eighteenth century the absolute values of taste (as exemplified by the Palladians) ceased to apply, to be replaced by eclecticism and relative values. Gradually there was a great range of choice: Athenian temples could co-exist with sham medieval ruins at Hagley Hall in Worcestershire, while architecture in the Chinese taste by Chambers could be seen at Kew with a 'Gothic Cathedral' by Müntz.

Humphry Repton, in *Fragments on the Theory and Practice of Landscape Gardening*,[3] demonstrated how the character of buildings could be completely changed by applied ornament: Repton was an eclectic who greatly influenced John Claudius Loudon (1783–1843). The latter's *Encyclopaedia of Cottage, Farm and Villa Architecture*, an immensely popular and influential work first published in 1833, contains many examples of identical buildings treated in numerous stylistic guises. The *Encyclopaedia* and Loudon's *The Architectural Magazine* were both intended to provide a taste for architectural beauties and comforts so that the dwellings of the great mass of society could be improved: Loudon's readership was not only found among the aristocracy, but also in great numbers among the middle classes. Loudon's publications had a singular importance in the creation of Victorian taste, especially in the suburbs and countryside, for he was not concerned with the niceties of architectural style: he was, on the contrary, interested in comfort, convenience, fitness for purpose and appropriate expression of use. Loudon was not doctrinaire in matters of style, and avoided dogmatic preferences that were based on the flimsiest of arguments: his acceptance of eclecticism was based on his view that the expression of architectural style 'was not an essential beauty in a building'.[4] He went on to observe that

> an edifice may be useful, strong, and durable, both in reality and in expression, without having any other beauties than those of use and truth; that is, of fitness for the end in view, and of expression of the end in view; or, in familiar language, of being suitable to the use for which it is designed, and of appearing to be what it is . . . *The Beauty of Architectural Forms* arises from . . . the expression of certain qualities which result from combinations of those forms, such as unity, variety, symmetry, &c.; and the expression of certain forms and details which have been con-secrated to architecture by long-continued use. The first may be called the universal and inherent beauties of all architectural styles; and the second, the historical or accidental beauties of particular styles. The first kind of beauty is . . . independent of any style . . ., its effect resulting entirely from organic impressions, and associations of a general nature; the second depends on the addition, to the first class of beauties, of the associations con-nected with the known forms and details of the different styles of Architecture . . .[5]

Repton had proposed different elevational treatments for different moods: Classical styles suggested formality, while Gothic was informal, a factor emphasised by its asymmetrical composition. There were even buildings which had elevations of different styles, or where styles were mixed: the mid-eighteenth-century Castle Ward, near Strangford in County Down, has an entrance-front that is pure Palladian, while the elevation to Strangford Lough is Gothick. In other instances Classical architraves and crenellated parapets co-exist. John Foulston (1772–1842), the leading architect in the Plymouth area during the second, third and fourth decades of the nineteenth century, went a step further in his designs for a group of buildings at Devonport. His intention was to build a 'series of edifices exhibiting the various features of the architectural world', and to produce 'a picturesque effect, by combining in one view, the Grecian, Egyptian, and a variety of the Oriental'.[6] Here was eclecticism indeed: a library in the 'Egyptian' taste, a 'Hindoo' Gothick chapel for Dissenters, a Doric town hall and monument, a pair of houses with Ionic details and a terrace of houses with Roman Corinthian enrichment. The whole ensemble was not completed until 1824 (*Fig 1*).

Such stylistic flexibility was apparent in the churches erected under the aegis of the Church Building Act of 1818 (known as Commissioners' or Waterloo churches) of which some 214 were built. Many of these churches were capacious preaching-boxes with galleries and

Fig 1 A group of buildings at Devonport of 1824 by John Foulston including a terrace of houses with an engaged Roman Corinthian Order on the left, a prostyle tetrastyle Greek-Revival Town Hall using the Doric Order, a commemorative Doric column, a Mount Zion chapel in the 'Indian' style of Brighton Pavilion and a Library in the Egyptian taste. (*Lithograph by T. J. Ricauti, printed by G. Lee*)

vestigial chancels (if there were chancels at all), and most of them were cheap. The important thing was that churches should be built, and that Evangelical dislike of show would prevail. Although the Commissioners left the matter of style out of early considerations, they were later to mention Roman, Greek and Gothic, with a preference for Gothic, largely on grounds of expense, for Classical architecture tended to mean porticoes of stone, which could not be done on the cheap. 'Neatness' was all, a word that signified approval where much building was concerned in the first decades of the last century, and stylistic matters initially were of little import except when it was thought appropriate to avoid show, encourage economy, and demonstrate a utilitarian medley that would be safe from any charge of partisanship. In the reign of William IV and during the first decade or so of the Victorian Age the choice of style began, to a certain extent, to be determined by building type. Greek was suitable for museums, galleries, public buildings; Gothic (usually Perpendicular) was chosen for churches; an Italianate *palazzo* style was regarded as appropriate for banks, certain commercial offices and gentlemen's clubs; Tudor was the style for schools, workhouses, almshouses and the dwellings of the labouring classes; and Romanesque could be found associated with certain County Halls, gaols, and court-houses. It must be emphasised, however, that the categories of style and type were not adhered to rigidly, and there was considerable room for manoeuvre. However, it is true to say that architects were obliged to be *acquainted* with all styles, but that, while architects of talent could produce respectable and scholarly essays in Classical or Gothic styles, their less competent brethren were likely to be uneasy with some styles, cautious with others, and hamfisted with the rest.

During the eighteenth and early nineteenth centuries knowledge of the architecture of Classicism increased. The newly excavated Pompeii and Herculaneum became familiar through publications, while ancient Roman buildings acquired new popularity through the views of Piranesi and others. Stuart and Revett's *Antiquities of Athens* and other sources provided architects with accurate illustrations of the architecture of ancient Greece, while the superlative illustrations in Denon's *Voyage* . . . and in the monumental publications that followed Napoléon's Nile expeditions increased understanding of ancient Egyptian architecture.[7] Designers therefore had reliable architectural 'dictionaries', 'grammar-books' and patterns from which to fashion their creations. One of the problems of applying the Greek Orders to, say, a church, was that a Greek temple was not intended for congregational worship. Architects had to take the rectangular box of the eighteenth century, put double rows of windows along the sides to light the spaces above and below the gallery, add a portico based on an ancient Greek exemplar to one end (usually the liturgical 'west'), and invent a tower using pile-ups of Greek Orders. While buildings such as W. and H. W. Inwood's new St Pancras Church in London (completed 1822) can be regarded as an ingenious, even beautiful, example of a Greek-Revival church using accurately observed motifs from a number of sources, they did arouse criticism, not only because they were Greek, but also because they were increasingly seen as inappropriate to a revival of 'Christian' architecture and because their forms lent themselves exclusively to Evangelical Protestantism at a time when interest in Ecclesiology was growing.

Every conceivable style could be used by architects in a free and eclectic manner in those heady days before style became confused with morals. George Wightwick (1802–72), who joined Foulston as a partner in the Plymouth office was also eclectic in his choice of styles, although his 'interest in ecclesiology was not sufficient to satisfy the High-Church party, which dominated the diocese of Exeter in the 1840s, and soon he began to lose his ecclesiastical patronage'.[8] Wightwick was staunchly Evangelical in outlook, and stuck to the principle of the form of an auditorium for a Protestant church, which was unacceptable to those of an Ecclesiological bent. A strange design by him for a *Palace of Architecture* of 1840 shows an entrance gate incorporating every conceivable style, put together with a clumsy disregard for any of the niceties of proportion or detail. In 1842 Richard Brown published his *Domestic Architecture* and in 1845 *Sacred Architecture,* both of which were, in the words of Howard Colvin, 'indiscriminately eclectic', and contain weird notions of what might be appropriate stylistically: some of his designs are perhaps nearer in spirit to the fairground than to serious architecture, in spite of the author's intentions. Joseph Michael Gandy (1771–1843) produced a number of superbly rendered drawings of buildings in which many styles were represented,[9] and recommended that architects should cull elements from every climate, age and taste. Gandy, in short, sought to explore the future development of architecture by means of discriminating eclecticism using a wide range of earlier forms and motifs that were linked in some elusive way. Like so many of his generation, he was unable to achieve this, for his vision was backward-looking: he was unable to make the leap away from the bondage of the Picturesque. The simple geometry of much of Neoclassical architecture, like that of Joseph Bonomi (1739–1808) at Great Packington in Warwickshire, the simplified stereometrically pure images of Étienne-Louis Boullée (1728–99) and Claude-Nicolas Ledoux (1735–1806), certain designs by Friedrich Gilly (1771–1800), Newgate Prison by George Dance the

Younger (1741–1825), and some canal and dockyard architecture seemed to point towards a new style where Classical relationships of proportion, solid and void, and integrity of geometry would be paramount, but stripped of all the tyranny of overt use of the Orders, and minus all decorative frippery. Only occasionally did Victorian architects achieve this: Jesse Hartley's Albert Docks in Liverpool, with its massive plain brick walls and huge cast-iron primitive Doric columns (*Plate 2*), is Sublime architecture indeed, while many warehouses, railway tunnels, viaducts and other buildings eschew the Picturesque in favour of something tougher, more Sublime, and unpretty. Picturesque architecture tended to be an architecture of illusion, subject to criteria of association, composition, dreamy silhouettes and apparent utility, although real utility was usually very remote.

The Victorian 'Battle of the Styles' was not a simple matter of opinion, nor was it a question of Greek versus Goth. The history of Neoclassicism shows among its main themes the archaeological rediscovery of

Plate 2 The Albert Dock Warehouses in Liverpool of 1843–5 by Jesse Hartley (1780–1860) with Philip Hardwick, who designed the Dock Traffic Office (not shown in the photograph). These are among the most Sublime of all nineteenth-century examples of commercial and industrial architecture, with their cast-iron unfluted Doric columns, massive undecorated brick walls, repetitive elements, and avoidance of ornament worthy of C.-N. Ledoux, the French Neoclassical architect and theorist, at his most uncompromising. (*JSC*)

Rome, Greece and Egypt, and the search for simplicity through stereometrically pure forms. The problem with Gothic at the beginning of the nineteenth century was that although there was a lot of medieval architecture about, and accessible (far more so than the ruins of Greek architecture, trapped within the decaying Ottoman Empire), systematic studies were thin on the ground. The studies of Milner, Rickman and Whewell helped to clarify the typology of Gothic, in spite of the gloriously Rococo attempts of Batty Langley (1696–1751) – the author of *Gothic Architecture . . .* of 1747 and many other works – to clarify and make Gothic intelligible to those brought up on the Classical Orders: Langley's Gothic 'Orders' are engaging, although he incurred later ridicule when knowledge of the style became more soundly based on archaeological observation. The 'Pointed Style' began to be seen as having three distinct parts, known as First, Second (or Middle) and Third Pointed, and attention was drawn by scholars to the distinctive character of mouldings and window tracery. Thomas Rickman (1776–1841) was both an architect and a writer who, in his *An Attempt to Discriminate the Styles of English Architecture from the Conquest to the Reformation* of 1817, produced the first systematic treatise on Gothic architecture in England. As a Quaker, Rickman was not interested in the niceties of Ecclesiological debate, but he was interested in the grammar and vocabulary of medieval architecture. Rickman's standard work went into several editions, and the importance of his *Attempt . . .* in the history of the Gothic Revival cannot be over-emphasised. Substantially, beautifully, and accurately illustrated, the work described Early English (First Pointed thirteenth-century), Decorated (Middle Pointed fourteenth-century), and Perpendicular (Third Pointed late fourteenth- to sixteenth-century) architecture. Rickman took every feature of a medieval building in turn and described it under the heading of that period with which he was dealing in chronological order. Thus by the ending of the first quarter of the nineteenth century architects had a useful source-book for Gothic styles. It is interesting that the Gothic Revival began with Perpendicular (the latest phase of real Gothic), and gradually worked backwards in time to Early English, then to Continental Europe, just as Neoclassicism sought ever earlier and more 'pure' and primitive precedents. Several distinguished Gothic-Revival churches are pre-Victorian, including St Luke's, Chelsea, St Dunstan-in-the-West in 9. The Strand, and some of Rickman's own work, but Gothic became something more than a mere style from the time of Pugin.

Pugin

Augustus Welby Northmore Pugin (1812–52) regarded Picturesque

Plate 3 The tower at Hadlow Castle in Kent by George Ledwell Taylor (1788–1873) of 1840 from the south, an example of Picturesque *effect* that did *not grow from necessity*, and would therefore be regarded by Pugin as a sham. The towers at Fonthill and Hadlow were extreme examples of the 'abbey' style of country house, so 'unnaturally natural', as Pugin put it, as to be ridiculous. Here was no beauty from necessity, but a building deliberately designed to be Picturesque and to create an effect by its silhouette, details, and extraordinarily exaggerated verticality. (*RCHME No AA51/5923*)

Gothic, such as at Wyatt's Fonthill Abbey, as depraved, dishonest and absurd. He was scathing about Regency 'castellated' houses with crenellations, decorative porticullises which would not lower, draw-bridges that did not function, minute turrets that an undersized dwarf could not ascend, guard-rooms *sans* guards, donjons which were in reality drawing-rooms, watch-towers which incorporated the maids' bedrooms, bastions for the butler's pantry, and the general deception of buildings like Fonthill or G. L. Taylor's Hadlow Castle Tower in Kent (*Plate 3*). The so-called 'abbey' style of country house was a mere toy,

35

devoted to luxury. In particular, Pugin denounced the cavalier way in which architects mixed profane and sacred architectural elements, confused structure and ornament, and distorted scale. To Pugin a real Gothic building had to express in its composition the asymmetry of a plan that actually worked on logical lines. He felt that a building consciously designed to be Picturesque, with decorative modelling, superfluous towers and pinnacles, was absurd and ridiculous. An old 'Catholic' house, like Haddon Hall in Derbyshire, or Penshurst Place in Kent, was 'truly Picturesque', however, because the beauty of the composition grew from necessity and function. The gate-house, hall and other parts looked like what they were, and were not concealed behind some contrived façade.

In April 1829 the *Roman Catholic Relief Act*[10] (known as 'Catholic Emancipation') was passed, partly as a result of pressure from Ireland, and many of the social and political restrictions were lifted. Following a Consistory in Rome on 29 September 1850 when Pope Pius IX named fourteen new Cardinals, including Dr Nicholas Wiseman, who was nominated Lord Archbishop of Westminster, a Roman Catholic bishop was enthroned in Birmingham, and in October England and Wales were parcelled up into dioceses. Further enthronements followed in 1851, and, such was the public outcry against 'Papal Aggression', that *The Ecclesiastical Titles Act*[11] was passed expressly prohibiting the assumption of territorial titles by Roman Catholic archbishops, bishops and deans relating to 'Pretended Provinces' under a penalty of a fine, but the Act was never enforced, and was repealed in 1871.

Many intellectuals seceded to Rome in the 1830s, partly as a result of matters discussed in the Introduction, and partly through an admiration of 'Catholic' art. Pugin himself was converted in 1834, and although he denied the primary motive for his conversion was architectural, he believed that the only way in which a 'grand' and Sublime style of architecture could be restored was within the Roman Catholic church, and under its influence. To Pugin, Gothic was the only style suitable for a 'Christian' (i.e. Roman Catholic) country, but the Roman Church in England was not enthusiastic about Gothic, preferring a watered-down Roman Baroque, if it had any stylistic preferences at all. In the climate of opinion following 1829 Pugin began to formulate notions about the forms of Gothic architecture as though they were the tenets of the Roman Church, and his arguments became more and more shrill. Architecture was 'true' or 'false', morally depraved or uplifting, and 'honest' or 'dishonest'. Natural materials were good, but stucco or faience were degenerate. In 1836 he published his *Contrasts; or, a Parallel between the Noble Edifices of the Fourteenth and Fifteenth Centuries, and Similar Buildings of the Present Day: Showing the*

Present Decay of Taste. It was an intemperate and powerful polemic, in which the works of the leaders of the architectural profession of his own day were compared with the works of medieval architects and found wanting. Everything grand or noble in architecture was only possible as a result of the Roman Catholic religion; destruction of art, irreverence, and loss of perception were due to the Renaissance and to Protestantism; and the degraded state of architecture was due to the absence of Catholic feeling among the practitioners and the loss of ecclesiastical patronage. *Contrasts* was followed by *The True Principles of Pointed or Christian Architecture* (1841), *The Present State of Ecclesiastical Architecture in England* (1843), and *An Apology for the Revival of Christian Architecture in England* (1843), in all of which the message was clear: Classical architecture was no better than Stonehenge in its structure, and it was pagan anyway, while Gothic was not a style, but a principle, a moral crusade, and the only mode of building possible for a Christian nation (*Fig 2*).

Pugin was vitriolic about the torrent of Roman-cement enthusiasts, who provided ornament by the yard, and capitals by the ton. Gothic, to Pugin, offered a way out of the confusion of what he termed a carnival of architecture in which every style was piled together in a confused manner. The reason for so much borrowing seemed to him to be that styles were adopted rather than arrived at by a series of logical steps, and that ornament and design were adapted to buildings rather than generated by the structure. Pugin warned against the study of prints of buildings, and the widespread custom of imitating parts of them: to his way of thinking the architectural books in the hands of practitioners were as dangerous as the Bible in the hands of Protestants.[12] Gothic would provide a symbol of regeneration and integration in society and architecture, and would be appropriate not only as a national English style, but as an indicator of the Catholic Revival itself. Gothic was a much more suitable style for the times than Classicism: Classical buildings put the elevations first, but in Gothic buildings the elevations were dependent upon and subservient to the plan. Gothic was more appropriate for public and secular buildings than Classical styles because it was more English, whereas Classical architecture was imported.

Pugin argued that, as most of the institutions of the country were essentially medieval, from the monarchy downwards, the Gothic Revival was appropriate for religious, governmental, climatic and social needs. While England was no longer the same England as it had been in the fifteenth century, Pugin and some of the great Catholic families yearned to bring the country back to that period, at least in terms of the universal religion.

Fig 2 'Catholic town in 1440' (above) showing the walled town, the fine array of church towers and spires, the great abbey in its own enclosure, the chapel on the bridge and the cross at the entrance to the bridge. The same town in 1840 (below) shows a marked change. The walls have gone, and have been replaced by warehouses. Many churches have been demolished, while spires, pinnacles and other embellishments have been cut down or are in a sorry state of repair. The abbey is in ruins. Instead of the medieval bridge with cutwaters and chapel there is an iron bridge and a toll-gate with lodges for the keepers, while the cross has been replaced by a column with a ball on top. Factory chimneys, pottery kilns and warehouses dominate the skyline instead of the church spires. A timber-framed inn has been replaced by the gas-works, while in the foreground is the new gaol built on the octagonal and geometrical principles of the hated utilitarian Benthamites and their fearsome *Panopticon,* with its cruel atheistic associations. Instead of the *sancte*-bell cote on the church on the right, two iron vents pierce the ridge. (*From Pugin's* Contrasts)

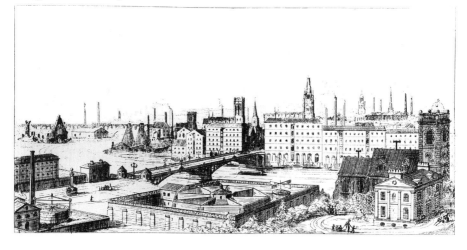

In his compositions for the Grange and St Augustine's at Ramsgate of 1843–52, St John's Hospital and Priest's House at Alton in Staffordshire, and the Castle at Alton (both 1840s), Pugin created buildings that were robust, 'true Picturesque' (rather than sham), and expressive of their function in the sum of their individual parts. Here utility was decorated, and the buildings were treated in a natural way, based on medieval precedent, without disguise or concealment. Pugin's insistence on a moral content in architecture and his claims that any building treated 'naturally' would look well provided nothing was hidden were potentially dangerous, for similar arguments have been used to justify some of the worst architectural travesties of recent times. When 'moral' values superseded 'visual and associative values'[13] ideas of beauty, context and charm went overboard, and notions of what was or was not 'true' became paramount.

As a designer Pugin's remarkable and rich details (including the interiors) of the Palace of Westminster, carried out with Barry from 1836, are among his finest work, but, although he built several places of worship for the Roman Church, very few of his designs were realised as he intended, partly because of lack of enthusiasm for the zeal (even fanaticism) Pugin brought to his arguments, and partly because Pugin's favoured style, Gothic architecture of the Decorated or Middle Pointed style (i.e. of the fourteenth century), was expensive to realise properly. The Palace of Westminster was Perpendicular, or Third Pointed, and by the 1840s this style was being regarded as too late, too decadent, and too near the beginnings of the hated Renaissance styles (and even associated with the Reformation and the Tudor split with Rome). St Marie's, Derby, and St Alban's, Macclesfield, are both early (1837–8) Pugin churches in the Perpendicular style, with western towers, large windows, Third-Pointed tracery, and small chancels compared with later developments. Pugin used Decorated tracery at St Chad's Cathedral in Birmingham (1839–46), the first Roman Catholic cathedral to be built in England since the Middle Ages, but the perforated brick walls, high roofs, and northern European appearance of the twin spires owe more to Continental Gothic. Inside (*Plate 4*), however, the glowing glass, richly gilded Decorated chancel screen, and other features, gave St Chad's a distinctively English flavour; it is appalling that this important landmark of the Gothic Revival had its interior ruthlessly mutilated in the 1960s, even to the removal of the lovely screen.

Perhaps only at St Giles's, Cheadle, Staffordshire, of 1841–7, did Pugin achieve a perfect and scholarly version of an early Decorated parish church, wondrously coloured inside, and embellished with details culled from England as well as from the Continent. The painted interior was inspired by Viollet-le-Duc's work at Sainte-Chapelle in Paris, and the whole ensemble was largely paid for by Lord Shrewsbury, Pugin's rich, aristocratic, Roman Catholic client, for whom Pugin had built Alton Castle and Hospital. At St Giles's, Cheadle, the creative genius and scholarship of the man blaze to delight us today (*Plate 5*), but much of his work, even his own once-wonderful St Augustine's (*Fig 3*) at Ramsgate (1845–50), has been altered in accordance with liturgical changes required by the Vatican. St Giles's soars, assures by its solidity, its beautiful proportions, and its attention to correct Gothic detailing of the fourteenth century. Even the enchanting *sancte*-bell cote is scholarly in its Second-Pointed form.

However, Pugin did not eschew First Pointed, or Early English Gothic. Early First Pointed, or the Lancet style, did not require tracery, so it was regarded as primitive, and it was much cheaper than Middle or Third Pointed. It was therefore a style suitable for remote and poor areas, like parts of Ireland, or where funds were very tight. Pugin used Early English Gothic at St Wilfred's Church, Hulme, of 1839–42, at the cathedrals of Nottingham (1841) and Killarney (1842), and at Mount St Bernard Abbey in Leicestershire, founded in 1835 for a community of Cistercian monks by Ambrose Lisle March Phillipps (later de Lisle) (1809–78), a Cambridge man who had been converted to Roman Catholicism, and who was an enthusiast for Roman Catholic art on the Continent. Phillipps received help from his friend the Earl of Shrewsbury, and Pugin gave his services free to produce a very severe group of buildings in the First Pointed style constructed of the local intractable Charnwood rock. This was the first abbey built in England since the Reformation (*Plate 6*).

The Ecclesiologists

Pugin's dreams of making a new Roman Catholic England, centred on the Church, and symbolised by Gothic architecture, were not realised, or were only realised in small pockets. The surprising thing about Pugin was that his influence lay far beyond his own Church, and struck all sorts of responsive chords among Anglicans: Pugin was the decisive influence on many Anglican Goths. The Ecclesiologists took up Pugin's ideas, and soon Middle-Pointed Anglican churches, complete with screens, sedilia, and all the marvellous details of Decorated Gothic, were being built by High Churchmen. The Gothic Revival was a visible expression of the revival of sacramentalism, and an affirmation of the continuity of the Catholic tradition within the Church of England. Middle Pointed was the approved liturgical and functional style for the Ecclesiologists: it was not only applied to new buildings, but also imposed upon genuine medieval churches that often lost their

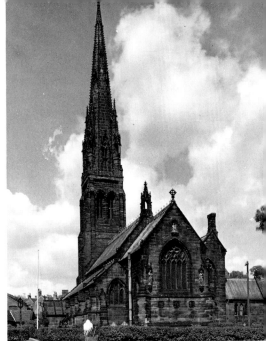

Plate 4 The interior of St Chad's Roman Catholic Cathedral in Birmingham showing the chancel screen with Pugin's Rood before mutilation in recent years. (*RCHME No A42/170*)

Plate 5 The Roman Catholic church of St Giles, Cheadle, Staffordshire, a superlative essay in Second-Pointed Gothic of 1841–7 by A. W. N. Pugin. Note the assured proportions of the tower and spire, *sancte*-bell cote over the chancel arch, and Decorated tracery in the windows. (*RCHME No AA56/8125*)

Perpendicular and Early English fabric to an invasion of Victorian Decorated. In this respect the achievements of the Ecclesiologists were phenomenal: by 1873 the battle seemed won, for about a third of all parish churches had been restored, while between the accession of William IV and the death of Prince Albert in 1861 about 1,500 new churches had been built in England.

The tyranny exercised by the Ecclesiologists was astounding: woe betide any architect who had the temerity to offend them! During the 1840s, when English Middle Pointed Gothic was *de rigueur*, the dominant theme of the Gothic Revival was that of copying bits of real medieval buildings. On the grounds that architects had to learn the alphabet, the grammar, and the basics of Gothic before original compositions could be achieved, the Ecclesiologists selected various buildings, or parts of buildings, that were regarded as worthy of emulation. St John's Roman Catholic Cathedral at Salford (1844–48) by M. E. Hadfield (1812–85) and J. G. Weightman (1801–72), for

41

Fig 3 Church of St Augustine, Ramsgate, by Pugin, another essay in Second-Pointed Gothic.

Plate 6 Mount St Bernard Abbey in Leicestershire, founded in 1835, an essay in First-Pointed or Early-English Gothic of the thirteenth century by Pugin. Here Pugin composed his buildings in the 'true Picturesque' style, in which the three-dimensional forms grew naturally from the plan. (*JSC*)

example (*Fig 4*, was agreeably eclectic, with a tower and spire based on St Mary's at Newark, the nave modelled on Howden, and the choir on Selby Abbey.[14] Salford attracted approving noises, while Benjamin Ferrey's (1810–80) Anglican Church of St Stephen, Rochester Row, Westminster, of 1846–50, was an early example of a Decorated building of the Gothic Revival to receive the imprimatur of the critics (*Fig 5*). Ferrey's fine church of St Mary at Chetwynde in Shropshire, of 1865, was admired for its scholarly allusions to the Early English or First-Pointed style of Gothic (*Fig 6*). Richard Cromwell Carpenter's (1812–55) churches of St Paul, Brighton (1846–8), and St Mary Magdalene, Munster Square (*Plate 7*), London (1849–52), were respectable Middle-Pointed Gothic Revival in style, and indeed *The*

Fig 4 Roman Catholic Cathedral of St John at Salford (1844–8) by Hadfield and Weightman, an eclectic work of the Gothic Revival with tower and spire based on St Mary's at Newark, the nave modelled on Howden and the choir on Selby Abbey.

Fig 5 Church of St Stephen, Rochester Row, Westminster (1846–50), by Benjamin Ferrey, a Second-Pointed work of the Gothic Revival. Its hardness, sharp details and smooth surfaces anticipate later interiors by Butterfield and others.

Ecclesiologist had its approved architects who were considered to be capable of designing churches in accordance with rules, principles and laws of something regarded as an exact science. Carpenter also designed in 1848 the remarkable group of buildings that comprise the College of St Nicholas at Lancing in Sussex: the college was begun in 1854 in the Geometrical-Pointed style of Gothic, and the chapel in 1868 (completed in 1978). The school buildings are by Carpenter, Slater and Ayrton, but the chapel was modified to designs by Richard Herbert Carpenter (1841–93), completed by Stephen Dykes-Bower. In terms of style, Continental influences were very strong by the time the chapel started on site, so the overall flavour is French Gothic of the thirteenth century, accentuated by the soaring vaulted interior and apsidal east end. Lancing comes very near the Puginian ideal, although it was an Anglican foundation (*Fig 7*).

Carpenter, Ferrey, and a few other Goths were smiled on by the Ecclesiologists, but architects who did not come up to scratch (including Barry and Blore) were denounced. Thus, during the first decade of Victoria's reign, the Ecclesiologists had achieved a consistency of style, form, and method, although the Evangelicals abhorred what appeared to be a headlong rush to build Anglican churches in the style of Papist Mass-Houses, while Roman Catholic commentators dismissed Anglican ecclesiology as an empty and fraudulent pageant, without any inner reality. It would be no exaggeration to state that controversy was bitter. When Newman seceded to Rome in 1845 the Ecclesiologists began to protest their distance from Rome, even to the extent of criticising Pugin, the man who had done so much for the Gothic Revival, and who was the acknowledged master of a new generation of Goths, including Burges and George Gilbert Scott. The early history of the revival of Gothic architecture was fraught with controversy, and Rome loomed ever, and apparently menacingly, over much debate at the time.

Rather than relying on criticism of work by various architects to improve standards the Ecclesiological Society determined to build an exemplar of all it held dear: this would be a model church which, in its design and detail, would fulfil the requirements of orthodox ritual

Plate 7 The church of St Mary Magdalene, Munster Square, London, of 1849–52 by Richard Cromwell Carpenter (1812–55), an example of a Middle-Pointed (Decorated) Gothic Revival church built of Kentish ragstone, a material more suited to rural than urban surroundings. It was a reaction against such materials that led architects to explore the possibility of using hard impervious materials that would stand up to the rigours of the nineteenth-century city climate. (*GLPL F 268 53[90] St Mar*)

Fig 6 Benjamin Ferrey's church of St Mary, Chetwynde, Shropshire: a competent essay in the Early-English or First-Pointed style of Gothic, using a broach spire based on Rutland precedents, geometrical tracery in some of the windows, and lancets.

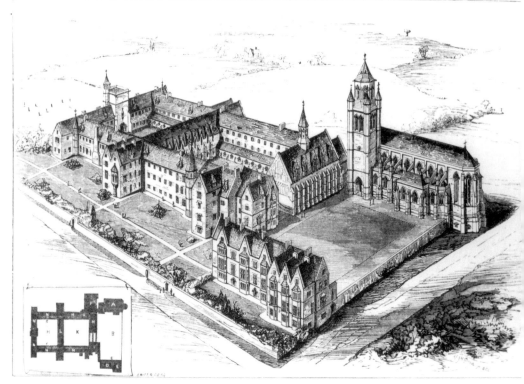

Fig 7 College of St Nicholas at Lancing, Sussex designed by R. C. Carpenter in 1848 and started on site in 1854. An Anglican college in which Puginian principles of Gothic design were observed. Here was the 'true Picturesque' manner in which the forms grew naturally from the plan.

as well as those of architectural beauty. It would also set ·standards for all Anglican churches of the future. Architectural and ecclesiological control would be vested in the Society, whose executive was Alexander James Beresford Hope (later Beresford-Hope) (1820–87), the son of Thomas Hope and Louisa Beresford. William Butterfield (1814–1900) was selected as the architect, and a confined site in Margaret Street, Westminster, was purchased. From 1849–59 rose the extraordinary

Plate 8 View from the south-east of the church, vicarage and school of All Saints', Margaret Street, London, of 1849–59 by William Butterfield (1814–1900). The Ecclesiologists' Model Church, of polychrome brickwork, it should be compared with Carpenter's St Mary Magdalene (*Plate 7*). With this ensemble Butterfield achieved a 'true Picturesque' composition in which his three-dimensional forms responded to the plan and the site. (*RCHME No BB65/4481*)

46

church, vicarage, and school of All Saints', Margaret Street (*Plate 8*). These buildings were very different from those of the previous generation of Gothic-Revival ecclesiastical buildings, for they were essentially urban in character, of polychrome brickwork, and considerably influenced by Continental Gothic precedents. The hard, shiny, exact and multi-coloured work of architects such as Butterfield must be seen against the muted architectural background of the context into which their buildings were slotted. During the 1850s Beresford Hope had played a very considerable part in moving Ecclesiologists away from a rigid insistence on English Middle Pointed towards early-Gothic precedents on the Continent. It began to be seen that the opinions and attitudes that held styles to be like plants, growing to perfection and then decaying, were absurd. Middle Pointed, which once was seen as Gothic Perfection, fell from favour, and a tougher, more authentic, and chronologically earlier prototype was sought. (A similar exploration backwards into time occurred with the Neoclassical movement: first Rome, then Greece, then the search for simplicity and the stereometric pure form, and finally Egypt were used from which to take precedents). Eventually the Gothic Revival was to seek its precedents in the massive architecture of early Burgundian First Pointed, as with the churches of James Brooks (1825–1901), and churches became more fortress-like as a result: bastions of faith in a sea of vice and squalor.

Before All Saints', Margaret Street, the search for a modern style suitable for the grimy atmosphere of a contemporary town had begun. George Edmund Street (1824–81) argued that a town church should have high, smooth walls of coloured bands, with panels: windows would be high and large to let as much light in as possible without inviting vandalism, while towers were to be set back from the line of the street, and a piling together of motifs, like those of a Continental town church, was to be sought.[15] Town churches, like those designed by Cundy and Carpenter in the 1840s, were usually of stone, such as Kentish rag, which is essentially a country material, looking very odd in the context of London (*Plate 7*). In 1848 Benjamin Webb of the Cambridge Camden Society wrote with enthusiasm about the brick churches of Venice,[16] while *The Ecclesiologist* had begun appreciations of Italian Gothic architecture as early as 1846.[17] By 1851 it was opined that new forms and materials suitable for the urban environment were indispensable for future developments,[18] and, as George L. Hersey has pointed out, the illustrations of buildings such as Benjamin Ferrey's St Stephen, Westminster, of 1845–7 in *The Builder* of 1850 gave an impression of hard, sharp details and surfaces that anticipate the interiors of churches by Butterfield and Street. Hersey also likens the arrival of All Saints' in the context of the muted tones of early-Victorian

London to that of a 'Congo chieftain' appearing in a performance of *Les Sylphides*. It is an apposite comparison.[19]

John Ruskin

George Gilbert Scott (1811–78) recognised the importance of Pugin and of John Ruskin (1819–1900) as influences on English architecture.[20] Both, however, were bigots: Pugin was anti-Protestant as only a convert can be, while Ruskin was obsessionally anti-Papist. Ruskin is associated with 'Ruskinian Gothic',[21] which seems to be a term associated with structural polychromy (colour in the material rather than applied), naturalistic sculpture and Italian Gothic, but Ruskin's *Seven Lamps of Architecture* only appeared in 1849, the year in which All Saints', Margaret Street, was commenced on site, so it appears 'Ruskinian influences' were coincident with changes of taste that were occurring already. His seven lamps were those of Sacrifice, Truth, Power, Beauty, Life, Memory and Obedience, and reflect Ruskin's concern for ornament, surface, qualities of light and colour, in which he discerned human emotions, joys and skills of the creative craftsman. He praised Continental Gothic, contrasting it with what he felt was the mean-spirited architecture of England: in fact, English medieval work did not escape his denunciations, for he saw much English Gothic as thin, wasted and insubstantial even since the thirteenth century. In Italian Gothic, colour and pattern, to Ruskin, were infinitely superior to English work, and it was this insistence that helped to contribute to a climate in which rich textures, strong modelling, and even violent colour were introduced to English Gothic Revival architecture in the High Victorian period. The fact that the colour in Italy is often of inlaid marbles set in smooth surfaces helps to explain much about post-Ruskinian 'structural polychromy', and indeed about the pronounced Italian influences that entered Gothic-Revival buildings from the 1850s.

In *The Stones of Venice* of 1851–3 Ruskin also advocated the emphasis of the various courses of masonry by means of differently coloured layers of stone (again structural polychromy) which he said was analogous to the principles of geological beds, and he advised against interrupting the purity of this horizontal-layered effect by means of vertical elements such as pilasters. Ruskin agreed that a new style was not needed, but that an appropriate style should be accepted that would eventually give birth to a universally acceptable new style. In *The Stones of Venice* Ruskin praised Italian more highly than French Gothic, because it seemed to be strongly constructed, simple in its massing, but infinite in its variety: by the late 1850s he was enthusing about Chartres and Nôtre Dame in Paris. Nevertheless, Ruskin and Venetian Gothic became firmly linked in the public imagination, and

Ruskin's name was invoked (not least by himself) as the imprimatur for a type of polychrome Gothic loosely based on eclectic motifs from Italy.

Many architects borrowed elements from the illustrations in Ruskin's works, and there are several outstanding examples of Gothic-Revival buildings with a pronounced Italian Gothic flavour, like E. W. Godwin's (1833–86) Town Hall in Northampton of 1861–4, George Somers Leigh Clarke's (1825–82) General Credit and Discount Company offices at 7 Lothbury, City of London, of 1866–8, and the same architect's Merchant Seamen's Orphan Asylum at Wanstead of 1861. Lanyon, Lynn and Lanyon's warehouse for Richardson Sons and Owden (*Plate 9*) in Donegall Square North, Belfast (1867–9), is a splendid design in Venetian-Florentine Gothic with roundels on the spandrels of the first and second floors. The corners of the building have naturalistic carved capitals, the foliage of which grows into the wall, a definite Ruskinian touch. Before damage in the air-raids of 1941, the tall roof had Gothic dormers with hipped roofs. Lanyon, Lynn and Lanyon were also responsible for the Clarence Place Hall, May Street, Belfast, originally a hall for the Church of Ireland (Anglican) Young Men's Society, a marvellous essay in polychrome (red, white and blue) brickwork, with stone dressings, of 1865–6: this superb building in the Italian Gothic style was probably influenced by the writings of Ruskin and of G. E. Street (*Plate 10*).

W. H. Lynn (1829–1915) developed remarkable skills in evoking Italian flavours in his Gothic architecture: his Town Hall at Chester of 1864–9 is particularly successful, but his charming little Venetian Gothic buildings for the Belfast Banking Company at Dungannon (1855) and Newtownards (*Plate 11*) are particularly felicitous. A variant of the Lombardo-Venetian style was used at Elmwood Presbyterian church, Belfast, by John Corry, of 1859–62, a remarkably rich design in which Romanesque and Gothic elements merge, but the inspiration is again Ruskinian (*Plate 12*). Lanyon and Lynn's Sinclair Seamen's church, Corporation Square, Belfast, of 1856–7, is another distinguished building in the Lombardo-Venetian style of Italian Gothic much influenced by the writings of John Ruskin, and certainly one of the best examples of the style (*Plate 13*).

More famous than the Ulster examples is the University Museum at Oxford of 1854–60 by Sir Thomas Deane (1792–1871) and Benjamin Woodward (1815–61) (*Fig 8*). The Oxford building mixes elements from northern Italy, Flanders and England, but the overall effect is Italian. More interesting, perhaps, is the internal arrangement of the Museum. Eastlake, in his *History of the Gothic Revival*, stated that the architects had endeavoured to realise beauty in their art not by literally

Plate 9 The former warehouse of Richardson Sons and Owden in Belfast of 1867–9 by Lanyon, Lynn and Lanyon, a fine example of Gothic Revival with a pronounced Italian flavour, probably influenced by the writings of Ruskin. (*JSC*)

Plate 10 Clarence Place Hall, May Street, Belfast, of 1865–6, by Lanyon, Lynn and Lanyon in the Italian Gothic style, and faced in polychrome brickwork with stone dressings. (*JSC*)

reproducing the decorative features of medieval work, but by investing with the spirit of the Middle Ages the skills of Victorian workmanship and the materials of the 1850s. The large quadrangle (*Plate 14*) had to be roofed with glass and iron, and the main difficulty was to accomplish this 'without limiting the design to the merely structural features of the Crystal Palace or condescending to the vulgar details of a railway terminus. Under these circumstances Messrs Deane and Woodward did their best to Gothicise their ironwork . . .'. The capitals were formed of beaten metal which was attached to the cast-iron columns, and so attracted criticism. Eastlake felt that the 'ornaments of leaves and flowers, however excellent in themselves, are mere additions having no sort of relation to the constructive feature which they adorn and claiming a raison d'être of scarcely higher pretensions than the plaster enrichments of a brick cornice. They appear unnecessary, not because they are simply decorative (a reason which would condemn half the old forms of ornamental iron-work), but because they are confessedly *applied* decorations to a feature whose very form is regulated by practical considerations'.

The whole effect of the court is stunning, skeletal, and extraordinary: the building could never be confused with medieval work. Around the court are two storeys of Gothic arcaded cloisters, the voussoirs of which are formed of alternate dark and light stones. The naturalistic carved capitals are exquisite and accurate, and are all different, while the shafts of the arcades on the first floor are all different samples of various kinds of hard stone, polished and labelled for educational purposes: the building itself was therefore intended as instructive, not

Plate 11 The former Belfast Banking Company's offices at Newtownards, County Down, in Venetian Gothic style, by W. H. Lynn. (*JSC*)

Plate 12 Elmwood Presbyterian church, Belfast, by John Corry, of 1859–62. A mixture of Lombardic and Venetian Romanesque and Gothic influences. (*JSC*)
Plate 13 Sinclair Seamen's Presbyterian church, Corporation Square, Belfast, by Lanyon and Lynn, of 1856–7, a remarkable essay in Lombardic Italian Gothic, much influenced by the writings of John Ruskin. (*JSC*)

only in terms of its artistic qualities, but also to demonstrate the colour and source of a great number of hard marbles, granites, and other stones. Indeed, the carved capitals above the labelled shafts also represent plants associated with the geographical areas from which the coloured shafts came, and were thus educational too.

Alfred Waterhouse's (1830–1905) Assize Courts in Manchester of 1859 mixed motifs from the medieval civic buildings of Flanders with elements from Italy (*Fig 9*). In this, Waterhouse was doing what Ruskin recommended in his *Stones of Venice*, namely a mingling of Middle Pointed from northern Europe with details from northern Italy. Both the University Museum in Oxford and the Assize Courts in Manchester were hailed by critics as fine secular modern buildings soon after they were built.

Fig 8 The University Museum, Oxford, 1854–60, by Deane and Woodward, mixing Gothic elements from Italy, Flanders and England.
Plate 14 Interior of University Museum, Oxford, showing the iron-and-glass structure. (*Rodney Roach*)

Fig 9 Entrance to the Assize Courts, Manchester, of 1859, by Waterhouse. An eclectic building incorporating Gothic from Flanders and Italy.

Ruskin emphasised the virtues of strong construction, fitness for purpose, and nobility of sculpture and decoration. He stated that delight in ornament and delight in structure or use were two very different things, for the most beautiful objects in the world, like peacocks and lilies, were also the most useless. The architect, he noted, is not bound to exhibit structure, and declared the argument that ornamentation should be decorated structure to be false. Ornament is simply ornamental, for architectural enrichment can be of any variety if it does not obscure utility or the idea of use. As a critic, Ruskin strayed into strange territory, for he took up a position as a moral censor: good architecture could be produced only if the designer were in a state of Grace, while bad architecture suggested Original Sin. Classical architecture was immoral and corrupt, and the social and intellectual climates of Victorian England were the sources of architectural confusion.

With Ruskin, the high moral tone, censorious denunciations of style, and absurd stances of 'approved' motifs culled from 'respectable' localities or periods, became even more shrill than under Pugin. Yet High Victorian Gothic was the climax of the Sublime, and it is associated with the hard, gritty, polychrome buildings of the 1850s and 60s, and with the period when Ruskin held sway as an arbiter of taste.

To the critics of the 1850s, All Saints', Margaret Street, seemed to be the ideal town church, free from the tyranny of antiquarian precedent (*Plates 8 and 15*). 'Passers-by gazed at the iron-work of the entrance gateway, at the gables and dormers of the parsonage, at the black brick voussoirs and stringcourses, and asked what manner of architecture this might be, which was neither Early English, Decorated, nor Tudor, and which could be properly referred to no century except the nineteenth.'[22] Butterfield's building was an attempt to create 'not a new style, but a development of previous styles; to carry the enrichment of ecclesiastical Gothic to an extent which even in the Middle Ages had been rare in England; to add the colour of natural material to pictorial decoration; to let marbles and mosaic take the place of stone and plaster; to adorn the walls with surface ornament of an enduring kind; to spare, in short, neither skill, nor pains, nor cost in making this church the model church of its day – such a building as should take a notable position in the history of modern architecture'.[23]

Butterfield was to develop a hard, even violent and strident architecture while remaining an unrepentant Goth. His work has a strong individual character, robust and uncompromising in its expression. At Millport, Greater Cumbrae, in the Firth of Clyde, he designed a spectacularly successful group of buildings. George Frederick Boyle, future sixth Earl of Glasgow (1825–90), had been Secretary of the Oxford Society for Promoting the Study of Gothic Architecture: like many of his generation, Boyle was deeply influenced by the Tractarians, and he returned to Scotland to build a Tractarian College on Cumbrae, encouraged by Lord Forbes of Medwyn, with whom he had founded the new Cathedral at Perth, the first Scottish cathedral built since the Reformation. It was the success of the secular college and theological seminary at Glenalmond, founded by W. E. Gladstone's father, that prompted Boyle to build his venture on Cumbrae. Such zeal might well be compared with the parallel development of colonial cathedral-building with which William Butterfield, Boyle's architect for the Millport College, was involved. The College of the Holy Spirit was founded in 1849 for the 'frequent celebration of Divine Service by a Collegiate Body under circumstances favourable to religious learning'. The siting is a triumph, and the 'true Picturesque' quality of the buildings is at once obvious (*Plate 16*). The eye is held by the tall tower and pyramidal spire, but there are three buildings in the asymmetrical composition: the chapel, the choristers' house to the north, and the canons' house to the south, each offering a contrast to its neighbours.

Plate 15 Interior view of All Saint's church, Margaret Street, London, showing the hard polychrome materials. (*RCHME No AA78/327*)

Plate 16 The College of the Holy Spirit and Cathedral of the Isles at Millport, Greater Cumbrae, by William Butterfield, of 1849–51, demonstrating 'true Picturesque' composition based on the grouping of forms and on the function of the plan, as opposed to the false Picturesqueness as shown in Plate 3. (*JSC*)
Fig 10 Church of St Alban, Holborn, of 1859–62 by William Butterfield. Hard, polychrome Gothic, influenced partly by the brick Gothic architecture of Northern Europe.

Characteristic Butterfieldian motifs of hipped dormers, chimneys, elongated windows, and hipped gables are composed in an irregular but tightly controlled ensemble.

Butterfield's oeuvre was vast, and only a few examples can be included here. The church of St Alban, Holborn of 1859–62 (*Fig 10*) aimed at 'originality not only in the form but in the relative proportion of parts', as Eastlake put it: much 'structural polychromy', diaper-work and other stridently colourful effects were employed. Other unmistakable Butterfield churches are the tall violently polychrome church of St Augustine, Queen's Gate, London of 1870–7, with its double bellcote at the west end; the church of St Mark, Dundela, Belfast of 1875–8, with its massive rectangular tower capped by a tall hipped roof; All Saints', Babbacombe (1865–74); Keble College, Oxford, of 1867–83 (the

58

chapel of which is an astounding *tour-de-force* of strident angularity, chequered, lozenge and stripey polychromy, and massive vertical thrusting buttresses); and Rugby School chapel (completed in 1872), one of Butterfield's finest compositions, the climax of which is the massive tower with octagonal belfry stage and huge gargoyles (*Plate 17*). All Saint's church, Margaret Street, London, however, remains Butterfield's undisputed masterpiece (*Plates 8 and 15*): there can be no question that the masterly handling of such a volume of buildings on a confined and almost square urban site, together with the startling polychrome brick of the exterior and the harsh, shining, machine-like quality of the interior, show Butterfield as a virtuoso of the Sublime. Here is no quaint, romantic reordering of the rural parish church: All Saints' is a bastion of the revived faith, expressed in Victorian Gothic using hard, modern, unrural materials, with an ingenious use of reinterpreted motifs from many sources.

Plate 17 Rugby school chapel of 1872 with pronounced polychrome brickwork by Butterfield. (*JSC*)

Butterfield, then, was a master of High Victorian Gothic, using materials with honesty of expression, glorying in harsh structural polychrome effects, expressing the plan in the three-dimensional forms, and thus obeying Pugin's call to build in the 'true Picturesque' manner. Butterfield also built many houses, some of which are humble cottages, but they are all planned for convenience, and features such as chimneys and windows are where they are needed. His grander houses include Milton Ernest Hall in Bedfordshire, built for Benjamin Starey between 1853 and 1856: it is a large house of stone enlivened with red brick, and has typical chimneys, the vertical accents of which are enhanced by the dressings. Windows are of the sash type and have glazing-bars, looking forward to the full expression of sashes in later work of the Domestic Revival, while there is a tall canted bay rising above the eaves level and capped with a timber-framed gable of startling boldness, again anticipating, perhaps, the gables of Shaw's Cragside and other examples later in the century. Gables have canted hips, and, set against the steeply pitched roof, have a pronounced Continental and unEnglish air. The whole effect is bold, uncompromising, stark and assured (*Plate 18*). Another instance where sash-windows were employed, this time in a building freely composed of French and Italian Gothic elements, and with much structural polychromy, can be found at Eatington Park, Warwickshire, designed by J. Prichard for E. P. Shirley in 1858 (*Fig 11*).

Yet even before Butterfield's All Saints', Margaret Street, had been consecrated, a further change of taste had occurred, reflecting growing concern with Continental Gothic, and producing an even tougher, more primitive type of architecture.

E.-E. Viollet-le-Duc

In 1854 the first volume of Eugène-Emmanuel Viollet-le-Duc's great *Dictionnaire Raisonné de L'Architecture Française du XIe au XVIe Siècle*[24] was published from which date the French architect became an important arbiter of the Gothic Revival with his championing of the architecture of medieval France. Viollet-le-Duc was supremely rational and Gallic compared with the intemperate emotionalism of Ruskin: the

Plate 18 Milton Ernest Hall, Bedfordshire, of 1853–6, by William Butterfield, an example of his uncompromising style. Elements of the design look forward to the work of Philip Webb at Clouds and of Norman Shaw at Cragside, while the sash-windows are perhaps pre-echoes of the 'Queen-Anne' style. The building also expresses different functions in its fenestration and so complies with Pugin's 'true Picturesque' requirements. (*RCHME No AA78/6827*)

Fig 11 Eatington Park, Warwickshire, by J. Prichard. Polychrome French and Italian Gothic.

Frenchman emphasised the importance of structure, purpose, dynamics, techniques, and the expression of these. However, it is probable that British architects learned from Viollet's illustrations rather than his rationalist theories, for it has long been the case (and still is) that architects copy the pictures, images and design motifs, without bothering to read the text. William Burges (1827–81) said as much.[25]

It was clear that reaction to the strong polychrome surfaces and aesthetic of 'Ruskinian Gothic' set in with the 1860s, and the models for a purer, more real, primitive and truthful Gothic were early French buildings. The monochrome, tough, primitive, even rough early French Gothic seemed to offer architects like Burges an escape from what were seen as difficulties. Stern French exemplars, such as those of Laon, seemed more vigorous, less effete, then the luxuriant Middle Pointed so beloved by the Ecclesiologists. Tough French First Pointed, with its massiveness, grandeur of scale and complete lack of frivolous frippery, was seen as more appropriate to the needs of designers of urban churches in the cities of the 1860s. The immense engineering works, machinery, ships and railways of Victorian England needed a style to match that was bold, broad, strong, stern, masculine and uncompromisingly tough: that style was early French Gothic.[26]

Waterhouse's Manchester Town Hall of 1868–76 (*Plate 19*) is a mixture of English and French First Pointed, but it is far more than that: it is a building that is of its period, a High-Victorian Gothic secular masterpiece that combines eclectic elements to form a style that can only be Victorian. The plan is beautifully related to the site, and the mass of the building grows from the plan in what appears to be an effortless way. Burges mixed many allusions to northern French Gothic at St Fin Barre's Cathedral (1866) in Cork. The same architect's muscular and uncompromising churches in Yorkshire, Christ the Consoler at Skelton (1871–2) and St Mary at Studley Royal (1872–8), are both in an early Gothic style, but almost over-heavy, and exceedingly rich in powerful ornament, vigorous sculpture and strong colouring.

Rich and heavy forms of early French Gothic, mixed with a wide range of decorative motifs, were realised by Burges at Cardiff Castle (1868–81) and Castell Coch (1876–81) for the Marquess of Bute (*Plate 20*), both buildings considerably influenced by the work of Viollet-le-Duc, especially his reconstructions of French medieval castles. An example of domestic architecture in which Continental Gothic is dominant, dating from 1857, is Quar Wood, Gloucestershire (*Fig 12*), by J. L. Pearson, who was to build many churches much influenced by his studies of French medieval architecture. Quar Wood, with its saddleback roof and open loggia of the tower, spirelet, and decorative ridges, is clearly derived from Burgundian prototypes, and the buildings at Beaune may be mentioned as sources. Eastlake speaks of the Gothic Revival as being retrogressive in regard to the chronological order of styles, moving backwards from Perpendicular through Decorated (Second Pointed) to Early English, then to Continental precedents, and searching for a primitive, early, 'pure' Gothic like that of the churches of Burgundy for inspiration.

George Edmund Street (1824–81) designed one of the last and greatest buildings of the Gothic Revival, the Law Courts in the The Strand of 1874–82, a wonderful eclectic mixture of architectural motifs culled from France, Italy and England. The striped exterior of part of the Carey Street elevation owes much to Italy, especially to Siena, while the marvellous series of vertical elements on The Strand frontage demonstrates not only the facility with which a great Victorian architect could mix French and English Gothic elements, but break up

Plate 19 Manchester Town Hall of 1868–76 by Alfred Waterhouse (1830–1905), a mixture of French and English First-Pointed Gothic adapted to secular building. (*JSC*)

Plate 20 Part of the interior of the chapel at Cardiff Castle of 1868–81 by William Burges (1827–81) showing that architect's hard, uncompromising use of early bold French Gothic. (*RCAHMW No AA56/8585*)

Fig 12 Quar Wood, Gloucestershire, by J. L. Pearson of 1857, a house much influenced by the medieval architecture of Burgundy.

the mass of what is a very big building by cunningly contrived changes in vertical and horizontal planes (*Plate 21*). Butterfield achieved a similar breakdown of an enormous mass of building at Keble College, Oxford of 1870–77, although he retained a harsh polychrome of brick and stone there, and an almost primary colour scheme in the chapel, while Street was far more restrained with his stone frontages to The Strand and the tough monochromes of the great hall of the Law Courts, probably the grandest secular room of the whole Gothic Revival (*Fig 13*). With the Law Courts Street seems to embrace both Ruskinian claims for Italian Gothic and Viollet-le-Duc's championing of early French medieval precedent. Street published his *Brick and Marble in the Middle Ages: Notes of a Tour in the North of Italy* in 1855, and his subsequent designs show pronounced Continental influences. His church of St James the Less at Westminster, for example, of 1859, mixes Continental and English Gothic (*Plate 22*), while SS Philip and James in North Oxford (1860–66) looks back to the thirteenth century, with a pronounced Burgundian flavour (*Fig 14*).

Eastlake identified Street's church of St James the Less as marking a revolt from a national style. 'Here the whole character of the building,' he asserted 'whether we regard its plan, its distinctive features, its external or internal decoration, is eminently un-English.' In particular Eastlake noted the semi-circular apse, plate-tracery, dormers inserted in the clerestory, the bold vigour of the nave arcade, and the 'chromatic decoration' of the roof. Street was respected by his contemporaries for his originality, but it was an originality 'secured by legitimate means', without recourse to 'that license which with the less accomplished designer' might result in 'extravagant proportions or *bizarrerie* of detail.' Eastlake praised the tower and spire of SS Philip and James (*Fig 14*), its natural colour, and the admirable restraint with which Street achieved his effects. Street's church of St John at Torquay of 1869 (*Fig 15*) is an admirable example of what Eastlake called his 'luxuriant fancy', with its structural polychromy, assured boldness, and toughness of detail.

Plate 21 The Strand frontage of G. E. Street's Royal Courts of Justice, London, of 1874–82, an eclectic mix of Gothic motifs culled from Italy, France and England. The vertical modelling cunningly breaks the frontage up, and disguises the mass of the building. (*RCHME No BB88/5488*)

Fig 13 The Great Hall of the Royal Courts of Justice in The Strand, London, by G. E. Street, in the First-Pointed style. One of the grandest secular rooms of the Gothic Revival. (*RCHME No BB71/1915*)

Plate 22 Interior of the church of St James the Less, Westminster, of 1859, by Street, showing the polychrome brickwork. (*RCHME No BB88/4066*)

Fig 14 Church of SS Philip and James, North Oxford, by G. E. Street, of 1860–66, an essay in thirteenth-century First-Pointed Gothic, with a pronounced Burgundian influence. Note the French apse with plate tracery and tough tower with broach spire and massive lucarnes.

Fig 15 G. E. Street's church of St John, Torquay, of 1869.

Yet Viollet had despaired that his own age would never leave an architecture of its own to posterity, but only pastiches and mixtures. Engineers who built railway-engines created impressive powerful machines that expressed power, energy and function: those engineers did not dress the locomotives up to resemble horse-drawn coaches. Style, therefore, was only appropriate to the object. Viollet perhaps forgot that the first railway-coaches looked like stage-coaches on smaller wheels (just as later the first automobiles tended to look rather like hybrid horse-drawn coaches before they developed styles of their own). To Viollet-le-Duc Gothic architecture was diagrammatic, dynamic and rational, and furthermore could express aspects of a secular society: in other words Gothic could be an architectural and structural system serving secular needs because it was rational. Gothic could be the beginning of a language that would be built on the dynamic aesthetics of medieval French architecture, but which would evolve beyond recognition into something new,[27] not based on images or on style, but on the logic of structure, the properties of materials and the function of the buildings.

George Gilbert Scott's (1811–78) distinguished architectural career clearly was influenced by Pugin, Ruskin, and Viollet-le-Duc. At first, his buildings were based on English models: the archaeologically respectable Martyrs' Memorial in Oxford, for example, of 1841–4, recalls English medieval crosses, especially the Eleanor Crosses, and, as Eastlake said, 'contributed in no small degree to establish his reputation as a Gothic architect' (*Plate 23*); and the church of St Giles at Camberwell, designed by him in 1841, was considered at the time to be of the purest English style and with the most orthodox arrangement of any early Revival ecclesiastical building. Gradually, however, Scott was to respond to influences from other countries, and his work became bolder, more eclectic, and often extraordinarily assured. His design for the church of St Nikolaus, Hamburg, of 1844–5 is a scholarly evocation of German Gothic, a style that appears in the spire of the University of Glasgow, Gilmorehill, added in 1887 by John Oldrid Scott (1841–1913) to his father's main building of 1866–70. The latter incorporates elements from Scottish, French, and Italian medieval architecture (*Plate 24*), as does the elder Scott's Albert Institute in Dundee, of 1865–7, with its crow-step gables and circular turrets. George Gilbert Scott's Midland Grand Hotel at St Pancras, London, of

Plate 24 The University of Glasgow, Gilmorehill, by George Gilbert Scott of 1866–70, showing how Scott introduced bartizans and a Scottish flavour to his Gothic. The spire in the German Gothic style was added by John Oldrid Scott in 1887. (*RCAHMS No GW/3153*)

Plate 23 The Martyrs' Memorial in Oxford, a Middle-Pointed essay by George Gilbert Scott of 1841–3. It was devised by a group of Churchmen to commemorate Cranmer, Latimer and Ridley who were burned at the stake in the reign of Queen Mary. The Memorial was thus a challenge to the High-Church party, but it served to cause many divines to question the Anglican position, and more secessions to Rome took place as a result. (*JSC*)

Plate 25 The Midland Grand Hotel at St Pancras Station, London, by George Gilbert Scott of 1868–74, incorporating polychromatic elements, English and French First-Pointed, Flemish motifs, and Venetian Gothic parts in one building of the Gothic Revival. The advantages of Gothic for asymmetrical compositions incorporating functional plans were apparent. (*GLPL No 67/ 7870 27.315 StPan*)

Plate 26 Kelham Hall, Nottinghamshire, another eclectic work by Scott showing how Gothic based on Italian, French and English exemplars could also be used for domestic architecture in a grand country house. Note the free fenestration and adherence to Pugin's 'true Picturesque' principles of composition. (*RCHME No A45/1074*)

1868–74 (*Plate 25*), is an extraordinary tour-de-force of eclectic Gothic treated with tremendous assurance: it is built of brick with stone dressings, and incorporates polychrome elements, English and French First Pointed, Flemish motifs and bits of Venetian Gothic, all in the one building. Pre-echoes of the Midland Grand can be found in the same architect's Kelham Hall, Nottinghamshire (1858–62) (*Plate 26*), a country mansion that responds to Pugin's demands for 'true Picturesque' methods of composition, and again quotes Continental Gothic (including several elements culled directly from Venetian prototypes), uses a hard polychrome scheme of elevational treatment, but employs English Decorated sculptural detail, perhaps in deference to the celebrated carvings in the Minster at Southwell, not far away.

With Scott's Albert Memorial (*Plate 27*) in London of 1863–72, High-Victorian Gothic reached its apogee. The canopy is in the Italian Gothic style of the thirteenth century, based on a combination of the superstructure of the Scaliger tombs in Verona and on other canopied features of Italian Gothic tombs, monuments and reliquaries: it is a *ciborium,* richly coloured, carried on polished granite piers (polished granite was used by Scott in several buildings, including Kelham Hall and the Midland Grand Hotel), so the colour is in the material used. Another precedent for the Albert Memorial, of course, was George Meikle Kemp's (1795–1844) Sir Walter Scott Memorial in Edinburgh, that huge Gothic shrine dominating Princes Street, which was actually designed in 1836, but completed in 1846, two years after the unfortunate Kemp, son of a Border shepherd, and a carpenter by trade, was found drowned in the Union Canal. Kemp's shrine has its precedents in the unrealised Gothic shrines designed by many early nineteenth-century architects, including Schinkel, but he introduced archaeologically correct eclectic themes, including parts of Melrose Abbey, the western towers of the Cathedral of Rheims, and the Cathedral of Antwerp. The Sir Walter Scott Memorial introduced a spectacular type of Gothic canopied memorial reminiscent of a medieval *cathedra,* or bishop's throne, to civic art: it was the precedent for Thomas Worthington's Albert Memorial in Manchester of 1862 (the year before G. G. Scott's design for the London Albert Memorial was accepted), a Gothic canopy in the Second Pointed style sheltering a statue by Noble. Scott's achievement was to introduce hard and ravishing polychrome in his free interpretation of Italian *ciborium,* reliquary and canopied tomb, judiciously mixed and forming the canopy over Foley's statue of the Prince.

Plate 27 The Albert Memorial, London, of 1863–72: George Gilbert Scott's High-Victorian Gothic monument with a pronounced Italian influence. (*GLPL No 70/10351 45. 5ALB*)

3 THE QUESTION OF STYLE II

**Introduction; Neoclassicism and the Egyptian Revival;
Tudor and Seventeenth-Century Revivals; Romanesque Revival;
The Italianate Style; The Scottish-Baronial Style;
The Rundbogenstil; Rogue Goths and the Later Gothic Revival;
The Domestic Revival, Vernacular Revival, Arts-and-Crafts
movement, 'Queen-Anne' Style and Renaissance Revival; Free
Eclecticism; The French Taste; The End of the Century and the
Classical Revival**

Style is the dress of thoughts
Lord Chesterfield, Letters, 24 November 1749

*Oratio certam regulam non habet; consuetudo illam civitatis,
quae numquam in eodem diu stetit, versat*
(Style has no fixed laws; it is altered by the usage of the citizens,
and is never the same for any length of time)
Seneca, Epistulae ad Lucilium, 114 13

Introduction
The Victorian era falls into three periods, each of which has a distinct
architectural flavour, and each of which lasted about two decades.
These might be described as the Early Victorian, High Victorian and
Late Victorian phases. However, several styles were used for building
at the same time, and although most of the polemics, high moral tone
and shrill dogma emanated from the Gothic camp, Classicism was
certainly not dead during the period when the Goths appeared to
triumph.

Neoclassicism and the Egyptian Revival
In the first decades of the nineteenth century, in spite of the
predominance of formal Neoclassical public buildings, variety began to
be sought, partly as a reaction against the dull severity of so many
Greek-Revival structures by Wilkins, Smirke and others. C. R. Cockerell
(1788–1863) was responsible for two of the most distinguished
Classical buildings of the early Victorian era, the Taylorian Institute and
the Ashmolean Museum in Oxford of 1839–45, in which Greek and
Roman elements are combined (*Plate 28*), and the Bank of England in

Liverpool of 1844–7, a powerful essay in Classicism that suggests strength, grandeur and security. Soane's pupil George Basevi (1794–1845) was responsible for the noble pile of the Fitzwilliam Museum in Cambridge of 1834–45 (*Plate 29*), an opulent exercise in Roman Corinthian, which Cockerell helped to complete, as he did St George's Hall in Liverpool of 1839–40 designed by Harvey Lonsdale Elmes (1814–47), and probably the finest Neoclassical public building in England (*Plates 30–31*). Classicism was the dominant architectural language of Newcastle-upon-Tyne as developed by John Dobson (1787–1865), of Edinburgh (where Thomas Hamilton [1784–1858] and William Henry Playfair [1790–1857] were the most important of the Classical architects of the period), of Glasgow (where Alexander 'Greek' Thomson [1817–75] developed themes of the Prussian Schinkel in his brilliant buildings), of Leeds (where Cuthbert Brodrick [1822–1905] created the extraordinary Town Hall [*Plate 32*] of 1853–8), of Halifax, and of other northern cities. It was Barry who produced the strangely eclectic Town Hall of Halifax of 1859–62, although the building was completed by Edward Middleton Barry (1830–80): it is an interesting mixture of Gothic silhouette (especially in the extra-

Plate 28 The Taylorian Institution and Ashmolean Museum, Oxford, of 1839–45, by C. R. Cockerell, in which the Greek Ionic Order from the Temple of Apollo Epicurius at Bassae is mixed with Roman and Italian Renaissance themes. On the left is part of G. G. Scott's Martyrs' Memorial. (*JSC*)

ordinary tower) and Renaissance themes derived from Venetian prototypes by Sansovino, from English Baroque and from French Renaissance precedents (*Plate 33*).

The Classical temple theme (also used by Hansom at Birmingham Town Hall of 1832) returned at Todmorden Town Hall, Yorkshire, designed by John Gibson (1817–92) and erected between 1860 and 1875: Todmorden has a podium on which the Roman temple of engaged columns rises (*Plate 34*). The fact that Classicism survived in the north was due partly to the association of the Gothic Revival with the High-Church and Roman Catholic parties in the south, and especially the geographical and other associations with Oxford, Cambridge and London. Scotland, with its Presbyterianism, and the north of England with its Dissenting connections, did not respond wholeheartedly to the blandishments of the Goths. Classicism survived throughout the period, although it went through various metamorphoses. William Wilkins's (1778–1839) National Gallery in Trafalgar Square and Sir Robert Smirke's (1781–1867) British Museum, two

Plate 29 George Basevi's Fitzwilliam Museum in Cambridge of 1834–45, an opulent exercise featuring the Roman Corinthian Order. This building shows how Victorian Classical architecture was tending to distance itself from the severity of Neoclassicism (as typified by Smirke's British Museum, Wilkins's National Gallery, or Playfair's Royal Scottish Academy), and become more showy and luxuriant (*RCHME No BB88/1866A*)

Plate 30 St George's Hall, Liverpool, from 1839, perhaps the finest Neoclassical public building in England. Designed by H. L. Elmes, it was partially completed under the direction of Cockerell and others. The overall effect of the exterior is temple-like, and this allusion to important buildings of Antiquity gives it a firm place in the Neoclassical pantheon. (*RCHME No CC73/2985*)

Plate 32 (above) Leeds Town Hall of 1853–8 by Cuthbert Brodrick. The showiness of this building, while using the Classical language of architecture, reflects the taste for opulence of the period, yet the Town Hall is not an essay in Neoclassicism, and is nothing like the temple forms of St George's Hall in Liverpool. It owes something to Brongniart's Bourse in Paris and to Tite's Royal Exchange in the City of London, while the urns that crown the balustrades recall the work of Sir Charles Barry at his most exuberant. The building is an eclectic interpretation of nineteenth-century French precedent (Brongniart) mixed with themes from Barry's *palazzoesque* designs, and with a mausoleum-like tower capped by a Baroque domed form that recalls the work of Thomas Archer at Birmingham. (*JSC*)

Plate 31 (left) Interior of St George's Hall, Liverpool, showing the pronounced Roman influence based on the Imperial Baths of Caracalla. In spite of its allusions to Antiquity, the interior is much more showy and luxurious than the severity of the exterior, and signals the beginnings of a Victorian taste for greater richness and opulence than anything the sparse and refined language of purist Neoclassicism could offer. (*RCHME No BB/2849*)

Plate 33 Halifax Town Hall of 1859–62, by Sir Charles Barry and E. M. Barry. A mixture of Gothic silhouette and eclectic detail from French Renaissance, English Baroque and Venetian precedents. (*JSC*)

Plate 34 Todmorden Town Hall of 1860–75, a Roman temple by John Gibson set in a northern town. (*JSC*)

important Greek-Revival buildings, were completed in the early years of Queen Victoria's reign, but with the work of Cockerell and others Classicism became richer and less aridly severe than during the fashion for the Greek Revival style.[1]

There was also a recurring interest in Egyptian architecture in the first part of Victoria's reign. Publications such as Denon's *Voyage dans la Basse et la haute Égypte . . .* (1802), coupled with Nelson's victory over Napoléon at the Battle of the Nile, had aroused considerable fervour for *Égyptiennerie* in the first decades of the century. Thomas Hope had encouraged a taste for Egyptian objects, and there had been some Egyptian Revival buildings, such as Foulston's Egyptian library at Devonport of 1823 (*Fig 1*). The Egyptian Temple Mills in Leeds of 1842 by Joseph Bonomi Jr (1796–1878) and James Combe was a scholarly work based on the Temples of Antaeopolis and Horus at Edfu (*Plate 35*). In Egypt flax was produced for linen, therefore a flax-mill in Leeds was in the Egyptian style partly as allusion and partly as advertisement. Egyptian elements recur in designs by Wightwick, in speculative housing in Islington, in the scholarly Egyptian Courts by Owen Jones

Plate 35 The Temple Mills in Leeds, an example of the Egyptian Revival by Joseph Bonomi Jr and James Combe of 1842. (*JSC*)

and Joseph Bonomi at the Crystal Palace at Sydenham, and in the remarkable Freemasons' Temple in Boston, Lincolnshire, of 1860–63. The full details of the Egyptian Revival can be found in the present author's *The Egyptian Revival* of 1982 and in Richard Carrott's book of the same title (1978).[2]

Tudor and Seventeenth-Century Revivals

During the reigns of George IV and William IV, and in the first decade of Queen Victoria's reign, the Goths did not have things all their own way. First of all there was a powerful continuity of Classicism in the hands of the leaders of the profession, but before Pugin's *Contrasts* and before the Palace of Westminster there were signs of the increasing interest in Elizabethan, and seventeenth-century styles, and even in Romanesque. Anthony Salvin (1799–1881) designed many houses in which Elizabethan, seventeenth-century and Tudor Gothic motifs were mixed with ideas of Picturesque composition and a scholarly attention to medieval domestic and military features.

Salvin's Peckforton Castle in Cheshire (1844–50) is a fine example of a revival of thirteenth-century castle architecture mixed with nineteenth-century planning (*Plate 36*), while the same architect's Scotney Castle in Kent (*Fig 16*) of 1835–43 employs mullioned and transomed windows, an asymmetrical composition, gables, some crenellations, and a cunningly contrived massing that made the building look as though it had been added to at various times for the sake of convenience. In fact, it is this very 'naturalness' (it is, of course, nothing of the sort) that is one of the most significant of English contributions to architecture, and which achieved its zenith with the Arts-and-Crafts Domestic Revival in the decades before the catastrophe

Plate 36 Peckforton Castle, Cheshire, by Anthony Salvin: a nineteenth-century house in which convenience and the Gothic Revival combine. (*JSC*)

Fig 16 Scotney Castle, Kent, of 1835–43, by Anthony Salvin (1799–1881). Note the asymmetrical composition, the mullioned and transomed windows, gables, crenellations, and other features of early seventeenth-century revival.

of 1914. Salvin's Harlaxton Manor in Lincolnshire is perhaps more Elizabethan than Elizabethan architecture, yet it dates from the reign of William IV, although William Burn was to design the extraordinary Baroque Cedar Staircase (1838–55) in the reign of the new Queen. William H. Playfair (1790–1857) designed a splendid Elizabethan-Jacobean palace for Donaldson's School (*Plate 37*), West Coates, Edinburgh, of 1841-51 which has elements based on Burghley House at Stamford, Audley End in Essex, Linlithgow Palace, and Edinburgh Castle, which, with Harlaxton and Mentmore, represents a stylistic alternative to earlier Gothic.

Mentmore Towers, Buckinghamshire (1851–4), by Sir Joseph Paxton (1803–65) and G. H. Stokes, was probably the greatest of all the Elizabethan-Revival houses (*Plate 38*), although Barry's Highclere Castle in Hampshire of 1839–42 runs it a close second. A Tudor-Gothic gabled style with mullioned and transomed windows was adopted for

Plate 37 Donaldson's Hospital, West Coates, Edinburgh, of 1841–51, by W. H. Playfair. It includes elements of Renaissance architecture from Burghley House at Stamford, Audley End in Essex, Linlithgow Palace and Edinburgh Castle. An alternative to the Gothic Revival. (*RCAHMS No ED/5839*)

Plate 38 Mentmore Towers, Buckinghamshire, of 1851–4 by Sir Joseph Paxton and G. H. Stokes. An example of the Elizabethan Revival applied to a country house. (*RCHME No BB76/3683*)

a number of country houses by the architect Henry Roberts (1803–76) including Norton Manor, Norton Fitzwarren, in Somerset of 1842–3, and Toft Hall, Knutsford, of 1851.[3] At Orchardleigh Park, Somerset, Thomas Henry Wyatt (1807–80) designed a house for W. Duckworth in the 1850s that incorporated mullions and transomes, gables, and other features common in seventeenth-century domestic architecture (*Fig 17*): it also included some Elizabethan Renaissance details, so it is an example of late sixteenth- and early seventeenth-century eclectic revival. William Eden Nesfield's (1835–88) Cloverley Hall, Shropshire, for P. Heywood of 1862, mixed architectural motifs from French late-Gothic and late-Tudor styles in an assured composition (*Fig 18*).

Romanesque Revival
A revival of Romanesque architecture began with the Castellated style. Thomas Hopper (1776–1858) had used Romanesque at Penrhyn Castle, Caernarvonshire (now Gwynedd), in *c* 1825–44 and at Gosford Castle, Co Armagh, *c* 1820–*c* 50 (with a new entrance front by G. A.

Fig 17 Orchardleigh Park, Somerset, by T. H. Wyatt, of 1855–8: a free mix of late-Tudora and Jacobean architectural motifs.

Fig 18 Cloverley Hall, Shropshire, by W. Eden Nesfield, of 1862: French and English late-Gothic forms.

Burn of 1859), and the style received further exposure in George Ernest Hamilton's *Designs for Rural Churches,* published in 1836. Hamilton himself designed Christ Church, Stafford, in 1838–9 in a Romanesque style, J. Donthorne created the Norman Gaol in Peterborough of 1842, and John Plowman (*c* 1773–1843) built Shire Hall, Oxford, in a massive Norman manner between 1839 and 1841. Even earlier, between 1830 and 1832, William Joseph Booth (*c* 1795–1871) had built St John's church at Moneymore, Co Londonderry, for The Drapers' Company,[4] possibly in deference to Hibernian Romanesque precedent, and partly to differentiate between an Anglican church and the simplified Classical preaching-boxes preferred by others sects such as the Presbyterians. Romanesque was again chosen for St Patrick's church at Kilrea, Co Londonderry, of 1839–44, which George Smith (1783–1869) and William Barnes (1807–68) designed for The Mercers' Company. Henry Roberts's church of St Mary of 1840–41 at Elvetham Hall, Hampshire, is a further Neo-Norman ecclesiastical building.

The church of St Mary at Wreay in Cumberland, consecrated in 1842, was designed by Sara Losh as a memorial to her sister, Katherine. It is one of the most extraordinary monuments of Victorian Romanesque architecture, mixing French and Italian elements with a strong dose of Rhenish Romanesque. The strange and wonderful apse (*Plate 39*) with its arcade of tough columns, the carvings of William Hindson that look like Arts-and-Crafts work of about 1900 (but which date from the 1840s), and the sheer originality of this marvellous and little-known building make Wreay church one of the most interesting examples of the English Romanesque Revival.

Other examples of the Romanesque style include Walton Prison in Liverpool (a tough, chunky building by John Weightman of 1848–55) and the enchanting Hiberno-Romanesque parish church of St Patrick at Jordanstown in Co Antrim (*Plate 40*) which has a round tower and a rich brick interior: it was designed by Lanyon, Lynn and Lanyon, and dates from 1865–8. Two years earlier London acquired an Italian Romanesque office block by George Aitchison Junior (1825–1910) at 59–61 Mark Lane (*Plate 41*). Henry Clutton (1819–93) chose Italian Romanesque for the cloisters at the Oratory in Birmingham of 1860, and there were other manifestations of the style that recurred even during the triumphant progress of Gothic.

Plate 39 Church of St Mary, Wreay, Cumberland, of 1840–2 by Sara Losh, in Free Romanesque style. (*JSC*)

Plate 40 St Patrick's Church, Jordanstown, County Antrim, of 1866 by Lanyon. An essay in the Hiberno-Romanesque style, complete with round tower. (*JSC*)

Plate 41 Nos 59–61 Mark Lane, London, of 1864 by George Aithison Jr. An example of the Italian Romanesque style applied to an office block. (*GLPL No 74/ 10995. OMAR*)

The Italianate Style

Classicism remained a powerful force to be reckoned with, especially in parts of the country far from London and the two ancient universities. Leeds, Newcastle, Glasgow and Edinburgh have been mentioned, but Liverpool, with its Sublime Albert Docks of the 1840s by Jesse Hartley and Philip Hardwick (*Plate 2*), St George's Hall (*Plates 30–31*), the Bank of England by Cockerell of 1844–7, the Picton Reading Room by Sherlock of 1875–9, and the Walker Art Gallery of 1874–7, can boast some of the most distinguished Classical buildings in Britain. Belfast, too, has many noble Classical structures including the Crumlin Road Gaol (1843–50), the County Courthouse (1848–50), the Union Theological College (1852–3) and the Head Office of the Northern Bank (1851–2), all by Sir Charles Lanyon (1812–89), who could turn his hand to pretty Tudor-Gothic (as at Queen's University of Belfast [1849]) (*Plate 42*). He was also no mean hand when it came to essays in the Italianate *palazzo* style made fashionable by Sir Charles Barry (1795–1860) (as at the former Head Office of the Belfast Bank) (*Plate 43*). This *palazzo* vogue was favoured for secular architecture: as it was astylar (that is, without columns or pilasters on the exterior) it avoided the unfashionable use of colonnades that had been associated with the Neoclassical styles, and especially with the Greek Revival. Barry, like Cockerell, abandoned Greek prototypes for a more Italianate manner, producing first the Travellers' Club, Pall Mall, in London of

Plate 42 The Queen's University of Belfast of 1846–9 by Sir Charles Lanyon, one of the three Queen's Colleges founded in Ireland in 1845 to provide non-denominational higher education. A fine essay in the Tudor-Gothic style, with a central tower modelled on the Founder's Tower at Magdalen College, Oxford. Tudor Gothic seems to have found favour for use in educational buildings, workhouses, almshouses and the like. (*JSC*)

1829–32 and then the Reform Club of 1837–41 (*Plate 44*), the latter based on the Palazzo Farnese in Rome. For the second Duke of Sutherland Barry also built Cliveden House (1850–51) in Buckinghamshire and remodelled Trentham Hall (1834–42) in Staffordshire, but he did not always confine himself to an Italianate mode of design.

The Italianate style was given royal approval by its use at Osborne House (*Plate 45*) on the Isle of Wight of 1845-51, designed by Thomas Cubitt (1788–1855) and Prince Albert (1819–61). Like Osborne House, the new London Bridge railway terminus (*Plate 46*) of the Croydon, Brighton and South Eastern Railway Companies had an attractive campanile-like tower, the top stage of which was pierced by triple round-arched openings on each face: it was designed by Henry Roberts (1803–76), George Smith (1783–1869), J. V. Rastrick (1780–1856)

Plate 43 The Northern Bank, formerly the Head Office of the Belfast Bank, Belfast, remodelled in 1845 in the Italianate *palazzo* style by Sir Charles Lanyon from Sir Robert Taylor's Old Exchange and Assembly Rooms of 1769–76. Note the rusticated ground floor and aediculated windows at the first-floor level clearly derived from precedents established by Sir Charles Barry in his London Clubs. (*JSC*)

Plate 44 The Reform Club, Pall Mall, London, by Sir Charles Barry of 1837–41, a sumptuous essay in the Italian *palazzo* style with, on the left, Barry's Travellers' Club of 1829–32 and the Athenaeum of Decimus Burton to the far left of 1828–30. (*JSC*)

Plate 45 Osborne House, Isle of Wight, of 1845–51, a palace in the Italianate style. (*RCHME No BB452/772*)

Plate 46 'The London Terminus of the Brighton and Dover Railroads' by Henry Roberts of 1841–4. The Italianate style used for a London railway station. (*Guildhall Library, City of London*)

and Thomas Turner, but the Italianate front appears to have been mostly Roberts's work, and dates from 1840. The building was completed in 1844.

Descendants and relatives of the Barry *palazzo* style can be found in many banks, commercial buildings, offices and the like in several cities throughout the Kingdom. The extraordinarily fine Custom House in Belfast, for example, is a marvellous study in the Italian Renaissance *palazzo* style by Lanyon and Lynn of 1854–7, adapted to a Palladian plan and set on a high battered podium. As distinguished is Belfast's Harbour Office, the original structure of which was designed by George Smith in an Italianate *palazzo* style (Smith's elevation to the harbour is still as he designed it with a beautifully handled clock-tower capping the whole composition). Smith was surveyor to The Mercers' Company (he and his pupil, William Barnes, designed St Patrick's church, Kilrea, Co Londonderry, for the Company). He appears to have obtained his commission to design the Harbour Office through his connections with the City of London. (The Harbour Office was extended most sympathetically by William Henry Lynn in 1891–5 [*Plate 47*].)

Other examples of the Italianate style include Edward Walters's (1801–72) building for the Manchester and Salford Bank (later Williams Deacon) in Mosley Street, Manchester, of 1860, David Hamilton's (1768–1843) Western Club in Buchanan Street, Glasgow, of 1840–41 (which is a remarkably original interpretation of the

Italianate style, and which demonstrates how completely Victorian architects were to break with the earlier styles of Georgian Britain), J. T. Rochead's Bank of Scotland (1869) at the corner of George Square and St Vincent Place in Glasgow, and the Head Office of the Commercial Bank of Scotland in Glasgow's Gordon Street by David Rhind (1801–83) of 1857, a tour-de-force of Italian Renaissance Revival which has elements from Sangallo, Michelangelo (Farnese), and

Plate 47 The Harbour Office, Belfast. The portion on the right, with clock-tower, was designed by George Smith and built 1852–4. It was enlarged to designs by W. H. Lynn in 1891–5. Beyond is the Sinclair Seamen's Presbyterian Church of 1856 by Lanyon and Lynn in a Lombardic-Venetian style of Gothic. (*JSC*)

Raphael (Vidoni Caffarelli) in it, loosely interpreted (*Plate 48*). Rhind had already built the Commercial Bank of Scotland in George Street, Edinburgh (with its Giant Order and prostyle hexastyle Corinthian portico suggesting more a Graeco-Roman temple than an Italianate *palazzo*), in 1843–7, and there are many distinguished variations of Italian *palazzi* façades in Victorian commercial buildings based on Roman, Florentine, Venetian and other prototypes. Edinburgh's Bank of Scotland in George Street by J. M. Dick Peddie (1824–91) of 1883–5 is a late example of the restrained astylar *palazzo* style with aediculated first-floor windows, while the Bank of Scotland (formerly the British Linen Bank) in St Andrew Square in the same city of 1846 by David Bryce (1803–76) is perhaps one of the showiest examples of the Italianate commercial style, although it is not astylar, for it is embellished with a Giant Corinthian Order standing forward of the façade in the manner of the Roman buildings at Baalbek or the great Baths of Rome itself (*Plate 49*): it suggests memories of Palladio's work in Vicenza or some of the grandest Roman Baroque work. Jacopo Sansovino (1486–1570), the architect of the Library of St Mark in Venice and of the Palazzo Corner della Ca' Grande in the same city (1537), was the begetter of an even more sumptuous *palazzo* style such as that found at Edward Walters's Free Trade Hall in Manchester of 1853–6. Sir George Gilbert Scott's Government Offices in London (1862–73) combine Picturesque asymmetry with an Italianate *palazzo* style of the grandest type based on precedents in Genoa and Venice: Matthew Digby Wyatt (1820–77) also contributed to the design. In terms of composition the asymmetry of Osborne House is similar.

The *palazzo* style of Barry had many progeny, including the banks, clubs and grand houses mentioned above. 'Millionaires' Row', or Kensington Palace Gardens in London, also had examples of this style in the splendid houses built to embellish this exclusive residential area: No 15, by James Thomas Knowles of 1854–5, is a fine example with its heavily rusticated ground floor, aediculated first-floor windows and massive *cornicione* (*Fig 19*).

Barry's Reform Club set standards of opulence and taste outside and in (*Plate 50*), but as the century progressed the comparative plainness of the Travellers' and Reform Clubs (*Plate 44*) began to pall, and a more sumptuous architectural expression of the Italianate style was sought. Basevi and Sydney Smirke's Conservative Club in London's St James's of 1843–5 was one of the first of the Tory replies to the Whigs, but even grander was Sydney Smirke's Carlton Club of 1854–6, an essay in Venetian Renaissance Revival based on Sansovino's Library of St Mark of 1537 (*Plate 51*). Like the Reform Club the Carlton had its main rooms grouped around a covered *cortile*, but its elevational treatments

Plate 48 The National Commercial Bank, Gordon Street, Glasgow, of 1857, by David Rhind, a tour-de-force of Italian Renaissance Revival in which there are quotations from Sangallo, Michelangelo and Raphael. (*RCAHMS No GW/164*)
Plate 49 Bank of Scotland, St Andrew's Square, Edinburgh, of 1846, by David Bryce, one of the showiest examples of the Italianate commercial style. (*RCAHMS Ed/12023*)

were more ornate, incorporating polished granite engaged columns in the pursuit of a structural polychrome version of Venetian Renaissance architecture. Nearly opposite was the Army and Navy Club of 1848–51 by Charles Octavius Parnell (d.1865) and Alfred Smith which also used Sansovino's St Mark's library façade on the upper storey, but elements from his Palazzo Corner della Ca' Grande (1537) on the lower, a much plainer treatment not unlike that used by Edward Walters in his Mosley street bank.

The Scottish-Baronial Style
One of the first Victorian examples of this style was the work of Charles Barry who, with Leslie, remodelled Dunrobin Castle for the Duke of Sutherland between 1844 and 1850. Barry adapted circular corner towers capped with conical roofs, and these became hallmarks of what came to be known as the Scottish-Baronial style, although Dunrobin owed more, perhaps, to French precedents than to dour Caledonian examples (*Plate 52*).

Scottish-Baronial seems to have been associated with a desire to find

93

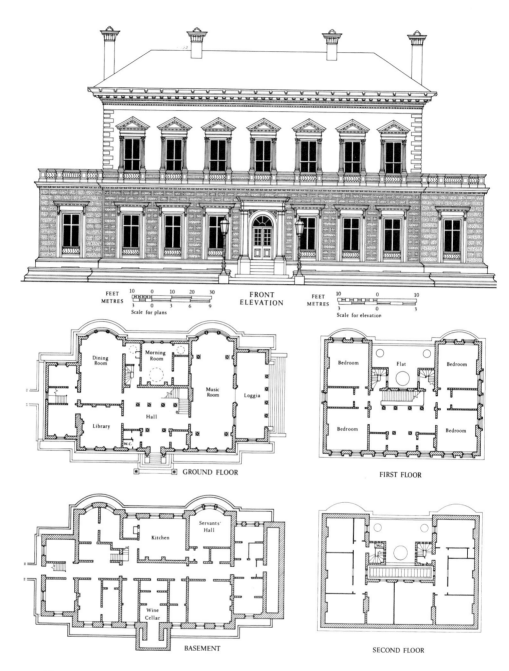

FEET 10 0 10 20 30 FRONT FEET 10 0 10
METRES 3 0 3 6 9 ELEVATION METRES 3 0 3
Scale for plans Scale for elevation

Dining Room   Morning Room
Music Room   Loggia
Library   Hall
w.c.
GROUND FLOOR

Bedroom   Flat   Bedroom
Bedroom   Bedroom
FIRST FLOOR

Kitchen   Servants' Hall
Wine Cellar
BASEMENT

W.C.
SECOND FLOOR

Fig 19 No 15 Kensington Palace Gardens, of 1854–5, by James Thomas
Knowles. It is an astylar composition in the manner of Charles Barry.
(*Drawing by John J. Sambrook, reproduced by kind permission of the
General Editor,* Survey of London)

Plate 50 The central 'saloon' or *cortile* of Barry's Reform Club in London, showing the opulence and grandeur of the Italianate style. (*RCHME No BB86/8419*)

Plate 51 The Carlton Club, Pall Mall, by Sydney Smirke. It is an essay in Venetian Renaissance revival incorporating elements from Sansovino's Library of St Mark. (*RCHME No BB85/3068*)

Plate 52 Dunrobin Castle, Sutherland, of 1844–50, by Barry and Leslie. An essay in the Scottish-Baronial style. (*RCAHMS No SU/344*)

an expression of some form of 'national' style rooted in the medieval, sixteenth- or seventeenth-century periods, and was paralleled by English searches for Elizabethan, Jacobean or Gothic modes that would satisfy the yearning for an architecture of indigenous character. In Ireland there were similar turnings to stepped crenellations, round towers, Celtic crosses, Hiberno-Romanesque forms and other motifs.

George Gilbert Scott, always keen to introduce some nod towards national sentiment (as in his designs for St Nikolaus at Hamburg), introduced circular corner *tourelles* with conical roofs at Glasgow University (1866 onwards) (*Plate 24*), and again mixed Franco-Scottish motifs at the Albert Institute, Dundee, of 1865–7. As with much else, the royal imprimatur given to the Scottish Baronial style when Balmoral Castle, Aberdeenshire, was remodelled between 1853 and 1855 by Prince Albert and William Smith (1817–91) of Aberdeen greatly extended the popularity of this style, especially in Scotland and Ulster where numerous examples may be found. Scrabo Tower, spectacularly sited on a hill near Newtownards, Co Down, is a fine Ulster example of the style, and dates from the 1850s when it was erected in memory of the third Marquess of Londonderry who died in 1854. It has bartizans, machicolations and a circular tower containing the stair

96

(*Plate 53*). At Balmoral the tower with *tourelles* was a precedent for many later buildings including Belfast Castle (Lanyon, Lynn and Lanyon of 1868–70), the University of Glasgow (*Plate 24*), and Fettes College in Edinburgh by David Bryce of 1864–9 (a strange composition that combines Scottish 'Baronial' elements with parts of Tolbooths, quotations from Roslin Chapel, and sundry French châteaux and public buildings of the late-Gothic style [*Plate 54*]).

Scottish-Baronial elements also occurred far from Scotland: two London buildings where they were used are the Royal College of Music of 1890–94 by A. W. Blomfield and the Prudential Assurance Building in Holborn by Alfred Waterhouse.

The Rundbogenstil

In the first half of the nineteenth century other styles, including Early Christian and Byzantine, as well as the Romanesque Revival, were exploited by designers, and these found particular favour in Germany among architects such as Friedrich von Gärtner, Georg Friedrich Ziebland and many others.[5] The German term *Rundbogenstil* is applied

Plate 53 Scrabo Tower, on Scrabo Hill near Newtownards, Co Down, built in the 1850s. It is an assured composition in the Scottish-Baronial style with machicolations, crenellations and bartizans. (*JSC*)

to all these 'round-arched' styles, many of which can be traced to a German enthusiasm for Italy that goes back to the Dark Ages, but which received a new impetus thanks to Winckelmann, Goethe and Schinkel. The *Rundbogenstil* is therefore related to Germanic precedent, to Italian architecture, notably Early-Christian and Romanesque buildings in Italy, to the passion for Italy found in the writings of Ruskin, Street and others, and to the interest in Italian architecture fostered by the Italianate buildings of Barry and his contemporaries. G. E. Hamilton, in his *Designs for Rural Churches*, published in 1836, advocated a Romanesque style. A convincing exercise in the Italian Basilican manner (*Plate 55*) with a free-standing campanile was built by Thomas Henry Wyatt (1807–80) and his partner David Brandon (1813–97) at Wilton, Wiltshire (in 1840–46) as the church of SS Mary and Nicholas, while the contemporary Christ Church, Streatham, of 1840–42 (*Plate 56*), with its fine brick exterior, elaborate colour-scheme inside by Owen Jones (1809–74), and brick campanile, is reminiscent of German re-workings of the Italian basilican type, such as the Allerheiligenhof-kirche in Munich designed in 1826 by Leo von Klenze, and other buildings by Persius and Hübsch. Christ Church was designed by James William Wild (1814–92). An early example of the round-arched style based on precedents in Ravenna was used by J. Hungerford Pollen (1820–1902) for the university church in Dublin of 1856.

Plate 54 Fettes College, Edinburgh, of 1864–9, by David Bryce. A combination of Scottish-Baronial, French châteaux, Roslin chapel Gothic, and a general mixture of Franco-Caledonian medieval styles, strongly flavoured with the Balmoral manner as arrived at by Prince Albert and William Smith. (*RCAHMS No ED/9986*)

Plate 55 The Church of SS Mary and Nicholas, Wilton, Wiltshire, of 1840–46. by T. H. Wyatt and D. Brandon, a fine exercise in the Italian Romanesque Basilican style, with authentic detached *campanile*. It was built for Sidney Herbert, and cost £20,000. (*RCHME No AA51/11903*)

During the 1850s a further impetus was given to a growing enthusiasm for the *Rundbogenstil* in England. Karl Friedrich Schinkel (1781–1841) had experimented with motifs derived from Italian vernacular villas at the Court Gardener's house at Charlottenhof in Potsdam in 1829: these motifs included towers, low-pitched roofs, round-arched openings, pergolas and loggias. Leo von Klenze (1784–1864) was to use elements from the Palazzo Cancellaria and the Vatican Belvedere at the Alte Pinakothek (1826–36) in Munich, and from the Palazzi Rucellai and Pitti in Florence at the Königsbau of the Residenz (1826–35) in the same city. He also used Italian models for churches, including St Dionysus in Athens of 1844–53. Schinkel's Italianate villa style unquestionably influenced Alexander Thomson of Glasgow (1817–75), especially at Pollok School (1856), 25 Mansionhouse Road, Langside (1856–7), and Tor House, High Craigmore (*c* 1868).[6] The

99

Plate 56 Christ Church, Streatham, of 1840–42, by J. W Wild. A noble essay in *Rundbogenstil* influenced by German precedent. (*Ingrid Curl and Jonathan Taylor*)

Plate 57 North side (1866) of the quadrangle of the South Kensington Museum in *c* 1872, by Fowke and Sykes, an example of the round-arched Italianate style. (*V & A No 9774*)

Plate 58 The Royal Albert Hall (1867–71), London, by H. Scott and F. Fowke. (*JSC*)

most important manifestations in Britain of the round-arched Italianate style occurred in the Victoria and Albert Museum Quadrangle (*Plate 57*) of 1860–72 by Captain Francis Fowke (1823–65) and Godfrey Sykes (1824–66), the Royal Albert Hall (1867–71) by Lt. Col. Henry Scott (1822–83) who based his scheme (*Plate 58*) on a design by Captain Fowke,[7] and the Huxley Building, formerly the Science Schools, Exhibition Road, Kensington, of 1867–71 by General Henry Scott with J. Gamble, J. W. Wild, and others.[8] That these red-brick and terracotta-faced buildings were influenced by German exemplars cannot be doubted, for German ideas were very much in the air through the influence of the Prince Consort and his artistic adviser, Professor Ludwig Grüner (1801–82), who encouraged the use of polychrome façades and grotesques as as South Kensington.[9]

Other examples of the *Rundbogenstil* include Fowke's Royal Scottish Museum in Edinburgh (1861), the Prince Consort Library at Aldershot of 1860, and, of course, the Royal Mausoleum at Frogmore near Windsor of 1862–71 which is in the form of a Greek cross with an octagonal clerestory and low convex ambulatories designed by Grüner that would not look out of place in the Munich of King Ludwig I

(*Plate 59*). The interior of the mausoleum is in a richly coloured High Renaissance manner which is curiously at odds with the *Rundbogenstil* of the outside, and has a pronounced Raphaelesque flavour in accordance with the prejudices of Prince Albert and Professor Grüner.[10]

The fashion for *Rundbogenstil* found sympathetic response in numerous buildings: one of the most successful instances in which a Lombardic-Romanesque composition using polychrome bricks was realised is the Methodist church, University Road, Belfast, by William J. Barre, of 1864–5. Barre's Italian campanile with spectacular machicolations and fully expressed stair in the subsidiary turret are especially fine (*Plate 60*).

One of the largest and last of the round-arched public buildings, in which a German-Romanesque flavour (imparted by quotations from Andernach, Bamberg and Worms) is judiciously mixed with Fowke's Germano-Italianate Renaissance materials and style, was the Natural

Plate 59 The Royal Mausoleum, Frogmore, near Windsor, Berkshire. (*JSC*)
Plate 60 Methodist church, University Road, Belfast, by W. J. Barre, of 1864–5, a fine example of the *Rundbogenstil* in a Lombardic Romanesque manner. (*JSC*)

Plate 61 The Natural History Museum in South Kensington of 1870–81 by Alfred Waterhouse, a blend of Germanic Romanesque and other *Rundbogenstil* elements. (*Kindly provided by the General Editor,* Survey of London)

History Museum in South Kensington of 1870–81 by Alfred Waterhouse, who faced his building with a Neapolitan yellow terracotta relieved with bands of blue-grey (*Plate 61*).

Rogue Goths and the Later Gothic Revival

The Gothic Revival was still going strong while all the buildings mentioned above were being conceived and built. The High-Victorian Gothic period of about 1850 to 1875 is quite distinct in manner from the earlier styles dominated by Pugin, Carpenter, Cundy and Second-Pointed English Gothic, for it is violently vigorous, often raspingly harsh, strongly coloured and concerned with a structural emphasis that can best be appreciated in the churches of Enoch Bassett Keeling (1837–86), Edward Buckton Lamb (1806–69), Samuel Sanders Teulon (1812–73) (*Fig 20*) and William White (1825–1900). Lamb and Keeling both designed for the Evangelical persuasion, and it shows:

103

Fig 20 Church of St Stephen, Hampstead, by S. S. Teulon, 1869; a powerful example of Continental Gothic, freely treated.

Fig 21 Church of St George, Campden Hill, of 1866 by Enoch Bassett Keeling. (Building News, *22 July 1864*)
Fig 22 Interior of church of St George, Campden Hill, by Bassett Keeling. showing the rasping, jagged quality of his harsh, uncompromising, angular Gothic, 'freely treated'. During the 1860s and '70s the clustered piers so uncompromisingly displayed at St George's were to be regarded as over-fussy, thus later Gothic architecture became tougher, more archaic, and simpler. (Building News, *1864*)

both attracted the displeasure of the Ecclesiologists, both gloried in repetitive notchings and chamferings, both expressed their roof structures in an outlandish, even ugly way, and both seemed to want to jar the beholder with the sensation of saw-tooth arrises, scissor-shaped trusses and barbaric, harsh polychromy. Their most extraordinary churches are St George's, Campden Hill (1866) (*Figs 21–22*), St Mark's, Notting Hill (1863) (*Fig 23*), and St Paul's, Anerley Road, Norwood (1866) (*Plate 62*) (all by Keeling), and St Mary Magdalene's, Addiscombe, Croydon (1868), and St Margaret's, Leiston, Suffolk

(1853) (by Lamb).[11] St Mark's was a startling building, with arcades of spindly cast-iron piers and spiky arches of red, black and white voussoirs, the arrises of which were notched, like those of the scissor-trusses that carried the roof (*Fig 23*). St George's, Campden Hill, was less thin, but it was even more lively in its polychrome treatment (*Figs 21–22*). St Paul's had a glorious interior enriched by painted stencilled patterns over the whole of the wall-surfaces (*Plate 62*). Lamb and Keeling were both in the 'Rogue Goth' camp, as defined by Harry Stuart Goodhart-Rendel (1887–1959), and, like Teulon, were not approved of by the Establishment figures who sought severity, unmoulded planes, and a more primitive, early-Gothic style based on Continental precedent. Street, for example, used a massive and austere style in his first rural churches, but by the mid-1850s he was experimenting with structural polychrome techniques as at St James the Less in Westminster (*Plate 22*) and at the belfry of St Mary Magdalene, Paddington, of 1867–73 (*Plate 63*).

William White's great church of St Michael at Lyndhurst, Hampshire, of 1858–70, a massive structure of brick with stone dressings (*Fig 24*), has much structural polychromy as well as notched arrises so beloved by Keeling, and led *The Ecclesiologist* to regret the 'affectation of originality'. The interior of the church contains much fine Victorian work, including a reredos by Lord Leighton, excellent glass by William

Plate 62 Church of St Paul, Upper Norwood, London, by E. Bassett Keeling. The entire interior, including the solid chancel screen of heroic proportions, was covered with stencilled designs. Note the delicately detailed cast-iron columns. (*RCHME No BB70/6702*)

Fig 23 Church of St Mark, Notting Hill, by Keeling, in his most stripey, notched and jagged Gothic. (Building News, *18 September 1863*)

Morris and others, and a lovely Easter Sepulchre by Street. Nevertheless Lyndhurst lacks an insistence on robustness, muscularity and primitive Gothic that were to be features of the more advanced work. From the 1860s clustered piers (like those of St George's, Campden Hill [*Fig 22*]) were replaced by huge cylinders, polychrome surfaces became plainer, and a restless, violent jaggedness was superseded by something more austere, archaic and tough as the Gothic Revival moved through the 1860s and '70s. Burges produced primitive heavy forms in his churches in Yorkshire, but the Ecclesiological argument for city churches encouraged the design of large, tall, town churches with bold, clear interiors and high clerestories, like John Loughborough Pearson's (1817–98) church of St Peter, Vauxhall (1860–65), with its massive apsidal east end (*Fig 25*), brick vaulting, and vestigial aisles.

Wide, high naves, tiny, almost vestigial aisles, lofty clerestories, and a return to Continental Gothic of the thirteenth century characterise the churches of James Brooks (1825–1901), who used brick, wide short lancets of the Burgundian type, plate tracery, and apsidal east ends. His great churches are St Andrew's, Plaistow, Essex, of 1867, a fine essay in French First-Pointed Gothic (*Fig 26*); St Columba's, Kingsland Road, London of 1865–74, which is joined to a school, clergy house and mission house (*Fig 27*); St Chad's, Haggerston, started in 1867 (*Fig 28*); and the Transfiguration at Lewisham of the 1880s. Brooks was perhaps the greatest of the designers of complexes for 'town churches' following the successful precedent of Butterfield's All Saints', Margaret Street, and his massive assured compositions must have seemed like citadels in the parts of London where they towered over the surrounding buildings. With the primitivist architecture of James Brooks the Gothic became Sublime in its aesthetic.

Pearson was to follow St Peter's, Vauxhall, with a number of

Plate 63 Church of St Mary Magdalene, Paddington of 1867–73, by G. E. Street. Note the structural polychrome on the belfry and the austere early Gothic style. (*RCHME No BB56/2256*)
Fig 24 Church of St Michael, Lyndhurst, Hampshire, of 1858–70, by William White.

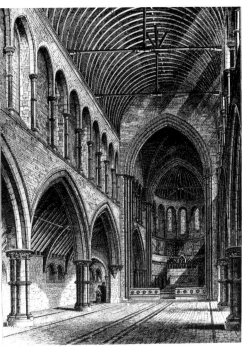

Fig 25 The apsidal east end of the church of St Peter, Vauxhall, by J. L. Pearson of 1860–5, an example of how the Gothic Revival was turning to Continental precedents of early thirteenth-century Gothic.
Fig 26 Church of St Andrew, Plaistow, Essex, by James Brooks, of 1867–70, a tough essay in French First-Pointed architecture.

churches, including St Augustine's, Kilburn, of 1871–7, a huge vertically accented building of great elegance, lightness and grace (quite unlike Brooks's work). His largest church is Truro Cathedral (1880–1910), completed by his son, in an Early-English Gothic style with the spires in Northern French Gothic based on Coutances (*Plate 64*). The interior is vaulted in the sexpartite French manner, and the baptistery is complex, rich, and perfectly First Pointed in manner. Pearson was to influence Edward Goldie in the latter's church of St James, Spanish Place, London, of 1885–90.

In the last decades of the Victorian era something of the violence of the Gothic Revival was dissipated. The 1850s and 1860s had seen a profusion of polychrome work, some of it bizarre when carried out by the architects Harry Goodhart-Rendel called 'Rogue Goths'. Gradually, however, architects abandoned structural polychromy and early Continental exemplars, returning to English late-Gothic motifs. The Revival was to turn from colour and to concern itself more with early-

Fig 27 Church of St Columbia, Haggerston, London, by James Brooks, of 1865–74, showing how the Gothic Revival returned to a primitive First-Pointed Continental style in that period. Note the robust composition, plate-tracery and fortress-like character, implying a citadel of faith.

Fig 28 Church of St Chad, Haggerston, London, by James Brooks, commenced in 1867, another lofty building faced internally with brick. Note the massive, simple piers, lack of elaboration in the mouldings, and apsidal east end, all typical of Gothic Revival in the late 1860s when the Revival turned back to early French precedent. As a town church, the nave was illumined from the clerestory lights.

Gothic forms, notably in the work of Pearson and Brooks, but towards the end of the century a further reaction occurred in favour of late English Gothic: in this respect George Frederick Bodley (1827–1907) was one of the first architects to return to English Second Pointed, much refined and deliciously serene, in his designs for St Augustine's church, Pendlebury, near Manchester, of 1870–74. In that building, significantly in the 1870s, the Sublime is nowhere to be experienced, while exquisite Decorated furnishings were even more in evidence at Bodley's other great church of the period, that of Holy Angels at Hoar Cross, Staffordshire, of 1872–6, which he designed with Thomas Garner (1839–1906). Holy Angels is sumptuous, with elaborate tracery and vaulting, and a blocky Perpendicular tower based on Somerset precedent (*Plates 65 and 66*).

Bodley's work was ultra-refined, delicate, intricate, and late in its

Plate 64 View from the south-east in 1895 of Truro Cathedral, Cornwall, designed by J. L. Pearson in 1880, in which Early-English Gothic merges with Northern French Gothic of the thirteenth century. The low aisle on the left is the south aisle of the former Parish church of St Mary, dating from 1504–18, an example of late-Perpendicular or Third-Pointed work which Pearson retained when he commenced building the Cathedral. The large traceried windows of the sixteenth-century *Echt*-Gothic contrast with Pearson's revival of thirteenth-century First-Pointed, with its typical lancets, wheel windows and soaring verticality. (*RCHME No BB69/1119*)

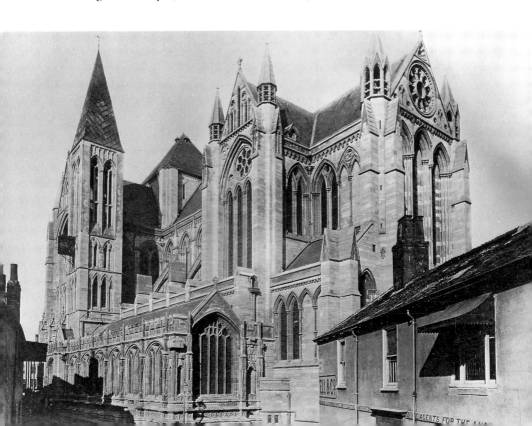

Gothic chronology. At the end of his career Bodley was to design Holy Trinity, Prince Consort Road, Kensington, an essay in English Second-Pointed of the fourteenth century, a drawing of which was exhibited at the Royal Academy in 1901. It is a sumptuous work of great serenity, anticipating a return to English precedents of the late-Decorated and Perpendicular styles by twentieth-century designers such as Sir John Ninian Comper (1864–1960) at St Cyprian's, Clarence Gate, London (one of his most felicitous achievements), and Comper's scholarly work at Eye in Suffolk.

As the century drew towards its close, then, English Gothic grew once more in favour, but the Gothic Revival itself was losing momentum. John Francis Bentley (1839–1902) had designed some of the most exquisite early Continental Gothic features for the tiny church of St Francis of Assisi, Notting Dale, London, of 1859–61 (*Fig 48*), and had built the church of the Holy Rood at Watford in the 1880s in a Perpendicular style influenced by Bodley. By 1894 Bentley was designing Westminster Cathedral (1895–1903) in a stripey Byzantine style mixed with Italian elements (*Plate 67*): such a curious choice of style is associated with other contemporary moves towards free eclecticism mixed with the desirability of building in hard impervious materials suitable for the London atmosphere, and a throw-back to the *Rundbogenstil* of South Kensington. It is odd to realise that this extraordinary building is almost contemporary with the church of the Holy Trinity, Sloane Street, London, by John Dando Sedding (1838–91), who had designed the church of the Holy Redeemer in Clerkenwell in an Early-Christian round-arched style in 1887. Holy Trinity, begun in 1888 and completed in the 1890s, the era of the Yellow Book and the arrest of Oscar Wilde, is a case where a late Gothic-Revival style, incorporating Decorated and Tudor elements of English medieval work, was furnished with a huge wealth of Arts-and-Crafts detail (*Figs 29–30*).

Bodley's love of tracery and of extremely fine furnishings had obviously influenced Sedding to some extent, and also provided an inspiration to later designers such as Comper and the young Giles Gilbert Scott (1880–1960), George Gilbert Scott's grandson, who was to create one of the grandest and last of the great monuments of the Revival (although competent, scholarly, and sensitive practitioners such as Stephen Dykes-Bower kept the Gothic lamps alight during the dark decades of recent times) with his stupendous and Sublime Anglican Cathedral at Liverpool of 1903, completed in the 1970s. The Lady Chapel of Liverpool Cathedral has delicate late-Gothic treatment of fenestration and detail, with tracery of an elaborate Second-Pointed type much influenced by Continental (especially German) precedent,

Plate 65 Church of the Holy Angels, Hoar Cross, Staffordshire, of 1872–6, by Bodley and Garner, an assured essay in Decorated Gothic Revival. (*RCHME No BB88/4339*)

Plate 66 Interior of the church of the Holy Angels at Hoar Cross, showing the sumptuous refinement of the late Decorated work. It should be compared with Plate 22 or with some of the interiors of Keeling and Brooks. (*RCHME No BB69/2244*)

Plate 67 Westminster Cathedral, Victoria, London, by J. Bentley, commenced in 1894: an example of the Byzantine style. (*RCHME No CC73/1951*)

Fig 29 Exterior of the church of the Holy Trinity, Sloane Street, London, by J. D. Sedding, commenced in 1888. It is in the English Gothic style, mixing Decorated and Perpendicular features. (*RCHME No BB88/1866*)

Fig 30 Interior of the church of the Holy Trinity, Sloane Street, by J. D. Sedding, showing the late Gothic-Revival style and the sumptuous Arts-and-Crafts detail. (*RCHME No BB88/1865*)

✠ CHVRCH·OF·THE·HOLY·TRINITY·VPPER·CHELSEA· Now in Covrse of Erection· J·D·SEDDING·ARCH·

and, unquestionably, by the example of Bodley's taste, although Scott is said to have reacted against the older man who was appointed to keep an eye on the precocious Scott. At Liverpool the jewel-like qualities of the best of Gothic-Revival scholarship co-exist with the mighty spaces and soaring forms of the main body of the building: the wheel of the Revival had come full circle.

The Domestic Revival, Vernacular Revival, the Arts-and-Crafts movement, 'Queen-Anne' Style, and Renaissance Revival
Richard Norman Shaw (1831–1912) began to practise in the 1860s. With Leys Wood in Sussex of 1866 he introduced vernacular elements to the design, using mullions and transoms, timber-framed gables, and other details that were not High Gothic at all (*Fig 31*). Free, asymmetrical compositions for domestic architecture had been a feature of the Gothic Revival, for Pugin, Butterfield and Street had all designed Picturesque groupings that were also derived from a strict utility. Windows of different types and sizes were placed in façades where they were needed, as at Alfred Waterhouse's new block for Balliol College, Oxford, of 1867 (*Fig 32*). Philip Webb's (1831–1915) Red House at Bexleyheath in Kent for William Morris of 1859–60, although having certain Gothic features, also incorporated aspects not associated with Gothic in particular (*Plate 68*). By the time Webb built Clouds in Wiltshire in 1879–91 he was mixing stylistic features quite freely (*Plate 69*), and with Standen in Sussex of 1891–4 'Queen-Anne' fenestration, tall chimneys, vernacular gables, Classical detail and a stylistic pot-pourri were to mingle in a remarkable and original free composition. Webb, like Gandy, was searching for a means by which he would eschew style, and his method was to mix different elements from various periods and precedents with a variety of materials. By combining medieval, eighteenth-century, and vernacular elements in a carefully contrived way he sought to free his buildings from stylistic labels and historicist straitjackets.

Eden Nesfield (1835–88) and Shaw were to adopt Picturesque compositions and vernacular styles, and to mix them in a new manner known as Old English. In this style tall chimneys, gables, tile-hanging,

Fig 31 Leys Wood, Sussex, by R. N. Shaw, an example in which elements from vernacular architecture, such as timber-framed gables with barge-boards, were introduced. It should be compared with Butterfield's Milton Ernest Hall (Plate 18).

Fig 32 Alfred Waterhouse's new buildings at Balliol College, Oxford, of 1867, showing the freedom of fenestration made possible by the Gothic Revival, and unthinkable in Classical architecture.

116

A Prospect of Leys Wood in Sussex:

Stable Court | Stables | Entrance Archway | Lodge & Gardeners House | Kitchen Offices | Servants Room | Butlers Pantry | Hall Entrance | Library | Drawing Room

March 1868

Plate 68 The Red House, Bexleyheath, Kent, by Philip Webb, of 1859–60. Although the house had certain Gothic features, it also incorporated segmental-headed openings with sash windows, pointing forward to the Domestic Revival and Free Eclecticism of the late Victorian period. (*RCHME B47/201*)

Plate 69 Clouds, East Knoyle, Wiltshire, by Philip Webb of 1879–91, a free mixture of stylistic features. It should be compared with Butterfield's Milton Ernest Hall (Plate 18). (*RCHME No BB69/2560 reproduced by kind permission of B. T. Batsford Ltd*)

mullioned and transomed windows, timber-framed elements and leaded lights combined in a revival of native English domestic forms, so that the Domestic Revival was born of the Gothic Revival. Of course vernacular elements from the sixteenth, seventeenth, and eighteenth centuries were available from which to copy, and Betteshanger in Kent of 1856–82 by George Devey (1820–86) is a good example of a house designed to look as though it had grown over the centuries: Devey used traditional materials and details, and in this he was followed by Nesfield and Shaw. The latter's Cragside (*Plate 70*) in Northumberland of 1870–85 is an extraordinarily accomplished Picturesque composition with mullioned and transomed windows, arrays of tall chimneys, timber-framed gables, and all the other features of the Domestic Revival.

Plate 70 Cragside, Northumberland, of 1870–85, by R. N. Shaw. A house composed in the 'true Picturesque' manner, with mullioned and transomed windows, arrays of tall chimneys, timber-framed gables, and other features of the Domestic Revival that grew out of the Gothic Revival. Compare with Fig 31. (*RCHME No BB81/1084*)

Plate 71 Kinmel Park, Denbighshire, commenced in 1868 to designs by Eden Nesfield. It is a mixture of the 'Queen-Anne', Dutch and French-Renaissance styles. (*RCAHMW No 860741, reproduced by kind permission of Sir John Cotterell, Bt*)

Nesfield's Kinmel Park in Denbighshire, built from 1868, is a vast house of a different character, constructed of red brick with a steeply pitched roof. The style is a mixture of 'Queen Anne', Dutch, and French Renaissance (*Plate 71*). Variants of the 'Queen-Anne' style occurred at Norman Shaw's Lowther Lodge of 1875–7, and at Newnham College in Cambridge of 1874–1910 by Basil Champneys (1842–1935). Shaw's 170 Queen's Gate in London (*Plate 72*) of the 1880s moved forwards from the so-called 'Queen-Anne' style to a type of Neo-Georgian manner that looked somewhat Colonial in detail and proportion, and that clearly influenced some designers of the twentieth century. Shaw had also mixed seventeenth-century bay-windows (complete with leaded lights and pargetting) derived from prototypes in Ipswich (*see Plate 73 for another example of this*) with brick façades pierced with 'Queen-Anne' windows at Swan House, 17 Chelsea Embankment (1875–7) and New Zealand Chambers, Leadenhall Street, London, of 1871–3.

Shaw was associated with the Arts-and-Crafts movement with which much of late-Victorian taste is concerned, and which developed from the Gothic Revival. It will be recalled that the demands of architects designing Gothic-Revival buildings had stimulated a change in and development of craftsmanship, for Gothic mouldings, Gothic carvings, stained-glass window design and manufacture, the making of encaustic tiles, the provision of elaborate metalwork and much else had to be learned, and craftsmen had to be trained to cater for this demand. Specialist firms were established to provide work of quality, among which that of Morris, Marshall, Faulkner, & Co. (established 1861 with

Plate 72 No 170 Queen's Gate, London, of 1888–9, by R. N. Shaw. A refined essay in which early eighteenth-century domestic features, such as the elaborate eaves-cornice, steeply pitched roof, segmental-pedimented dormers, tall sash-windows, carved doorcase, and brick walls with stone quoins acquired a slight Colonial flavour, looking forward to twentieth-century 'Colonial-Georgian' domestic architecture. (*JSC*)

Burne-Jones, Webb, Rossetti and Madox Brown as partners together with the three names of the title) was of considerable importance. Set up to produce well-made and well-designed decorative work, this firm produced celebrated stained glass, furniture, wallpapers and much else. Morris & Co. (as it became when William Morris [1834–96] took over full control from 1875) produced some of the best work that is loosely associated with the Arts-and-Crafts movement. In 1883 pupils of Norman Shaw formed a society, the aims of which were to debate art, architecture and craftsmanship. This later became an expanded group named The Art Workers' Guild, the purpose of which was to promote the unity of all the arts, and it held its first meeting in 1884. The Guild became a forum in which architects, artists, craftsmen and designers could discuss their work, ideals and aspirations. Support for an independent exhibition called Arts and Crafts was given by members of the Guild, and, with a catalogue designed by Walter Crane (1845–1915), the exhibition was duly held in 1888.

The Arts and Crafts Exhibition Society, of which William Morris was president from 1893 to 1896, was important in disseminating many of the ideas derived from the writings of Ruskin and Morris, and had an international reputation enhanced by the fact that British Arts and Crafts were promoted at various international exhibitions by the Society, which gave its name to a whole range of design and designers. Morris is also associated with the foundation of the Society for the Protection of Ancient Buildings (SPAB) which was formed in 1877 partly as a result of George Gilbert Scott's proposals to 'restore' Tewkesbury Abbey in a somewhat drastic way. Scott had carried out many works to the fabric of ancient buildings, some of which were more sensitive than others. At his worst he could be crassly banal and destructive, as at the church of St Mary de Castro in Leicester, and Morris's aim was to create public awareness of the need to conserve as much as possible of the original fabric so that the historic nature of the building would not be dissipated. Many of Morris's ideas concerning historic buildings are now accepted by conservationists.

It must be emphasised that the Arts-and-Crafts movement, the Vernacular Revival, the Domestic Revival and the 'Queen-Anne' style grew out of the Gothic Revival, and were connected with the so-called Aesthetic Movement, which is associated with Oscar Wilde, Whistler and others. The use of vernacular motifs, 'Queen-Anne' elements, timber-framing, and techniques of asymmetrical composition derived from ideals of Picturesque groupings gave British architecture, and especially domestic architecture, a distinctive flavour that was much admired by the rest of the world.

From 1875 a complete suburb was to be developed by Jonathan Carr

(1845–1915) at Bedford Park in Chiswick, connected to London by train. There, the 'Queen-Anne' style was to predominate, and the Aesthetic Movement's rejection of the overblown and overdecorated was to be a keynote. The salubrious qualities of the district were emphasised from the first. Norman Shaw, Maurice Adams (1849–1933) and E. J. May (1859–1941) built houses, mostly of red brick, set in gardens off tree-lined roads. Shaw designed the church (1880), which incorporated Perpendicular Gothic with seventeenth- and eighteenth-century domestic features, and the Tabard Inn with its tile-hung gables and bay windows (*Plate 73*). Bedford Park also has houses by Edward W. Godwin and C. F. A. Voysey (1857–1941) (*Plate 74*).

Godwin has already been mentioned in connection with Northampton Town Hall, but he is also associated with the Aesthetic Movement through his remarkable designs for furniture (which were strongly influenced by the art of Japan)[12] through his designs for the White House, Tite Street, Chelsea (for James McNeill Whistler of 1877–9),

Plate 73 A group of buildings at Bedford Park, London, by R. N. Shaw. The bank on the left, with four gables, incorporates Shaw's favourite feature of mullioned and transomed windows with a central circular opening derived from the seventeenth-century Sparrowe's House in Ipswich, Suffolk. Note the jettied upper floor and the projecting window-bays set under the jetties. To the right is a brick-fronted house with jettied gabled top storey, then the Tabard Inn with tile-hung gables and shallow bay windows. These important prototypes of the late 1870s and early '80s were the models for countless examples of domestic architecture for the next fifty years. (*JSC*)

and through his remodelling of 34 Tite Street for Oscar Wilde. So yet another strand – that of Oriental art – was threaded into the art movements of the 1870s. The White House was called thus because it was built of brick which was then whitewashed, a curious rejection of the return to brick that had been a feature of the 'Queen-Anne' style and the abandonment of stucco-faced façades.

Voysey's vernacular revival was different again, for he generally made his houses long and low with hipped roofs, battered buttresses, overhanging eaves, long ranges of mullioned windows and walls covered with rough rendering. Typical of his style are Broadleys (1898) and Moor Crag (1898–1900) by Lake Windermere, and Pastures House, North Luffenham, Rutland, of 1901 (*Plate 75*). Bowdlerised versions of designs by Norman Shaw and C. F. A. Voysey proved attractive to builders of detached and semi-detached houses until the outbreak of war in 1939, and the work of Ernest Newton (1856–1922) was to prove similarly attractive as a reservoir of precedent for styles of middle-class housing in the 1920s and '30s. Newton's Steephill, Jersey, of 1899–1901, Red Court, Haslemere, Surrey, of 1894 (which combined segmental-headed windows, gables and a mullioned and transomed bow-window) (*Plate 76*), and a house near Brockenhurst in Hampshire, of 1901, are among his best works.

Yet another curious revival of early-Renaissance architecture occurred as the Gothic Revival lost its momentum. It will be recalled that there was a revival of Elizabethan and Jacobean styles before the Gothic Revival entered its most furiously earnest phase, but as the century grew old a surprising enthusiasm for German and Netherlandish Renaissance architecture was apparent in the work of Ernest George (1839–1922) and Harold Peto. Their tall brick houses with stepped and scrolled Renaissance gables, elaborate moulded brickwork and terracotta details blended domestic architecture from northern Germany, the Netherlands and Flanders with elements of the 'Queen-Anne' style. Superb examples of Ernest George and Peto's eclectic designs can be found in Harrington Gardens and Collingham Gardens, South Kensington, of 1880–90 (*Plate 77*). Versions of this style, with much use of rubbed brick and terracotta, appeared in houses on the Cadogan Estate in London, notably in Pont Street. Architects such as John James Stevenson (1831–1908) favoured variants, using tall thin 'Queen-Anne' sashes, rubbed and contrasting bricks and early-Renaissance details, as at Pont Street and at the Red House, Bayswater Road, London, of 1871.

Edwin Lutyens (1869–1944) was a pupil of Ernest George, and imbibed from his master and from the exemplars of Norman Shaw's great houses techniques of asymmetrical composition, designing in

Plate 74 Bedford Park, showing Voysey's No 14 South Parade of 1889, designed to stand out from the red brick and steeply pitched roofs of most houses on the development. The house is roughcast rendered with stone dressings, and has a low-pitched roof with overhanging eaves on iron brackets. The wing on the left was added in 1894. Note the curved gables of the houses on either side, looking back to seventeenth-century precedent. (*JSC*)

Plate 75 Pastures House, North Luffenham, Rutland, of 1901, by C. F. A. Voysey. The battered buttresses, rendered walls with stone dressings, and ranges of mullioned windows with leaded lights are all typical of Voysey's domestic architecture. The semicircular entrance arch was copied in many suburban houses over the next thirty years. (*AFK*)

Plate 76 Red Court, Haslemere, Surrey, of 1894, by Ernest Newton. Pevsner, in his *Surrey* in the *Buildings of England* series, described this as an 'ominous house with sterile Neo-Georgianism just round the corner . . . (it) . . . has segmental windows combined with gables in an acid way . . .' Pevsner loathed the pre-echoes of the Neo-Georgian style, and singled out Red Court for criticism because, to Pevsner, the house had 'all the succeeding decades of sterility implicit in its purse-mouthed exactness'. Apart from the ingenuity and convenience of the plan. Newton's architecture is interesting for its use of canted bays, segmental-headed sash-windows, gables and slightly off-centre door set under a segmental bay-window. (*From Ernest Newton's* A Book of Country Houses, *London, B. T. Batsford, 1903*)

brick and using tile-hanging. Lutyens's Arts-and-Crafts houses in Surrey (Crooksbury House [1889], Munstead Place [1891], and Munstead Wood [1896–7]) all incorporate Surrey vernacular features. His Orchards of 1897 and Tigbourne Court (*Plate 78*) of 1899, also in Surrey, are among the most brilliant of all essays in the vernacular revival Arts-and-Crafts manner in which seventeenth-century southern English vernacular styles and materials are used as the envelope for ingeniously planned fanciful houses, the planes and volumes of which show a first-class architectural mind at work.

A northern European Renaissance Revival, as seen in the assured

Plate 77 Nos 39–45 Harringtron Gardens, Kensington, London by Ernest George and Peto. They were built between 1881 and 1884 and are strongly influenced by North-European Renaissance architecture of Flanders and North Germany. (*JSC*)

productions of Ernest George and Peto, had smaller scale versions at Port Sunlight in Cheshire, but the same architects could also produce excellent work in which the main accents were English vernacular, as at the Ossington Coffee Tavern of 1882 at Newark, Nottinghamshire, one of those ambitious 'inns' intended to promote the temperance cause. The building has oriel windows based on prototypes in Ipswich similar in design to those popularised by Norman Shaw.

Free Eclecticism
In the last decades of Queen Victoria's reign various styles became mixed, and planning became ingenious, less rigid and highly complex. The free use of vernacular, 'Queen-Anne', Renaissance, medieval and other elements became usual, and many important public buildings were erected that showed little trace of an overt Gothic Revival except in the freedom of composition. Gothic freed architects from the tyranny of symmetry, and it enabled picturesque asymmetrical compositions to emerge even when no Gothic details were used. Informal planning, expressions of function and materials, and elaborately sculpted silhouettes were very much in evidence during the 1870s to the end of the reign. Leicester Town Hall of 1873–6 by F. J. Hames is an example of a 'Queen-Anne' style public building, very much influenced by Eden Nesfield, with moulded and cut brickwork, stone dressings, hipped roof with dormers, tall chimneys, sash-windows, seventeenth-century Renaissance gables and a tall elegant clock-tower (*Plate 79*). The precedent for much of Leicester Town Hall is Nesfield's Kinmel Park in Denbighshire (*Plate 71*), mentioned earlier.

Both Sheffield Town Hall of 1890–7 (*Plate 80*) by Edward W. Mountford (1855–1908) and Oxford Town Hall (*Plate 81*) of 1893–7 by Henry T. Hare (1860–1921) are in a pronounced Renaissance Revival style: the former has elements from French, Flemish, English and Spanish Renaissance architecture (although the architect claimed it was English in character), and the latter has Elizabethan gables and windows although the overall style owes much to Sir Thomas G. Jackson (1835–1924) and especially to his Examination Schools in Oxford of 1876–82 (*Plate 82*). Hare used late-Tudor Gothic and a strange low tower with cupola at Westminster College, Cambridge, of

Plate 78 Tigbourne Court, near Witley in Surrey, of 1899–1901, by Edwin Lutyens. Early seventeenth-century Classicism is mixed with vernacular elements. (*AFK*)
Plate 79 Leicester Town Hall of 1873–6 by F. J. Hames, a building much influenced by the work of Eden Nesfield and especially by his Kinmel Park (see Plate 71). (*JSC*)

Plate 80 Sheffield Town Hall of 1890–7 by Edward Mountford, with elements taken from Renaissance architecture of France, Flanders, Spain and England: an example of the 'Free-Renaissance' style. (*JSC*)
Plate 81 Oxford Town Hall of 1893–7 by Henry Hare. The Elizabethan gables derived from Kirby Hall in Northamptonshire and the mullioned and transomed windows make this building more English in character than the Sheffield Town Hall, but the style is still a free adaptation of Renaissance motifs. (*JSC*)

1899, and it is apparent that a free eclecticism was emerging during the last decades of the nineteenth century. The significant thing was, however, that the pointed arch had quietly been abandoned, but Picturesque compositions were retained minus the tedium of old-fashioned Gothic detailing. Sensible sash-windows made Gothic openings redundant, and architecture was on its way back to Classicism, tentatively at first, via early Renaissance forms, but back to Classicism all the same. It was this use of the tall sash-widow in segmental-headed openings with brick dressings, that conjured the term 'Queen-Anne' style, from its superficial resemblance to the real thing.

The certainties of the Gothic Revival had given way to a confusion of eclecticism: the vacuum left by the end of the Revival was, in fact,

Plate 82 Sir Thomas Jackson's Examination Schools in Oxford of 1876–82 is fashioned from motifs culled from Elizabethan and Jacobean architecture. The mullioned and transomed windows derive from Kirby Hall in Northamptonshire and the entrance is of the Venetian Window or Serliana type. (*JSC*)

131

a loss of principle. Some thought that architectural confusion was caused by a loss of faith: one critic noted that it took a God to bring order out of chaos.[13] Synthesis was seen to be an answer, a synthesis of Gothic and Classical forms, that would give birth to an architecture appropriate for the late nineteenth century. In the Queen's Jubilee Year of 1887 the School Board Offices (*Plate 83*) on London's Embankment of 1871–9 (a strange eclectic building composed of mixed Netherlandish and Northern French motifs) by George F. Bodley (1827–1907) and Thomas Garner (1839–1906), the Alliance Assurance Office in St James's Street of 1881–8 by Norman Shaw (a hybrid mixture of striped façades with tall Renaissance stepped and scrolled gables) (*Plate 84*), and the Examination Schools in Oxford (*Plate 82*) mentioned earlier were singled out as triumphs of eclecticism in free Classical forms mixed with Gothic principles.

Alfred Waterhouse, in his National Liberal Club in London of 1885–7, mixed Romanesque, Italian and French Renaissance elements (*Plate 85*) which were said to reflect the uneasy pot-pourri of disparate opinion in the party.[14] The National Liberal Club was an oddity, for Waterhouse had declared that Gothic was suitable for building types in the nineteenth century, and that new materials could be adapted to that style. His harsh red terracotta and red-brick Prudential Assurance Buildings in Holborn, London, of 1878–1906 (*Plate 86*) has a central tower with bartizans and stepped gables, giving the building an oddly Scottish flavour that, if the building were translated into Aberdeen granite, would be very much more obvious. Waterhouse also used a hard type of Gothic at St Paul's School, Hammersmith, built of red brick with terracotta dressings in 1881–4 (*Figs 33–34*).

Shaw's striped frontages of the Alliance Assurance Office in London's St James's (*Plate 84*) of 1881–3 had shown pronounced Anglo-Netherlandish-Renaissance leanings in the gables. His New Scotland Yard of 1887–90 was also striped (shades of Ruskin's affection for Italy!), but this time had a granite base rising two and a half storeys before the banded effects of brick and Portland Stone rose two storeys

Plate 83 The School Board Offices, Victoria Embankment, London, by Bodley and Garner of 1871–7, a Free-Renaissance style building incorporating Netherlandish and Northern French motifs. (*RCHME No BB85/2080*)
Plate 84 Alliance Assurance Offices, St James's Street, London, of 1881–8 by R. N. Shaw, a hybrid building incorporating Renaissance scrolled gables and other Northern European features. (*JSC*)
Plate 85 National Liberal Club in Whitehall Place, London of 1885–7 by Alfred Waterhouse. A mixture of Romanesque and Italian and French Renaissance elements. (*RCHME No BL 25326*)

Plate 86 Prudential Assurance Building in Holborn, London, by Alfred Waterhouse, of 1878–1906. A Gothic building of harsh red terracotta and brick. Note the stepped gables and Scottish flavour of the tower. (*RCHME No BL 18220*)

Fig 33 St Paul's School, Hammersmith, by Alfred Waterhouse. (*RCHME No BB88/5487*)

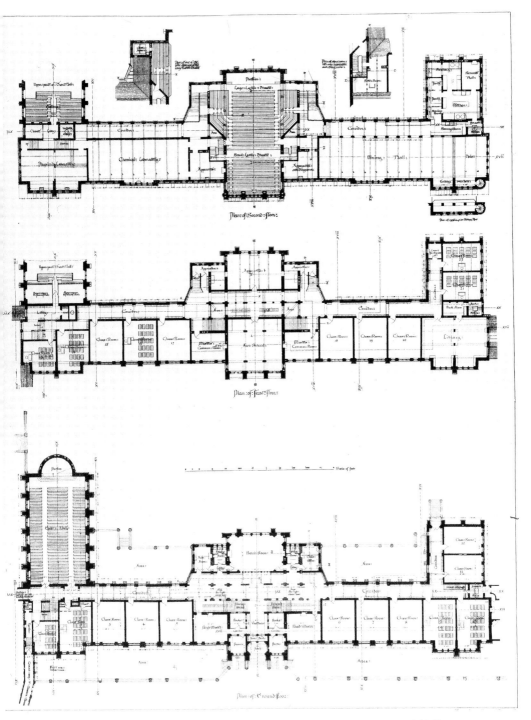

Fig 34 Plans of St Paul's School, Hammersmith. (*RCHME No BB88/5486*)

135

to the eaves and two more into the gables. At the corners of the building were bartizan-like *tourelles*,[15] and at the tops of the gables aedicules supported supplicant open segmental pediments through which obelisks thrust skywards. At Scotland Yard, therefore, Baroque devices mingle with Ruskinian stripes, late-medieval *tourelles*, and certain English and Netherlandish motifs (*Plate 87*). The former White Star Line offices in The Strand, Liverpool, by Shaw with J. Francis Doyle of 1896 have some similarities in style to New Scotland Yard.

Plate 87 New Scotland Yard, Westminster, by R. N. Shaw, of 1887–90, in which many eclectic elements mix. In spite of the striped Northern European Netherlandish flavour, the form of the building owes much to smaller French châteaux like that of Azay-le-Rideau. Stylistically Scottish Baronial elements mix with French and Netherlandish themes. (*RCHME No CC73/2584*)

Plate 88 The Imperial Institute in South Kensington of 1887–93 by T. E. Collcutt. Here Renaissance features from Dutch, Spanish, French, German and Flemish buildings merge with vestiges of late Gothic. (*RCHME No BB71/ 11530*)

Probably the last and greatest of late-Victorian eclectic buildings was Thomas Edward Collcutt's (1840–1924) Imperial Institute in South Kensington (1887–93), a wonderful amalgam of late Gothic and Dutch, Spanish, French, German and Flemish Renaissance styles. Collcutt had been a leading protagonist of the 'Queen-Anne' style, yet the architectural languages used in the Imperial Institute seem to embrace the best of the free Renaissance styles, pulled together and given a new, assured coherence (*Plate 88*).

The French Taste
A brief note is necessary on a curious aspect of Victorian taste in architecture. French furniture was much prized, but there were a few cases where overt copying or covert allusions to French Renaissance architecture took place. Of course there had been strong French influences in much Gothic-Revival architecture from the 1850s, notably at the hands of Street, Brooks and others, while the *tourelles* of some of the Franco-Caledonian buildings such as Dunrobin Castle had more than a Gallic touch.

Waterhouse's Eaton Hall, Cheshire, that huge palace of the Duke of Westminster, had more than a whiff of a French château about it, and

137

E. M. Barry built a Loire castle in the 1870s at Wykehurst, Bolney, in Sussex. An exterior stair at Belfast Castle by Lanyon, Lynn and Lanyon is straight from a Loire château, and there are other examples.

The four most extraordinary buildings in Britain in the French château style are the Bowes Museum, Barnard Castle, Co Durham, begun in 1869 to designs by Jules-A.-F.-A. Pellechet (1829–1903); Château Impney, Droitwich, Worcestershire, built for John Corbett to designs by Tronquois of Paris and the local man, Richard Phené Spiers, between 1869 and 1875; Waddesdon Manor, Buckinghamshire, built for the Rothschilds by Gabriel-Hippolyte Destailleur (1822–93) between 1874 and 1890; and the Royal Holloway College, Egham, Surrey, of 1879–87, by William H. Crossland (1823–1909). The College (*Plate 89*) is a strange Victorian attempt to recreate the architecture of a Loire Valley château of the time of François Ier. All four are vast piles: that at Barnard Castle was erected to house a curiously eclectic collection of furniture, pictures and *objets d'art* as a museum; Waddesdon was built as a house, as was Château Impney; and Holloway College was built as an educational establishment for women.

Very late French Gothic of the *Flamboyant* style was rare in Victorian Britain: early, robust Burgundian and Norman Gothic were favoured. Destailleur, however, was responsible for one extraordinary exercise using the *Flamboyant* Gothic style in the mausoleum of the Emperor Napoléon III, his Empress and the Prince Imperial at Farnborough in Hampshire (*Plate 90*), of 1887.

French Renaissance styles were employed in some of the grander groups of terrace-housing in parts of Kensington, and especially on the Grosvenor Estates between Hyde Park Corner and Victoria Station. Grosvenor Gardens and Grosvenor Place were spectacular examples. The ranges of terraces at Lancaster Gate, London, once known as Upper Hyde Park Gardens, designed by Sancton Wood (1815–86) for Henry de Bruno Austin on either side of Christ Church, were much admired for their elegance and their resemblance to features of the Tuileries Palace in Paris. Such French allusions were to be found, but the overwhelming influence on most of the stucco-faced housing of the Victorian period was that of Italy, or the free interpretation of Italianate motifs.

Plate 89 Royal Holloway College, Egham, Surrey, by W. H. Crossland, of 1879–87, an essay in the French château style of the Loire Valley. (*RCHME No BB84/3110*)

Plate 90 Mausoleum of the Emperor Napoléon III, the Empress Eugénie and the Prince Imperial at Farnborough in Hampshire, designed by Destailleur in the French *Flamboyant* style of Gothic. (*JSC*)

The End of the Century and the Classical Revival

While there were aspects of Art Nouveau in Britain visible while the Gothic Revival was in full spate (certain wispy decorations and the capitals of Blackfriars Railway Bridge), the style never became as popular in the British Isles as it was in France, Spain, Belgium and Central Europe. When it became associated with Oscar Wilde, the Yellow Book, and fin-de-siècle decadence its future was not assured in Britain, although it continued to flourish on the Continent for some time. Oddly enough, the style was used by Alfred Gilbert for three of his memorials: the Shaftesbury Memorial Fountain with Eros in Piccadilly Circus, the tomb of the Duke of Clarence in Windsor and the Queen Alexandra Memorial in St James's, all of which were almost posthumous Art-Nouveau examples.

C. Harrison Townsend (1851–1928) used terracotta and other materials in his remarkable designs for the Bishopsgate Institute (1892–4) (*Plate 91*), Whitechapel Art Gallery (1895–9) and Horniman Museum (1898–1901): all display Art Nouveau motifs, and even certain sub-Gothic and Romanesque allusions, but they were rarities.

Certainly Charles Rennie Mackintosh (1868–1928) had been closely involved with the attenuated style known as Art Nouveau in much of his interior design. His Glasgow School of Art north front of 1896–9 has certain Art-Nouveau elements judiciously mixed with a tough Scottish native style of building and motifs taken from factories, warehouses and the buildings of the Arts-and-Crafts Domestic Revival (*Plate 92*).

Arts-and-Crafts elements merged with Gothic architecture at Holy Trinity, Sloane Street, of 1888, finished in the 1890s, but perhaps an even more exquisite example of Arts-and-Crafts Gothic can be found at the John Rylands Library, Manchester, of 1890–1905, by Basil Champneys (1842–1935) with its marvellous spaces, extraordinary atmosphere, and lovely detail (*Plate 93*).

Yet in spite of the Free Styles, Vernacular Revival, 'Queen Anne', late Gothic, Arts and Crafts, Art Nouveau and various experiments in Renaissance architecture all having their day, Classicism never really died: as the century drew to its close architects seemed to be returning to Classicism. As early as 1885–7 John McKean Brydon (1840–1901) had built Chelsea Town Hall in a 'Free-Classic' style not uninfluenced by the architecture of Wren (*Plate 94*). In 1898–1912 followed his Government Offices, Whitehall, in a style based on Somerset House by

Plate 91 The Bishopsgate Institute of 1892–4 by C. H. Townsend. Art-Nouveau, Renaissance and other features are incorporated. (*RCHME No BB82/8306*)

Plate 92 The north front of C. R. Mackintosh's Glasgow School of Art, of 1896–9: a blend of many elements, freely treated. (*AFK*)

Plate 93 Basil Champneys's John Rylands Library in Manchester, of 1890–1905, a fine example of Arts-and-Crafts Gothic with elements from Decorated and Perpendicular styles. (*RCHME No BB69/6271*)

Plate 94 Chelsea Town Hall of 1885–7 in a 'Free-Classic' style influenced by the work of Wren. J. M. Brydon, architect. (*JSC*)

Sir William Chambers, bits of Wren designs and fragments of motifs by Gibbs. With these influences, of course, it was not pure Classicism to which architects were to turn, but the Baroque. Wren, Hawksmoor, Vanbrugh and Gibbs had all contributed Baroque designs, and it was these masters, more and more, who became the heroes of late-Victorian designers. There were odd intruders, such as the Roman Baroque front of the London Oratory of St Philip Neri and the Church of the Immaculate Heart of Mary (1892–5) by Herbert Gribble (1847–94) (*Plate 95*), but the main source of fin-de-siècle Baroque was English. William Young's (1843–1900) New (now Old) War Office in Whitehall of 1899–1906 shows Palladian, Mannerist and Baroque tendencies (*Plate 96*), which also occur in one of the most modern educational buildings of the era – the Belfast College of Technology (1900–07) by Samuel Stevenson, which was similar to Young's building in composition and elevational treatment (*Plate 97*). Young had previously designed the Municipal Chambers for Glasgow of 1883–8, an opulent symmetrical pile of French, Flemish, Venetian and Spanish Renaissance styles: the influences of Sansovino and even of Alexander Thomson

Plate 95 The Roman Baroque façade of the Brompton Oratory, London, of 1892–5 by Herbert Gribble. (*JSC*)

Plate 96 William Young's New (now Old) War Office, Whitehall, London, of 1898–1906: a mixture of Palladian, Mannerist, and Baroque features. (*RCHME No CC73/2589*)

were mixed with motifs from a bewildering variety of sources (*Plate 98*).

Norman Shaw had moved from the use of medieval and vernacular motifs to experiments with northern European Renaissance, then to Franco-Netherlandish-Scots-Baronial with Scotland Yard and the White Star Line offices in Liverpool. In the late 1880s he began to experiment with Classicism based on Italian Renaissance precedents, and by the end of the Victorian era he was firmly in the Classical camp with his Alliance Assurance Building of 1901–5 on the opposite corner of Pall Mall and St James's Street to that on which he had built his striped red-and-white northern Renaissance block for the same company in 1881–3 (*Plate 84*). There could hardly be a more startling contrast (*Plate 99*).

Plate 97 Belfast College of Technology of 1900–7 by Samuel Stevenson. A design very similar in form and elevational treatment to William Young's War Office, but no less splendid for its eclecticism. (*JSC*)

144

In the 1890s many architects were flocking to the Classical standard, albeit with a Baroque flavour. Aston Webb's (1849–1930) huge frontage for the Victoria and Albert Museum (1891–1909) employs many motifs from a number of sources including early-Renaissance elements, some Baroque ideas and sundry eclectic pieces from earlier styles. Baroque, and especially the Baroque of Wren, was used by Sir Alfred Brumwell Thomas (1868–1948) in his designs for Belfast City Hall, a sumptuous essay in the grandest manner of 1898–1906 (*Plate 100*). Both St Paul's Cathedral and the cupolas of Greenwich Hospital were the exemplars for Thomas's extraordinarily rich designs. John Belcher (1841–1913) and J. J. Joass (1868–1952) at the Moot Hall, Colchester (1898–1902), produced a marvellous Baroque composition that borrows elements from Wren and Hawksmoor. Similar sumptuous Baroque designs and an extraordinary mixture of Continental Baroque styles were produced for Cardiff City Hall by Lanchester, Stewart and Rickards in 1897. Rickards went on to design the equally Baroque Deptford Town Hall of 1900–03, and the stage was set for the Edwardian Baroque period which, like the architecture of Austria-Hungary, of Wilhelmian Germany and of the Republican United States of America, was as proud, as bombastic and as magnificent as it could

Plate 98 The Municipal Chambers, George Square, Glasgow, by William Young of 1883–88. An opulent pile of French, Flemish, Venetian and Spanish Renaissance styles. (*RCAHMS No GW/1890*)

Plate 99 R. Norman Shaw's Alliance Assurance Office of 1901–5 opposite his earlier block in St James's of 1881–3 (Plate 84). Classicism is firmly re-established. (*JSC*)

147

Plate 100 Belfast City Hall of 1898–1906 by Sir Alfred Brumwell Thomas. Sumptuous late-Victorian Baroque architecture much influenced by the work of Sir Christopher Wren. (*JSC*)

possibly be. Mountford's Old Bailey (started 1900) and John Belcher's Ashton memorial at Lancaster of 1907–9 were to epitomise the splendours of Edwardian Baroque. Classicism was once more triumphant, though in its proudest and most stupendous form, and eventually, by the end of the Edwadian era, a more austere Neoclassicism was to prevail.[16]

Sir Christopher Wren, in *Partentalia*, wrote that 'architecture aims at Eternity; and therefore is the only thing uncapable of Modes and Fashions in its Principals'. It is a matter for agreeable speculation to reflect on what he would have made of the free eclecticism, even confusion, of much of architecture in the Victorian age, or of the sorry state of affairs that has prevailed in more recent times.

4. PHILANTHROPIC HOUSING AND THE CONCERN FOR THE UNDERDOG: MODEL DWELLINGS AND MODEL VILLAGES

Introduction; Henry Roberts and the Society for Improving the Condition of the Labouring Classes; The Model Village; Saltaire, Yorkshire; Copley, Akroydon and Bournville; Port Sunlight, Cheshire

To contribute to the welfare of our fellow-creatures, with a view to the glory of God, carries with it that durable happiness which the pursuit of wealth, of fame, or of fleeting pleasure, cannot afford.

> Henry Roberts, *The Dwellings of the Labouring Classes*
> (London, 1867) 28

Introduction

The growth of the Evangelical Conscience played a major rôle in changing the climate of opinion in Britain, as discussed in Chapter 1. The problem of housing in the nineteenth century was most obvious in urban centres, although there were appalling conditions in the housing of the rural poor. An unprecedented growth of the proletarian population in towns caused severe difficulties to which the free-market system and *laissez-faire* did not offer satisfactory solutions: the drift to the towns was putting stresses on what public amenities there were. Not until the first cholera epidemics of the 1830s did it dawn on politicians that an enormous problem existed, for choked burial-grounds, evil-smelling streams and rivers (which were often little more than open sewers) and foul cess-pits were thought to exude a 'miasma' that was the cause of cholera. Housing and public health were major concerns of the Victorian age: overcrowding, ill-health, disease and mortality statistics were themes that haunted the period.

From 1836 the national network of Poor Law Boards of Guardians was obliged to register births, marriages and deaths, and Edwin Chadwick, first Secretary of the Poor Law Commissioners, by analysing these, was able to arrive at factual conclusions concerning the health of the nation. As a result of his efforts a Select Committee was set up in 1840 to inquire into the 'circumstances of large towns, with a view to improving sanitary arrangements for their benefits'. This committee made many recommendations for ameliorating conditions in towns,

149

including legislation to control the quality and standards of building and the provision of adequate sewers. A Royal Commision on the Health of Towns was established, and its report of 1845 confirmed what Chadwick and his colleagues had noted, while making recommendations for improvements including the building of tenement blocks to house the poor in a hygienic, decent and convenient way. There were endless debates about how the working classes were to be housed in an acceptable manner, and by whom this was to be achieved. The Evangelical Conscience recognised the need for standards that would give back dignity to the labouring classes by improving their dwellings. One of the great problems, of course, was the acquisition of land near town centres where prices were high, thus early attempts to provide philanthropic housing were necessarily built to high densities to keep rents low and make the whole exercise economically possible.

Just as the temperance movement sought to warn the young of the dangers of drink and to wean the drunkards off the bottle by example and by admonitory stories or pictures, so the Evangelical Conscience attempted improvements in working-class housing by means of exemplars. The key figure in the early Victorian philanthropic housing movement was Anthony Ashley Cooper, Lord Ashley, later the seventh Earl of Shaftesbury (1801–85), who, very early in his career had 'become profoundly impressed with the important influence of the dwellings of the people on their habits and character. To the miserable condition of their homes he attributed two-thirds of the disorders that prevailed in the community'.[1]

Henry Roberts and the Society for Improving the Condition of the Labouring Classes

The Victorian philanthropic housing movement developed from an organisation founded in 1830 by Benjamin Wills under the title of The Labourers' Friend Society, which had grown from the earlier Society for Improving the Condition of the Labouring Classes founded in 1825. The original society foundered shortly after its publication of a book of exemplary cottage and farm designs and the erection of twelve model cottages of 'Doric simplicity' at Shooters' Hill, which J. C. Loudon described and illustrated in his influential *An Encyclopaedia of Cottage, Farm, and Villa Architecture.*[2] The resurrected and re-named society of 1830 aimed to provide allotments of land for labourers to cultivate during leisure hours in order to encourage freedom from dependence on charitable assistance and the Poor Rate. By 1835 allotments had been granted to seventy thousand families, branch societies had been formed throughout the land, and a journal, *The Labourers' Friend*, was circulating at the rate of about 1,400 copies per month. The Society also promoted benefit societies, clothing clubs, loan funds, schools and dispensaries, the latter following the examples of the London Livery Companies in their Model Towns in Ulster.[3] At meetings throughout the country the improvement of the construction and design of labourers' cottages was proposed in order to benefit the health and morals of the inhabitants.

In 1844 a number of eminent people, previously unconnected with the Society, changed its direction[4] by pointing efforts towards the amelioration of the condition of the labouring classes. Among this 'body of gentlemen' were Lord Ashley, Dr Thomas Southwood Smith (1788–1861), the sanitary reformer (who had worked with Chadwick, who advocated facilities for dissection in a paper on 'The Use of the Dead to the Living',[5] and who traced epidemic fevers to the impoverishment of the poor, and thus showed that they were preventible), and the successful architect and Evangelical, Henry Roberts (1803–76). Ashley and his colleagues realised that an existing society with an established journal and branches nationwide would be an ideal starting-point for their ambitions to create exemplars in housing for others to follow. Among the aims of these eminent persons were the improvement of the dwellings of the poor, the extension of the cottage allotment system, and the introduction of friendly loan societies. Roberts was elected to the committee, and the Society was re-named first the Society for Improving the Condition of the Poor, and shortly afterwards the Society for Improving the Condition of the Labouring Classes (SICLC hereafter). The Queen and Queen Dowager transferred their patronage from The Labourers' Friend Society, and the Prince Consort was approached regarding the Presidency. Thus, using the vehicle of an established headquarters, branches, and a journal, the SICLC came into being as a dynamic force with the support of the highest in the land. It quickly gained fame as a first-rate philanthropic society, and the allotment and loan ideas soon became secondary considerations.

Vice-presidents included the Archbishop of Canterbury; Lord Ashley; Samuel Gurney (1786–1856), the bill discounter, philanthropist, Quaker, banker, prison reformer and treasurer of the British and Foreign School Society; William Alexander Mackinnon (1789–1870), MP, legislator, Tory who became a Liberal around 1852, burial reformer, abater of smoke nuisance and a leading figure in the promotion of health in towns; the sixth Duke of Manchester (1799–1855), who built many model cottages on his estates; Sir John Dean Paul, Bart, Chairman of the General Cemetery Company, banker (whose bank, Snow, Paul & Paul, crashed in 1855) and Evangelical (when the bank failed he said, complacently, 'This is the Lord's doing, and it is wondrous in our eyes');[6] and Lord John Russell (1792–1878), statesman, parliamentary reformer and future Prime Minister. The committee included Roberts, F. L. Wollaston and Joseph Toynbee.[7] Wollaston was a merchant-banker and had connections with the Clapham Sect; while Joseph Toynbee (1815–66), surgeon, anatomist and promoter of dissection, was founder of the Samaritan Fund. Roberts had entered the Royal Academy Schools and had trained in the offices of Fowler and Smirke: after winning the competition to design the new Hall for the Fishmongers' Company in 1832 he was able to develop a successful private practice, specialising in country houses for Evangelical members of the aristocracy, with a few churches and schools thrown in. His Destitute Sailors' Asylum in the East End of London of 1835 was his first venture in designing for a philanthropic society, and marks the beginning of an important series of buildings by him, some of which became exemplars of world-wide influence.

The aims of the Society included the building of model dwellings in order to demonstrate that commodious and healthy housing could be provided at moderate yet remunerative rents; to issue plans calculated to promote the construction of improved dwellings for the working classes; and to correspond with the landed gentry, with clergymen and others, in order to assist in the building of dwellings and the promotion of branches of the SICLC. Individual members of the Society were not to derive personal profit from the rents received in respect of properties purchased or built by the Society, and dividends were restricted to a maximum of four per cent per annum, a restraint which was to have an adverse effect on the work of the Society because greater returns on investment could be found elsewhere. Chadwick himself warned against the dangers of low rates of interest as they were commercially unwise and suggested a whiff of charity, two factors which were to damage the philanthropic societies, both from the financial point of view and from that of attracting desirable tenants.[8]

Much worse from the point of view of the SICLC was the presence of prominent advocates of dissection in influential positions within the Society. Ever since the reign of King Henry VIII[9] surgeons were granted four bodies of executed malefactors per year for dissection, and the number was increased to six under King Charles II, hardly a sufficient supply of corpses. By *An Act for Better Preventing the Horrid Crime of Murder*[10] of 1752, by which time the death penalty was applied to many crimes against property, the bodies of murderers were subjected to the additional indignity or 'punishment' of dissection, referred to as a further 'Terror and peculiar Mark of Infamy'. With the rise to power of various Benthamite and utilitarian factions in the 1820s and '30s the scene was set for further enactments that would create two classes of the poor: the 'deserving' and 'undeserving'. The *Representation of the*

People Act[11] of 1832 (the Great Reform Bill and Act) overshadowed the passing of another Act of Parliament that was of the greatest moment in degrading the poorest of the poor: this was *An Act for Regulating Schools of Anatomy*[12] of 1832 which pursued the 'punishment' of the destitute after death by enabling anatomy schools to be supplied with the corpses of those who died in institutions. This Act and the *Poor Law (Amendment) Act*[13] of 1834 were aimed at the destruction of more humanitarian and kindly methods of alleviating poverty by smashing the 'paternalism' of the traditional Tory land-owners and by degrading poverty and failure even further.

Executed murderers provided insufficient bodies for the needs of anatomists, so demand encouraged the supply of corpses obtained from burial-grounds by the 'resurrection-men'. Risks attached to 'body-snatching' were considerable, so an alternative was found by the murderous Burke, Hare, Bishop and Williams, who obtained fresh bodies without having to go to the trouble of digging them up first.[14] Before 1832 the anatomists got their subjects from the foot of the gallows, from graveyards and vaults, from murderers and from a trade in imported bodies, but from the passing of the new laws the poor who died in the workhouses were made into criminals in the minds of their contemporaries. This compulsory 'criminalisation' was a most signifi-cant factor in the problems of housing the poor by the philanthropic societies, for barrack-like tenements and any suggestion of charity were associated with the detested workhouses. Working-class burial-clubs testify to the widespread fear of the anatomists and of the social stigma associated with the fate of a body subjected to the dissectionist's knife.[15]

Private charity contrasted with the utilitarian cruelty of the work-house is a theme pursued in Dickens's *Oliver Twist* of 1837–8 and in Pugin's *Contrasts* in the edition of 1841: Pugin specifically shows the bodies of those dying in a Benthamite *Panopticon*-prison-like work-house being taken for dissection in his *Contrasts* (*Fig 35*). What Dickens, Pugin, traditional Tories and Radicals all sensed was that social balance was being threatened by the godless utilitarians who mas-queraded as liberators, democrats and rationalists. Even Dr Southwood Smith, who had been in the vanguard of Benthamite ideas concerning dissection, appears to have become concerned about the implications of using bodies of destitute 'unclaimed' poor for anatomical demonstra-tion.[16]

It began to be apparent during the 1850s that *laissez-faire* would not help to solve the problem of housing the poor, in spite of the Liberals' interest in representation of the people, in administration and in town-hall bureaucracy: Roberts himself saw that there was a point

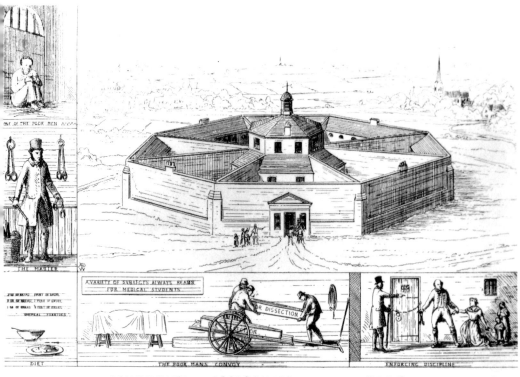

ONE OF THE POOR MEN

THE MASTER

FOR DINNER FIRST OF WATER, FOR SUPPER FIRST OF WATER, I AM OF BREAD A VERY OF BREAD.
OATMEAL PORRIDGE

DIET

A VARIETY OF SUBJECTS ALWAYS READY FOR MEDICAL STUDENTS

FOR DISSECTION

THE POOR MANS CONVOY

ENFORCING DISCIPLINE

CONTRASTED RESIDENCES for the POOR

ANTIENT POOR HOYSE

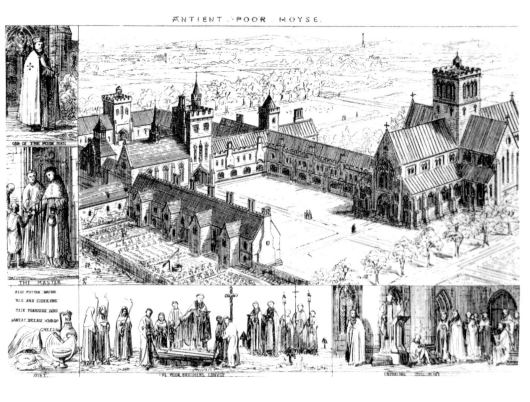

ONE OF THE POOR MEN

THE MASTER

BEEF MUTTON BACON
ALE AND CIDER FINE
MILK PORRIDGE ALSO
WHEAT BREAD VERY GOOD
CHEESE

DIET

THE POOR BROTHERS CONVOY

ENFORCING DISCIPLINE

at which intervention by government, private enterprise, or individuals was essential to provide help in housing the very poor, and in this he has been proved right. As Honorary Architect to the SICLC he was to produce a variety of designs for different types of accommodation: from the beginnings he made it clear that he was aware of the magnitude of the problem, and was critical of his fellow-professionals for not having given much attention to the design of housing for the working classes. To Roberts it was obvious that only a small proportion of the working class could help itself.

The Evangelicals sought to improve dwellings through 'Christian principles' in the same way that Howard had improved prisons. Indeed Roberts contrasted the domiciliary comforts enjoyed by those who had 'forfeited their freedom as the penalty for crime' with the wretched hovels from which too many members of the labouring classes were tempted to escape by entering the 'portals of domestic misery and moral ruin' (the gin-palace and the beer-shop).[17] Child-abuse, incest and violence were not phenomena of the 1980s, as Roberts and others make clear: such problems were widespread in the 1840s, and it was one of the aims of the Society to produce model family dwellings that would be dry, well-ventilated, and have at least three bedrooms, each with distinct and separate access. The SICLC published designs for improved dwellings, but it was soon clear that no amount of description or reasoning would suffice: an actual building as an experiment was necessary. In 1844 a site was found at Bagnigge Wells, Lower Road, Pentonville, at the top of Gray's Inn Road, and contracts were let to build a double row of two-storey houses to accommodate twenty-three families and thirty single females. Suitable attention was paid to ventilation, drainage and an ample supply of fresh water.[18] The Bagnigge Wells scheme[19] was the first in London to provide the working class with specially designed housing under the aegis of a philanthropic society. Unfortunately Roberts's designs were confined to a long, narrow site, and were regarded as drab and mean by the architectural critic George Godwin (1815–88), editor of *The Builder*.[20] Nevertheless, the fact that the SICLC had actually built some model dwellings attracted financial support from the public, and the influence of the Society began to grow.

There was a demand for properly managed lodging-houses for the itinerant labourers who flocked to the cities from the countryside,

Fig 35 Contrasted Residences for the Poor. A Benthamite *Panopticon-*Workhouse with corpses being taken for dissection shown with an 'Antient Poor House' of Catholic England, where dignity, kindliness, and serenity prevailed. (*From Pugin's* Contrasts)

155

but run-of-the-mill accommodation was a 'reproach to the Christianity of England'. The SICLC purchased in 1847 three existing 'doss-houses' in Charles Street, Drury Lane, and these were renovated and provided with suitable conveniences, although the nightly charge was no more than that for the less wholesome places. Roberts thus gained valuable experience, so when the Society purchased freehold land in George Street, Bloomsbury, he was able to design a new five-storey 'Model Lodging-House', complete with kitchens and laundries, common-room and superintendent's flat. The dormitories were sub-divided into cubicles, and there were communal wash-rooms (but only one water-closet for every twenty-five people), ventilated pantries and a small library. Ventilation to the cubicles was by means of shafts, the draught assisted by gas convectors: gas was also the means of illumination throughout the building. The provision of such models encouraged Parliament to pass two important enactments relating to lodging-houses, both promoted by Ashley, the *Common Lodging Houses Act* and the *Labouring Classes Lodging Houses Act.*[21]

Further experiments for conversion of lodging-houses to Roberts's designs were carried out at Hatton Garden in 1849, this time for fifty-seven women, but demand was so limited that it was reopened in 1855 as a lodging-house for men. A second purpose-built block, Thanksgiving Buildings, Portpool Lane, Gray's Inn Road, for twenty families in self-contained flats, and 128 single women (mostly poor, single semp-stresses on barely subsistence wages), was erected to designs by Roberts:[22] it was a large barrack-like block, with a Classical cornice and huge semi-circular-headed openings to the staircases (*Fig 36*).

'The question of lodging a large number of families in one lofty pile of building' occupied the SICLC for some time, and in 1850 the Model Houses for Families were erected on a site at Streatham Street in Bloomsbury leased by the Duke of Bedford at a very moderate rent. Roberts's scheme was to be the Society's most important contribution to the design of tenements, for it was dignified, consisted of self-contained flats, and had communal open space, workshops, and other amenities (*Plate 101*). Standards of construction were greatly in advance of their day, and access to each apartment was by means of galleries or open corridors approached by an open staircase. When the Model Houses were assessed for Window Tax on the grounds that they were one dwelling, the Society appealed against this charge: in due course Roberts's argument that the galleries were in effect elevated 'streets' leading to individual dwellings too small to be liable for tax was accepted, and in 1851 Window Tax was abolished, and a financial burden on the philanthropic societies was removed. This was a personal triumph for Henry Roberts.

Fig 36 Thanksgiving Model Buildings, Portpool Lane, Gray's Inn Road. Henry Roberts, architect. (*From Henry Roberts's* Dwellings of the Labouring Classes . . . *of 1867*)

Plate 101 Two framed architectural perspectives, rendered with water-colour, from the office of Henry Roberts, and probably by him, showing the Model Houses for forty-eight families at Streatham Street, Bloomsbury. On the left is a view from George Street, and on the right is a view of the internal quadrangle. (*The Peabody Trust*)

157

A   Sink, with Coal Box under.
B   Plate Rack over entrance to Dust Shaft, D.
C   Meat Safe, ventilated through hollow bricks.

E   Staircase of Slate, with Dust Place under.
F   Cupboard warmed from back of Fireplace.
G   Linen Closet in this recess if required.

Scale of   feet.

Fig 37 Model Houses for Four Families. Erected by Command of His Royal Highness, Prince Albert, K.G., at the Exposition of the Works of Industry of All Nations, 1851, and subsequently rebuilt in Kennington New Park, Surrey. Henry Roberts, architect. (*From Roberts's,* Dwellings . . .)

158

The most important and celebrated scheme of the SICLC was that for the Model Houses for Families erected at the Great Exhibition of 1851 (*Fig 37*): it won the highest award of the Exhibition (the Council Medal), and was one of the earliest attempts to bring the latest concepts of advanced housing for the working classes before as wide a public as possible. This 'Model Lodge' consisted of four flats for families, and was erected by command of Prince Albert, who put up the money to build the exhibit. Roberts was again the architect, and he produced an ingenious and economical plan with an open staircase which was the central feature of the design. Although the style was in a vaguely 'Jacobethan' mode, the construction (of hollow blocks patented by Roberts previously, fireproof floors and standardised components), was very advanced, and indeed the elevations could be treated quite freely. The Model Dwellings, having no windows in the side elevations, could be repeated infinitely as terraces, while the standard plan enabled tenements of several storeys to be constructed (*Fig 38*). This remarkable exhibit was seen by thousands of visitors to the Hyde Park site, and plans were sold in quantity.[23] The scheme was the basis for many variants (*Fig 39*), including those in an estate at Windsor, a terrace in the East End of London, and several other locations.[24]

Roberts was also the architect for a series of designs for cottages (*Fig 40*) published by the SICLC and erected under the aegis of local branches of the Society or by philanthropically-minded landowners. There are thousands of such buildings based on Roberts's plans all over Britain, sited individually, in groups, or even in entire estates. Here is pattern-book architecture on a grand scale, and it is no exaggeration to say that Roberts and the activities of the Society had a major impact on

Fig 38 Elevation of Two Pairs of Three-Storey Houses on the Plan of Prince Albert's Model Houses. A three-storey version showing how Roberts's plan could be built upwards and extended sideways as terraces. (*From* The Model Houses for Families, built in connexion with the Great Exhibition of 1851 . . . *[London, 1851]*)

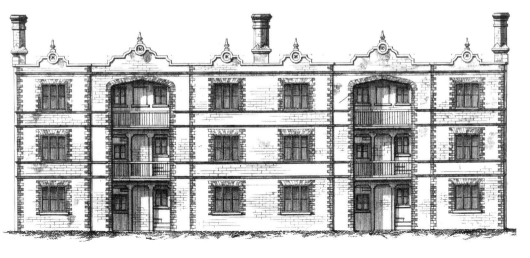

PLAN OF THE CENTRE BUILDING FOR EIGHT FAMILIES.

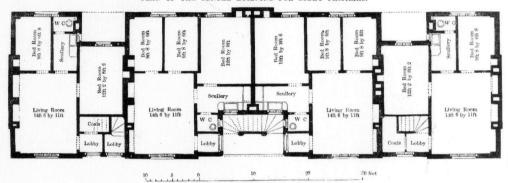

Fig 39 The Windsor Royal Society's Cottages. The centre building is an adaptation of the Prince Consort's Model Houses at the Great Exhibition of 1851, and the elevation shows how Roberts's Exhibition apartments could be joined to other buildings. Note the simplified treatment of the architecture. (*From Roberts's,* Dwellings . . .)

housing in rural areas. Examples can be found at Windsor, Tunbridge Wells, Lyndon, and Cottesmore (both in Rutland), and Culmore (County Londonderry) (*Plate 102*). The style of most of these cottages was a simplified Tudor-Gothic with hood-moulds, but the association of this style with the hated workhouses led Roberts to reduce the direct allusions to historicism by stripping his buildings of all unnecessary ornament and creating a pleasing and robust cottage style of the 1850s that looked forward to the Vernacular Revival of the 1870s. His urban schemes for Model Dwellings were firmly Classical in inspiration (*Plate 103*), though astylar and relying on robustness of construction, good proportions, and clean detailing rather than on any overt reference to the Orders. Streatham Street is the most distinguished block in this Classical mode, but the 1851 Model Dwellings for the Exhibition revert to a Tudorbethan style that perhaps emphasised the philanthropic and 'deserving poor' aspects of the SICLC's work. At Windsor the Exhibition Model Dwellings plans are used, but the elevations are treated in a manner that owes nothing to Tudor or Elizabethan architecture: the buildings become almost style-less, and look forward to developments later in the century (*Figs 39 and 41*).

The SICLC was one of several groups dedicated to providing model dwellings for the labouring classes: these included the Metropolitan Association for Improving the Dwellings of the Industrious Classes, various Industrial Dwellings Companies, and the Peabody Trust, whose architect, Henry Astley Darbishire, was to design many of the tenements for estates in London as well as the Columbia Square scheme

Fig 40 Roberts's designs for pairs of cottages for the Society for Improving the Condition of the Labouring Classes. (*From Roberts's,* Dwellings . . .)

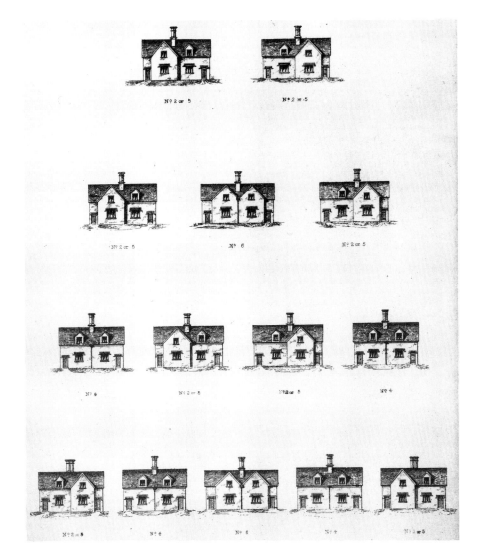

Plate 102 Model cottages identical to those Henry Roberts designed for the SICLC built under the aegis of The Honourable The Irish Society at Culmore, Co Londonderry. (*JSC*)

Plate 103 St George's Buildings (1852–3), Bourdon Place, London, built by John Newson to designs by Henry Roberts. A dignified tenement block with gallery access. (*Former GLC Dept of Architecture and Civic Design, No 77/ — 2828*)

Fig 41 The Windsor Royal Society's Cottages for the Working Classes, by Henry Roberts. The central block has an identical plan to that of the Great Exhibition Model Houses. (*From Roberts's,* Dwellings . . .)

of 1857–60 for Angela Georgina (later Baroness) Burdett-Coutts (1814–1906). Darbishire's designs for George Peabody (*Plate 104*) (who set up his trust to ameliorate the condition and augment the comforts of the poor of London in 1862) had developed by 1870 into a standard grey-brick tenement type of five storeys with a stripped-down Italianate character and an open stair-well based on Roberts's Exhibition prototype of 1851.

Roberts and others had realised that centralist intervention probably was necessary, and following the *Report* of the Royal Commission appointed to investigate the housing of the working classes of 1885 (a document which simply confirmed much that Roberts had been saying in the 1850s), the *Housing of the Working Classes Act* was passed that introduced the principle of state intervention.[25] The 'Jack the Ripper' murders in Whitechapel in the autumn of 1888 drew national attention to the dreadful conditions in London's East End and helped to create a climate of opinion for legislation[26] to be passed that organised sanitary and housing legislation and provided an armoury for slum clearance. While such schemes as the London County Council's Boundary Street Estate at Shoreditch of 1893 (*Plate 105*) and the Millbank Estate of 1897 were the immediate offspring of those enactments, realised in an eclectic late-'Queen-Anne' style with tall tenements, most local-authority housing thereafter tended to be modelled on the vernacular styles so favoured at Port Sunlight and Letchworth.

The Model Village
There had been precedents for the planned model villages of the

163

nineteenth-century industrialists. Chippenham in Cambridgeshire was developed by Lord Orford by 1712 with about fifty houses, a church and a school, and there were several other eighteenth-century planned villages such as New Houghton in Norfolk, Nuneham Courtenay in Oxfordshire, Milton Abbas in Dorset and Inveraray in Argyll. Some such villages were created as a by-product of enclosure and of the creation of new landscaped parks, but all offered reasonable standards of decent accommodation.

Nash and Pennethorne had developed Park Villages in the 1820s on the edges of Regent's Park, and these count among the first suburban Picturesque groupings of individually designed villas. Joseph Paxton and John Robertson planned Edensor in Derbyshire from 1838, a model village in which the Picturesque combines with a mixture of architectural styles, including the Italianate, the Gothic, the Swiss Châlet, and the seventeenth-century vernacular manner. At Edensor the stylistic freedom found in Loudon's *Encyclopaedia* is clear. Eden Nesfield used regional vernacular details at Radwinter in Essex and on the Crewe Hall estates in Cheshire, while Butterfield adapted the cottage style at Ashwell in Rutland. Bedford Park, of course, was to be one of the most celebrated of the consciously designed artificial 'communities', although it was predominantly middle-class, and it combines nostalgia for a Picturesque rural past with an Arts-and-Crafts architecture.

The Industrial Village was a variant of the rural Model Village. Early examples were Cromford in Derbyshire and Montagutown at Buckler's Hard in Hampshire of 1727. Planned villages with architectural pretensions were built by Moravians at Fulneck (near Pudsey), Gracehill (County Antrim) and Fairfield (near Manchester), all in a restrained Classical style, and all with foundations based on co-operation, discipline and brotherly love. Robert Owen probably derived some of his ideas for Villages of Co-operation from the Moravian settlements, although he replaced humility and brotherly love with French utilitarian notions of coercion and indoctrination. His New Lanark, near Glasgow, was one of the first of the nineteenth-century planned industrial villages, but its tenements, its communal experiments, and its authoritarian overtones were not to set the scene for what was to come. Indeed Owen had more in common with the Benthamites than with the real reformers who achieved kindlier, more humanitarian patterns for their experiments.

The Herdmann family developed Sion Linen Mills in County Tyrone from 1835 complete with cottages, schools and other facilities. The Herdmanns introduced social order, education, motives for improvement, and a knowledge of artistic taste to their Model Village. Much of Sion Mills was redeveloped later in an Arts-and-Crafts manner to

Plate 104 Typical Peabody Estate blocks at the Duchy Street Estate, Lambeth, by H. A. Darbishire. (*JSC*)

Plate 105 Part of the LCC Boundary Street Estate at Shoreditch, London, of 1897, clearly influenced by the late 'Queen-Anne' style and by the work of Norman Shaw. (*JSC*)

designs by William Frederick Unsworth (1850–1912), but the village is of great interest as a precursor of later and more famous examples: the buildings were in an appalling state in the late 1980s, which is an indictment of attitudes to a distinguished architect who had once worked with Burges and Street, no less.

One of the first of the enlightened industrialists of Victorian times to build a Model Village associated with his mills was John Grubb Richardson, whose Bessbrook, County Down, of 1846, was erected as a 'duty . . . to God in looking after the welfare . . . of a temperate population'.[27] Richardson was a Quaker, and his exemplary village was planned with ample open space, set in beautiful country, and contained buildings of a high standard of design. As with the London Livery Companies' planned villages in County Londonderry, dispensaries and other facilities were provided. Bessbrook was the model for later more famous experiments, including Bournville and Saltaire.

William Allen and other Quakers had been critical of Owen's apparent lack of religious principle, and, admiring the Moravian settlements, determined to establish self-sufficient communities of smallholders with schools, workshops and cottages. Allen's ideas influenced Feargus O'Connor (1796–1855), who established a series of Chartist Land Colonies between 1846 and 1850. One of these villages was O'Connorville, now Heronsgate, in Hertfordshire, built by the Chartist Co-operative Land Company.[28]

Saltaire, Yorkshire
When Benjamin Disraeli suggested, in his celebrated novel *Sybil*, that between employer and employees there should be a relationship more edifying than the payment and receipt of wages, he was reflecting an idea that was to grow in stature with the Victorian era, and that was to be taken up by several entrepreneurs. Not by far the least intelligent and humane of these industrialists, Titus Salt (1803–76) embraced such an ideal and put it into effect in a practical way.

His idea of using cheap alpaca fibres to make worsted cloth was to be the basis of a fortune which Salt partly used to create a Model Town outside Bradford. Experience in the courts, municipal institutions and industrial establishments had convinced Salt that, socially and morally, things were at a low ebb. Balgarnie, in *Sir Titus Salt, His Life and Lessons* of 1877, states that Salt originally intended to retire at the age of fifty in order to enjoy the life of a country squire, but decided instead to build a large factory and housing for the workers on a virgin site outside Bradford.

Like many of his generation, Salt opined that the troubles of the nation were due primarily to drink and lust: accordingly he decided to improve the condition of his workpeople by example so that family life would be strengthened and temptations would be removed. In 1850 he commissioned the architects Henry Francis Lockwood (1811–78) and Richard Mawson (1834–1904) of Bradford to design a new mill at Shipley Glen, some four miles away from the town. At one stage Salt had considered purchasing the Crystal Palace after the Exhibition of 1851, but instead he determined to build a new factory on the banks of the River Aire, the structure to be planned on the most advanced lines and to embody the latest inventions and constructional methods. The site was cleverly chosen, for, apart from its natural beauties, a railway and a canal existed to provide transport for raw materials and finished products.

Aware of the evils resulting from polluted air and water, Salt hoped to gather a well-nourished and contented body of workers together to form the nucleus of his model community. He declared that he had given instructions to his architects that nothing should be spared to render the dwellings exemplars for the country to follow, and in this aim he clearly was influenced by the Model Dwellings designed by Henry Roberts which he had seen at the 1851 Exhibition. Unlike Owen, whose religious views branded him as a Jacobin or worse, Salt was no experimenter with the bases of traditional life. Church-going and the family unit were to be respected, encouraged and maintained.

The factory, a large Italianate building (*Plate 106*), was commenced, and plans were drawn up for a model town to be laid out on a grid-iron pattern with ample open spaces, churches, a hospital, almshouses, schools, a club and an institute. Salt, though a devout Congregationalist, did not attempt to compel attendance at his own church. He granted sites to Methodists, Baptists, Roman Catholics and Swedenborgians with equal liberality, for he regarded religious belief of any variety as of great importance, while abstention from alcohol was essential to a godly, righteous and useful life. *The Saltaire Monthly Magazine* of March 1871 expressed its thanks to Salt for 'the stern exercise of his proprietorial rights, through which he preserved the residents . . . from the annoyance and temptation of public houses and beer shops'.

Salt's great factory was opened in 1853 with a banquet for 2,500 workers and over a thousand other guests. The Earl of Harewood, who attended the feast, was of the opinion that he had developed a high notion of the manufacturing classes as a result, while the *Bradford Observer* waxed lyrical on the splendours of the new six-storey stone building with its floors of arched brick construction carried on huge cast-iron members (a system used by Henry Roberts). The large plate-glass windows were designed to admit as much light and air as possible, and the huge chimney, reminiscent of an Italian campanile, was fitted

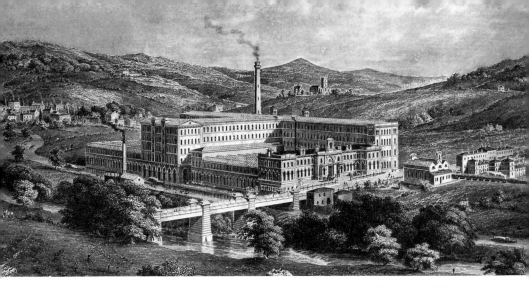

Plate 106 Prospect of the Mill at Saltaire, Yorkshire. Lockwood and Mawson were the architects. (*Bradford City Libraries*)

with patent fuel economisers to remove 'annoying effluvium'.

Lockwood and Mawson's work is solid and agreeably proportioned, and their mastery of style is demonstrated in the town itself. The Congregationalist church (*Plate 107*) of 1859, with its Corinthian Order of columns and pilasters, and its tall, elegant bell-tower, is an example of an assured Classicism far preferable than the halting and feeble Gothic found in some Nonconformist churches. Building continued to 1876, the various communal and educational establishments being erected as the dwellings went up, so there was no shortage of amenities. The existence of an agreed plan, and the control by the architects ensured an homogeneous character and a consistent style. Although the town is only a quarter of a mile square, it had over eight hundred houses built in terraces with back yards containing coal-stores and, originally, privies. The elevational treatment of the houses was distinguished, for Lockwood and Mawson favoured an Italianate style: the almshouses are particularly fine examples of their work in an Italianate Gothic manner (*Plate 108*). The architects introduced subtle variations of design, for houses are of differing sizes: Salt displayed an astonishingly enlightened approach when he conducted surveys of the housing needs of his workers. The result was that houses were provided which suited family functions, and contained two, three or four bedrooms. Monotony of architectural treatment was avoided, as was a rigid repetition of accommodation: these were major advantages over much housing of the period. Each house had a parlour, a kitchen, a store and a cellar in addition to the bedrooms, while even the smallest house was carefully detailed and soundly constructed, with adequate accommodation for a small family.

After a short period as a Member of Parliament Salt returned to Saltaire and commissioned a sturdy four-square mausoleum to be attached to his beloved Congregational church. Yet, despite the mausoleum, Salt still had fifteen years left to live in which he improved Saltaire further, and formed his firm into a joint-stock company. He was rewarded with a baronetcy in 1869. Eventually he was laid to rest in his tomb guarded by a hefty angel. It would be hard to name a more decent personification of the Victorian industrialist-benefactor than Sir Titus Salt, whose 'indomitable perseverence, resolute will, and patient toil' led to fortune, honours and the creation of the pleasant little Model Town that is his lasting memorial.[29]

Copley, Akroydon and Bournville

At Halifax Colonel Edward Akroyd began Copley in 1847 with shops and housing, while his Akroydon of 1859 onwards by George Gilbert Scott and W. H. Crossland (1823–1909) was built in the Gothic style to improve the taste of the inhabitants (*Plate 109*). This Model Village had advanced facilities, including gas, but its chief interest (apart from it stylistic aspects) lies in Akroyd's notions of a mix of housing so that the better-off and better-educated would improve the education, behaviour and taste of those further down the social ladder. Internal accommodation included single large living-rooms with sculleries, an improvement on the two-room plan including a little-used 'parlour'. The village was laid out around a large open square, while the Church

Plate 107 Congregationalist church at Saltaire, with Sir Titus Salt's mausoleum on the left. Lockwood and Mawson, architects, 1859. This firmly Classical building demonstrates the link between Nonconformity and Classical architecture. (*JSC*)

Plate 108 The almshouses at Saltaire in an Italianate Gothic style. Lockwood and Mawson, architects. (*JSC*)

Plate 109 The centre of Akroydon, laid out by G. G. Scott and W. H. Crossland from 1859. Note the Eleanor Cross memorial to Colonel Akroyd, similar to the Martyrs' Memorial in Oxford. (*JSC*).

of All Souls (described by Scott as his best church) is a sumptuous essay in the High Victorian Gothic Revival style (1856–9).

While Saltaire was taking shape George Cadbury (also a Quaker) developed his ideas for Bournville, which was to consist not only of improved housing for the industrious classes, but also was to contain dwellings suitable for office-workers. The first houses (1879) at Bournville were for foremen, and were set in large gardens, owing much to the ideal of an Arts-and-Crafts Domestic-Revival style for buildings set in a bushy landscape in the manner of Bedford Park. Only half of the houses at Bournville were to be let to employees, in order to leaven charges of 'benevolent paternalism', and there were ample recreational facilities. Bournville influenced later developments in other countries and in Britain.[30]

Port Sunlight, Cheshire

Industry and trade produced much of the wealth that made such experiments as Saltaire and Bournville possible, and it was industry that also produced goods that improved the lot of the masses of society. One of the most beneficial of products to be made widely available by industrial methods was soap, for it was cheap soap that did so much to raise standards of cleanliness and reduce the incidence of disease. Of all soaps Sunlight was by far the most successful as a product, and it was that product that gave its name to the most interesting and most attractive Model Village associated with an industry.

The idea of building Port Sunlight perhaps was suggested to William Hesketh Lever, later the first Viscount Leverhulme (1851–1925), by Saltaire. Like Salt, Lever believed in profit-sharing as he realised that part of his success was due to the surplus value produced by his workers. While he, like Krupp of Essen, Cadbury at Bournville and Richardson of Bessbrook, acknowledged the moral precept of returning some part of this profit to his work-force, he doubted the wisdom of the people in spending it. He could have paid a weekly cash dividend but, realising that too often the small monthly sums could be squandered, he used the sums to provide housing and other facilities for the use and enjoyment of workers and their families.

In 1888 Lever found the works at Warrington inadequate so he moved the factory to a new site on the west bank of the Mersey, three miles south of Birkenhead. There, he determined to build a town for his workpeople, and some thirty-two acres were initially reserved for residential purposes. The works were built on the remaining twenty-four of the fifty-six acres originally purchased. The site contained a number of ravines filled with slime and ooze, but these were filled in, and Lever decided to create formal vistas, avenues and spaces, representing the triumph of civilisation, progress and order over chaos, dereliction and waste. A culvert was built to channel the creek which ran from near the railway to Bromborough Pool, and the bridge over the stream was buried (hence the name of the Bridge Inn).

The first layout plan of Port Sunlight (1888) was Lever's own, and the first buildings and refinements of that plan were by the architect William Owen (1849–1909) of Warrington. It is clear that from the beginning the architects collaborated with Lever with the result that the settlement is, in the words of the official Ministry List, 'a large and complete museum piece, indicative of the thoughts and ideas of those fin-de-siècle architects working under the influence of the Pre-Raphaelites'. From its first foundations, Port Sunlight attracted favourable comment, and William Owen's designs for the first twenty-eight cottages and entrance lodge were awarded the Grand Prix at the 1910 Brussels exhibition.

Low density, a variety of architectural styles, and a boulevard-like approach adopted from France were to be the main features of the plan (*Fig 42*). The site, about one mile long by half a mile wide, is bounded on the south-east by the Works; on the north-east by the New Chester Road; on the south-west by the railway; and by Bebington Road on the north-west. The shape and the formality of the layout are immediately apparent from the plan, as are the large amounts of open space. The centrepiece of the development is the cruciform pattern of boulevards created by the intersection of The Diamond and The Causeway (*Fig 43*). This intersection is now marked by the magnificent granite and bronze War Memorial, designed by Sir William Goscombe John (1860–1952) and erected in 1921. The Diamond (conceived by James Lomax-Simpson) is a long formal garden, with ranges of houses and avenues on either side, disposed symmetrically: it has a raised garden with a stone arch stopping the vista at the south-east end, while the Lady Lever Art Gallery encloses the space at the north-western end.

Many of the houses are built in a Cheshire vernacular style, with half-timbered upper works, much influenced by the Arts-and-Crafts movement. There are brilliant forays into French *Flamboyant*, Flemish, North German and even colonial styles, as well as reinterpretations of the local vernacular. The symmetrical groups of gabled houses of 1913 facing The Diamond and designed by James Lomax-Simpson are noble compositions in themselves, and are admirable foils to the grander architecture of the Gallery and Memorial.

Other distinguished designs are those in Lower Road adjacent to the Gallery, by Charles Herbert Reilly (1874–1948); the *Flamboyant* Gothic group (1896) of hard terracotta and brick overlooking the Bowling Green in Cross Street by George Hastwell Grayson (1871–

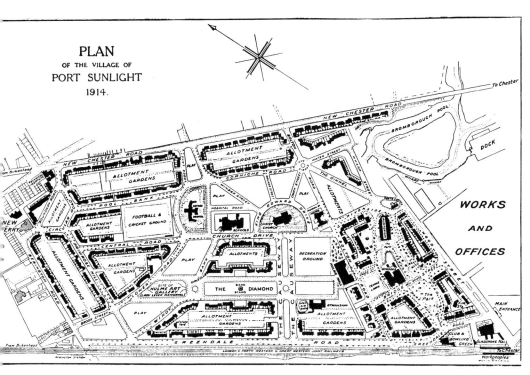

PLAN
OF THE VILLAGE OF
PORT SUNLIGHT
1914.

Fig 42 Plan for Port Sunlight as it had developed by 1914. Note the formal layout and axial planning. (*From T. Raffles Davison,* Port Sunlight *[1916]*)

Fig 43 Prospect of Port Sunlight from the north-west by T. Raffles Davison. The Works are in the distance, and the Art Gallery is the large building on the right at the end of The Diamond. (*From Davison,* Port Sunlight . . .)

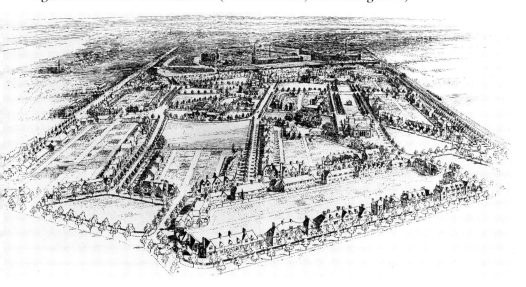

173

1951) and Edward Augustus Lyle Ould (1853–1909) (*Plate 110*); the gabled half-timbered cottages with elaborate pargetting in Park Road by W. and S. Owen (*Plate 111*); and the charming terraces of Flemish and North German-style houses of 1895 by Grayson and Ould in Wood Street (*Plate 112*). At the corner of Bridge and Wood Streets are distinguished houses of 1894 by the Owens with ogee gables, vitrified diaper work and walls of brick and terracotta (*Plate 113*). The eclecticism of these designs, coupled with craftsmanship of the highest order and an assured ingenuity of massing (notably in the treatment of chimneys and fenestration), show late Victorian design at its best: Port Sunlight is an ensemble of motifs culled from the finest precedents, put together with a professionalism and a panache that would put most work in the late twentieth century to shame. The range of designs for domestic buildings is considerable, and reflects stylistic fashions of the time.

The area around the Bowling Green is perhaps the social centre of the village. Beside the Green is the Lyceum of 1894–6, by Douglas and Fordham, now a Men's Club, and Hulme Hall of 1901, still used for functions, by W. and S. Owen. A major architectural focus is provided by the distinguished Christ Church of 1902, by William and Segar Owen (*Fig 44*) in an angular Edwardian Perpendicular style, realised in red sandstone. The richly vaulted narthex at the west end of the church shields the funerary effigies of Lord Leverhulme and Elizabeth Ellen, his wife (1850–1913). These beautiful and noble recumbent bronze figures are by Sir William Goscombe John.

Perhaps the grandest building in the village is the Art Gallery, designed in a severely logical Neoclassical style by Segar Owen. The foundation stone was laid by King George V in 1914, and the gallery was opened by Princess Beatrice in 1922. To the south-west of the

Plate 110 Houses in the *Flamboyant* Continental Gothic style, Port Sunlight, by Grayson and Ould, architects, 1896. (*JSC*)

Plate 111 Gabled half-timbered cottages, with elaborate pargetting in Park Road, Port Sunlight, by William and Segar Owen. In the distance is the Lyceum by Douglas and Fordham of 1894–6. A beautiful group of houses based on local Cheshire vernacular types, and therefore a mature example of the Domestic Revival. (*JSC*)

Plate 112 Houses with stepped gables of the Flemish and North-German type in Wood Street, Port Sunlight, designed by Grayson and Ould, of 1895. (*JSC*)

gallery is the Lever Memorial erected in memory of Lord Leverhulme by his fellow-workers in 1930, and designed by Sir William Reid Dick. Opposite the main entrance to the gallery in a pool at the end of The Diamond is a bronze fountain of 1949, designed by Charles Wheeler.

Other public buildings include the Bridge Inn of 1900, by Grayson and Ould, a gabled structure with galleries based on an old English coaching-inn type, and originally intended to serve non-alcoholic refreshments. Lever, like Salt, was aware of the evils of the demon drink, but an eighty-five per cent vote in favour of a licence made the Bridge Inn 'wet'. Lever said of Port Sunlight that the 'plan is most effective in elevating and bettering the conditions of labour, and has the additional advantage of ensuring that the wives and children shall share in it'. To Lever, the 'convenience and life of the people' could be achieved without any sacrifice of beauty or of 'inspiring vistas'. The success of Port Sunlight proved that philanthropy based on sound business principles actually worked, while improvements in the health of inhabitants soon became apparent. By 1917, Port Sunlight had a population of 4,600 with a death-rate some 4.6 per cent below the national average. Children attending Port Sunlight schools were pronounced heavier and taller than those attending classes of the same age-groups in Liverpool itself.[31]

Throughout the nineteenth century there were many experimental attempts to establish Model Villages with both agricultural and industrial associations.[32] Port Sunlight, Bedford Park and Bournville fixed the modes for architectural styles, Picturesque groupings and low densities that were later favoured at New Earswick, Hampstead Garden Suburb and the first Garden City at Letchworth. The vernacular styles of the Domestic Revival were important features of many attempts to build healthy dwellings in our own century, including the inter-war local authority housing estates and the speculative pseudo-timber-framed semi-detached and detached houses erected for renting to the private market in the 1920s and '30s. Both local-authority and private-enterprise Domestic-Revival housing suggested the rural retreat by their appearance, low density and style, and so demonstrated how far the ideal of the Picturesque had overcome that of the Sublime.

Plate 113 Houses of 1894 with ogee gables, vitrified diaper work and walls of brick and terracotta, at the corner of Bridge and Wood Street, Port Sunlight. W. and S. Owen were the architects. (*JSC*)
Fig 44 Drawing by T. Raffles Davison of William and Segar Owen's Christ Church, Port Sunlight, completed in 1902. (*From Davison*, Port Sunlight . . .)

5 DOMESTIC ARCHITECTURE APART FROM PHILANTHROPIC AND MODEL HOUSING

Introduction; The Ladbroke Estate; The Norland Estate; The Example of Glasgow and the Houses of Alexander Thomson; A Summing-Up

The number of modern houses in England that are artistically eligible for consideration is very large . . .
Hermann Muthesius in the Preface to the first edition of *Das englische Haus* (Wasmuth, Berlin, 1904)

Introduction

Urban developments in the Victorian age inevitably included an enormous amount of house-building. While census returns, literature and journals can tell us much about the social structure of the Victorian age, it is arguable that the most telling record can be found in the great legacy of Victorian domestic architecture which is significant not only for its quantity but because of its amazing diversity. Society and its strata are mirrored in that legacy, for the Victorian house expressed social status and aspirations: a 'good' address could show that a person had 'arrived', while a declining area could demonstrate a fall in fortunes. Stylistically, a development that exhibited unfashionable architectural features could be difficult to let, so it was often necessary for landlords to conform to current taste, even if it meant altering the façades of perfectly sound houses.

An example of this was in Bloomsbury, where Georgian brickwork, with windows and doors destitute of architraves of other dressings, was regarded as dull, tame and expressionless, and was being covered with cement rendering and Italianate detailing in the 1850s as the leases fell in. Further tinkering on the Bedford Estate occurred in the 1880s and '90s when terracotta dressings were applied to Georgian houses in order to attempt to bring them up to date. Reworking of interiors also occurred at intervals, so houses on the great estates, leased for fixed periods, accurately reflect prevailing taste at the time of the last alterations. It must be remembered that most houses were leased for fixed terms, or were rented: landlords therefore retained control over the appearance of their estates in a way far more comprehensive than later planning restrictions were ever capable of doing.

Nash had left a fashionable legacy in his huge unified architectural façades of stucco at Regent's Park and Street. Belgravia and South Kensington were also to acquire rendered elevations of considerable grandeur, and these made plain Georgian brick look very drab in comparison. It will be recalled that Gaius Tranquillius Suetonius had said in *Divus Augustus* that the Emperor had boasted he had found Rome brick and left it marble (*urbem . . . excoluit adeo, ut iure sit gloriatus marmoream se relinquere, quam latericiam accepisse*[1]): it was said of John Nash and his Royal patron that they had found London brick and left it plaster. Stucco-faced houses remained fashionable long after the death of Nash in 1835, even when advanced Victorian taste moved away from the predilection for a 'fatal facility of stucco' to a preference for brick and terracotta after 1870.

Nash himself was an accomplished designer of the asymmetrical country house of which Richard Payne Knight's (1750–1824) house at Downton in Herefordshire is the prototype, and he could turn his hand to Picturesque 'medieval' compositions as at Caerhays in Cornwall (1808), and Killymoon in County Tyrone (1801–03), but he also produced designs for asymmetrical Italianate houses as at Cronkhill in Shropshire (1802). From 1806 Nash and James Morgan began to lay out Marylebone Park which, from 1811, became Regent's Park, a fine landscaped area around which palatial terraces and villas were erected. Both the villas set in gardens and the great terraces facing the park were to influence many late developments throughout the country, and mention will be made of a few outstanding examples.

John Shaw (1776–1832) exhibited a design at the Royal Academy in 1803 for a 'British Circus, proposed to be built by subscription between the Paddington-road and Hampstead, on the freehold estate of H. S. Eyre, Esq.'. This great circus scheme, the formal crescents of Park Terrace (1812–22) and the Regent Street Quadrant (1818–20) by Nash, terraces such as Chester Terrace (1821–30), and the villas of Park Villages with its formal model suburbs (completed to designs by James Pennethorne), were all influential in different ways on Victorian domestic architecture, while Nash's designs for the planting of the Regent's Park area were also potent models for later developments. The circus and planting clearly influenced the planning of Kensal Green Cemetery, for example, while villas, terraces, crescents and other features recurred in the developments of many residential areas. Precedents for grand unified façades could be found in antiquity, but there were also British prototypes as at Bath and Buxton. However, the mixture of building types, terraces, semi-detached and detached houses, set in landscaped gardens, appears to derive from the model of Regent's Park and the Villages.

179

Two important estates in West London offer interesting exemplars of Victorian style and layout: the Ladbroke and Norland Estates of Northern Kensington, both of which developed as fashionable London moved westwards. The key, as always, was the location of the Court, for Kensington began to be desirable when Kensington Palace became an important Royal residence in the seventeenth century: Belgravia was near Buckingham Palace (which Nash had rebuilt for King George IV) and the clubland of Pall Mall and St James's, and the process of development continued in the vicinity of Hyde Park, the fringes of Kensington, Bayswater and Notting Hill.

The Ladbroke Estate

The maps of Northern Kensington show motifs of concentric curved roads that lie immediately to the west of Ladbroke Grove. The layout of this area is distinguished by these roads, terraces of houses and substantial villas, but there are great swathes of greenery also running in concentric curves between the bands of building (*Fig 45*). The long and involved history of the development of the Ladbroke Estate has been described, notably in Florence Gladstone's *Notting Hill in Bygone Days* and, very fully, in Volume 37 of the *Survey of London*.[2] The building of houses on this estate began during the lifetime of James Weller Ladbroke (died 1847) who, through a private Act of Parliament of 1821, acquired power to grant leases of ninety-nine years (not an unusual process in London developments). So that development of the estate would conform to an orderly overall plan, the distinguished architect, designer of landscapes and topographical artist, Thomas Allason (1790–1852), was appointed as surveyor. Allason (who was one of the first to observe the entasis on Greek columns)[3] drew up a design for the layout that took particular note of the rising ground, and the centrepiece of his proposals was an enormous circus bisected by a north-south thoroughfare that became the genesis of Ladbroke Grove. From the clauses of the Act and the character of the design, large detached or semi-detached villas were intended for the site, very similar to Nash's early designs for Regent's Park and clearly derived from the plans for the Eyre Estate at St John's Wood exhibited by Shaw at the Royal Academy in 1803 and based on an earlier scheme published in 1794.[4]

Building began on lands fronting the Uxbridge Road (now Holland Park Avenue), and almost all these houses are stucco-fronted, of modest scale, with the Classical tradition of the eighteenth century still strongly evident. Here, and in Ladbroke Terrace, the architect Robert Cantwell (1792–1858) designed several houses similar to those erected in Cheltenham by John Buonarotti Papworth (1775–1847). The

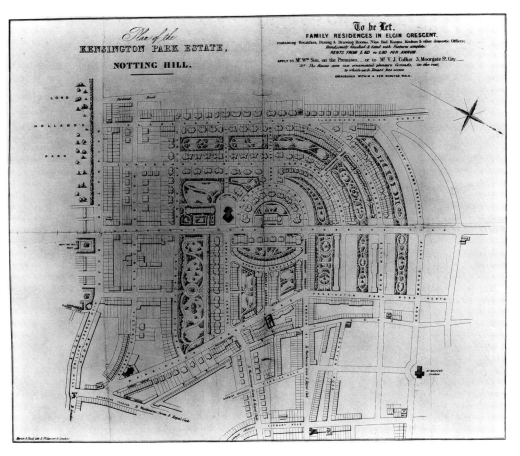

Fig 45 Plan of the Ladbroke Estate showing the concentric streets and swathes of greenery. (*Kindly provided by the General Editor, Survey of London*)

connection with Cheltenham is more than coincidental, however, for Pearson Thompson, the 'Maker of Cheltenham', commissioned Papworth to lay out the Montpellier Estate there, and that remarkable and prolific architect designed a house at Cheltenham for Richard Roy, one of the figures involved in the developments of the Ladbroke Estate. The curved sweeps alternating with straight roads, large landscaped gardens, and the positioning of churches and important architectural compositions as eye-stoppers at Cheltenham, provide many of the object-lessons of the Ladbroke Estate in terms of design. Many of the street-names occur in both places, including Lansdowne and Montpellier.[5]

Three elements from the Circus Plan of 1823 survived in the final layout of the Ladbroke Estate: the first was the north-south axis of

181

Ladbroke Grove; the second was the crescent on the western slope of the hill now crowned by the church of St John the Evangelist; and the third was the sequence of private 'paddocks' between groups of houses. An estate plan of the Kensington Park Estate, Notting Hill, of the 1850s shows how far developments had progressed by that time. The first revision of the original plan was by James Thomson (1800–83), a pupil of Papworth, and it was Thomson who designed a number of houses to the west of Ladbroke Grove.[6] Thomson was a master of assured and crisp Classical detail reminiscent of the grand display found in his work for Nash as executant architect for Cumberland Terrace and Cumberland Place, Regent's Park.

Variations of plan occurred as the layout of the estate took place, but these always included communal spaces: when John Hargrave Stevens (d 1875) produced his plan the 'paddock' idea came into prominence once more. Stevens and his partner George Alexander designed the church of St John the Evangelist, Ladbroke Grove, which was consecrated in 1845, and is built of Kentish ragstone in the Early English style of Gothic Revival, in marked contrast with the surrounding houses. The central tower with broach spire based on the church of St Mary at Witney is placed over the crossing. St John's is representative of that early phase of Gothic-Revival church building in which an inappropriately rural material was used: only a few years later the hard brickwork of All Saints', Margaret Street, and other urban churches was to supersede ragstone as a favoured material. Churches, of course, were necessary for the success of an estate, as they gave architectural and social focuses to residential areas at a time when church-going was *de rigueur* among the upper and middle classes. Apart from St John's and the later church of St Peter, Kensington Park Road, one other church on the estate deserves note: the very remarkable St Mark's church by Enoch Bassett Keeling (*Fig 23*) of 1863 (now demolished), described later as 'an atrocious specimen of coxcombry in architecture',[7] so violent and rasping was its jagged interpretation of polychromatic Continental Gothic. Wedged on a narrow site between the Ladbroke and Norland Estates is the exquisite little Roman Catholic church of St Francis of Assisi (1859–61) by Henry Clutton (1819–93) and John Francis Bentley (1839–1902) (*Fig 46*).[8]

By the time St John's was being built Thomson ceased to be involved in the development of the estate, although some of his designs were realised at 16–26 even and 31–39 odd Clarendon Road, 37–61 odd Ladbroke Grove, and 1–6 consecutive Lansdowne Walk, all relatively distinguished ranges of terrace-houses with pronounced Neoclassical features. All were actually built by William Reynolds, who played a considerable part in the development of the lands to the west of

Ladbroke Grove. Reynolds, who was a builder and surveyor, probably worked with Allason, and modified Thomson's scheme so that large numbers of single, paired, and tripleted villas replaced Thomson's designs for long terraces and villas in substantial gardens. Reynolds introduced a style of house much embellished with stucco dressings, of which the unusual pair at 43 and 45 Clarendon Road, unified with a Giant Order of Corinthian pilasters and a crowning pediment, provides a relatively distinguished example.[9]

The first edition of the large-scale Ordnance Survey maps of mid-Victorian times show individual garden-layouts together with the winding paths of the 'paddocks' or communal gardens. A comparison of what was actually laid out in the Ladbroke Estate with the ideas found in John Claudius Loudon's *The Gardener's Magazine and Register of Rural and Domestic Improvements* of the 1830s and '40s gives a clue as to the origin of these layouts. One of Loudon's correspondents, T. Rutger, produced a series of designs for laying out suburban gardens in 1835 in which he advised grass around clumps of planting rather than the gravel that was fashionable in the Regency period. He suggested a variety of evergreens, with holly, box, japonica, red cedar, privet, and a mixture of giant ivy, jasmine and clematis for individual gardens rather than large trees that would prevent anything else from growing underneath them. Ornamental vases and other

Fig 46 Baptistery of the Church of St Francis of Assisi, Notting Hill, London, by John Francis Bentley, of 1861.

objects from 'Austin's manufactory of artificial stone in the New Road' were suggested for positioning in strategic places to add interest to the gardens. At Brompton, Rutger noted that evergreens were being introduced into gardens where both 'common and Portugal laurels' were commonly planted. Indeed, he advised 'all persons about to lay out and plant' gardens to inspect the nurseries about Brompton and the New Road.[10]

One of the most successful nurserymen in Brompton was David Allan Ramsay who laid out and planted the cemetery of St James at Highgate for Geary and Bunning in the late 1830s and early '40s, and who subsequently worked on the landscaping of the West of London and Westminster Cemetery at Brompton for Geary and Baud. The circuitous paths of the 'paddocks' of the Ladbroke Estate owe their origins to Loudon, to the cemetery precedents, and to ideas promoted in *The Gardener's Magazine* and elsewhere.[11] Deciduous trees were recommended for parts of open gardens where leaves could be easily swept up and where they would not interfere with other plants or with buildings. It is not unlikely that Ramsay carried out works on the layout of the 'paddocks', to overall plans produced by the architects, for he was connected with the development of the Ladbroke Estate as a builder (and came to grief like so many others as a result).

It is known that Thomas Allom, the architect, who designed the most spectacular groupings of houses on the Ladbroke Estate, was responsible for many of the drawings in the second-premium design for the buildings of Brompton Cemetery where we know Ramsay was involved in the planting. Ramsay's association with Allom as builder of the latter's designs on the Estate and the style of landscape layout of the 'paddocks' would suggest that Ramsay may have been the landscape contractor responsible. This possibility is supported by the fact that Ramsay was one of William Reynolds's assignees in bankruptcy, and it was usually Reynolds who obtained sub-leases after covenanting to lay out the 'paddocks'.[12]

The lands to the east of Ladbroke Grove, including the spectacular Kensington Park Gardens, Stanley Crescent and Stanley Gardens, were laid out to a grand design by Thomas Allom. Stopped vistas are everywhere apparent, not least in Stanley Gardens, where the focus is provided by the symmetrical pair of 10 and 11 Stanley Crescent, designed by Allom and built by Ramsay (*Plate 114*). The focal point at the eastern end of Stanley Gardens is provided by Allom's church of St Peter, a rare example of an Anglican church built after 1837 in the Classical style (*Plate 115*). Indeed it is very late, dating from 1855–7, and reflects Allom's own Italianate tastes. The site for the church was provided by C. H. Blake, Allom's client, who was one of the few

Plate 114 Stopped vistas in Stanley Gardens, Northern Kensington, where the focus is provided by the Italianate 10 and 11 Stanley Crescent. Note the towers, fenestration and rich stucco-fronted blocks. (*JSC*)

Plate 115 Stanley Gardens, Northern Kensington, with Allom's church of St Peter, a rare example of an Anglican church built after 1837 in the Classical style, set amongst Italianate façades. (*JSC*)

speculators to benefit from the many efforts to develop the estate.

Allom was famed as an illustrator and artist, and his layout and individual designs for the Ladbroke Estate reflect his feeling for composition. There is nothing of the restraint and intimate scale of earlier developments on the estate in his work. Huge terraces, crescents and blocks were composed with elaborate stucco façades in a mixture of Italianate, French *Empire* and other styles, although the dominant architectural motifs are Italianate. The splendid composition of eclectic elements at 1 and 2 Stanley Crescent shows Allom at his most exuberant and assured: the buildings were begun by Ramsay who got into difficulties by 1854, so the work was completed by others (*Plate 116*).

As fashionable residential development expanded westwards it seemed that speculative building of houses on the Ladbroke Estate could hardly fail as a sound investment. Capital was cheap, the bank

Plate 116 Italianate houses by Allom at 1 and 2 Stanley Crescent, Northern Kensington. Stucco-faced speculative development of very high quality. (*JSC*)

rate was very low, plenty of builders were available, and excellent building materials were being manufactured and imported. The raising of the bank rate from two to five per cent in 1853 caused enormous problems concerning credit in the building trades, and, with good interest available from the banks and elsewhere (some cemeteries were paying excellent dividends), the public was not likely to risk its money by investing in builders. Indeed, until that date, cheap capital contributed to an over-supply of buildings on the Ladbroke Estate, and not until the 1860s were the half-completed houses finished and shells fitted out and occupied, a welcome upsurge of confidence, no doubt created partially by the developments of the passenger railways. It seems incredible to think of such vast and architecturally ambitious houses as those in Notting Hill lying as shells for several years in the 1850s, but that is what happened, and it was partly because of the systems by which estates were developed. In a nutshell, the method was that the ground landlord would lend money to developers to whom building leases were granted, but often the landowners themselves had to borrow capital which was obtained from private sources, from banks, from insurance companies and elsewhere. Much capital was raised on a mortgage principle by lawyers who often acted for the ground landlords, and indeed lawyers were mostly responsible for the means by which the Ladbroke Estate was developed, often coming a cropper as a result.

The Norland Estate
If the Ladbroke Estate development is a story of mixed fortunes, it also demonstrates how the ideas of Nash at Regent's Park were the catalyst for other estates. The Norland Estate lies to the west of the Ladbroke developments, and the Ordnance Survey maps also reveal it as having curved terraces and formal layouts: it is bounded on the west by the Kensington parish boundary, on the east by part of Portland Road and Pottery Lane, on the south by Holland Park Avenue, and by a zig-zag line north of Kenley Street.[13]

Building work began in 1839. Improved drainage of the Norland Estate in 1838–9 made possible by the diversion and partial covering of the surface-water sewer made the land a more attractive proposition for residential development. This improvement was occasioned by the construction of the Birmingham, Bristol and Thames Junction Railway, for the Westminster Commissioners of Sewers insisted that the creek be re-routed and improved by the Railway Company.[14]

At once the owner of the Norland Estate, Benjamin Lewis Vulliamy, saw the possibility for his lands, and started negotiations to sell to a builder, one William Kingdom, whose architect was Robert Cantwell:

the latter became surveyor to the Norland Estate in 1838. Kingdom did not actually buy the estate, but assigned the benefit of his agreement to Charles Richardson, solicitor, who purchased the freehold of the lands from Vulliamy.

Cantwell commenced work on the layout of the estate, and he was responsible for the southern half, including Royal Crescent, Addison Avenue and Norland Square. Addison Avenue is a broad street running north from Holland Park Avenue, and is the central axis of the estate. At right angles to Addison Avenue, parallel to Holland Park Avenue, is another thoroughfare, now called Queensdale Road, so the main arteries were in the form of a cross. In the south-west piece of the cruciform plan Cantwell sited his Royal Crescent to face Holland Park Avenue. From the centre of this crescent another road, St Ann's Villas, was planned to run north. In the south-east section of the cross he designed an elongated space, Norland Square, and so two grand and imposing architectural elements were provided to the north of the then Uxbridge Road. At the northern end of Addison Avenue a church was planned on axis.

A drawing of Royal Crescent was exhibited at the Royal Academy in 1839, and was credited to Cantwell as executive architect. Various prints of this drawing were produced, notably to attract custom to the estate, and show Cantwell's original conception to great advantage (*Plate 117*). The fashion for circuses, crescents and curved layouts, as we have seen, gained favour in the nineteenth century: Cantwell's crescent is composed of tall stucco-fronted houses of somewhat coarser detail than that favoured by Nash, but certainly recalls Nash's motifs in the provision of circular turrets at the corners, not unreminiscent of those at the junction of Adelaide Street and The Strand and those on another site at Victoria Square.

Cantwell may also have designed the terraces on Holland Park Avenue, and possibly the ranges in Norland Square, but he appears to have ceased his connection with the estate by 1840. Another surveyor, Joseph Dunning, was appointed in that year, and acted for Richardson until 1851.

Building began on the Holland Park Avenue frontage, naturally enough, and Richardson granted leases to several speculators and builders, as was the usual arrangement. Richardson also tried hard to attract persons of quality to the estate, which was thought to be inconveniently distant from central London. From 1841 the unfinished appearance of much of the estate and the difficulties in letting property actually built caused Richardson problems in the raising of further capital. The western half of Royal Crescent, for example, was not fully occupied until 1848, and 15–22 did not have residents until 1856.

Plate 117 Royal Crescent, Norland Estate, 1839, by Robert Cantwell, a grand essay of houses in the manner of Nash. (*Royal Borough of Kensington and Chelsea Public Library*)

Richardson did his best to make his estates attractive, lived there himself, got the Brentford Gas Company to light the streets, and obtained water supplies from the Grand Junction Water Works Company. In 1843 he promoted an Act of Parliament to enable paving, lighting, repair and cleansing of the streets as well as the maintenance of gardens to be paid for by raising rates.

In order to raise the tone Richardson gave the site for a new church to the Church Building Commissioners, and between 1844 and 1845 the new church of St James, Norlands was erected to designs by Lewis Vulliamy (1791–1871), and a district parish was assigned in 1846. The church tower, an elegant three-stage composition set in the centre of the south elevation, is on the north-south axis of Addison Avenue, and marks the natural centrepiece of the whole estate (*Plate 118*). St James's cost just over £5,000 and seated 750 people. The edifice is in the Early English Gothic Revival style, built of white Suffolk bricks with stone dressings, but, despite superficial acknowledgement of Gothic, St James, Norlands is really a Classical church.

In Addison Avenue itself a type of house that differed from the more conventional tall terrace-houses of Royal Crescent was built. Although the houses are joined, they do not appear to be in terraces, but in semi-detached pairs, with links in which the entrances are set (*Plate 119*). Precedents for this type occurred on the Lloyd-Baker Estate at Clerkenwell and elsewhere. The stucco façades are wide, elegant and beautifully proportioned: they may be by Frederick Warburton Stent, once articled to James Ponsford (an architect associated with the development of estates at St John's Wood). In spite of the building of the church, progress in developing Addison Avenue was slow and erratic, as was the case in Norland Square (which contains tall, narrow houses with segmental bays at basement and ground-floor levels).

189

Plate 118 The church of St James, Norlands, by Lewis Vulliamy, set in St James's Gardens, with paired houses designed by John Barnett. (*Guildhall Library, City of London*)

St Ann's Villas began as a development of Cantwell's Royal Crescent in the form of straight terraces, but, as with other ranges on the estate, these were not occupied at once. The northwards continuation was therefore planned to include pairs of semi-detached villas to attract custom, and these were built in a startlingly different style compared with the rest of the estate where the Italianate mode had prevailed. St Ann's Villas are of a Tudor-Gothic mould, of red and blue brick with stone dressings similar to designs in the architect Charles James Richardson's *The Englishman's House from a Cottage to a Mansion* of 1871 (*Plate 120*).

A plan of 1841 presented to the Commissioners of Sewers shows land north of Addison Avenue as leased for brick-making, which cannot have helped to attract the desired persons of quality. From 1847, however, part of this land around the church was developed as an elongated square to designs of John Barnett. The houses in the square, now called St James's Gardens, consist of linked pairs, with the links in the form of recesses that contain the entrances, a scheme not unlike that for the houses in Addison Avenue (*Plate 118 and Fig 47*).

Richardson was in trouble by 1848 and had to sell off the freeholds of most of his estate: this only postponed disaster, for further sales took place in 1851, and Richardson became a bankrupt dealer in patent medicines in Glasgow in 1855. This is yet another instance of the fearful risks that entrepreneurs took in order to develop their estates.

The Example of Glasgow and the Houses of Alexander Thomson
Glasgow cannot be considered in terms of the eighteenth century,

Plate 119 Addison Avenue, Norland Estate, with terraces cunningly designed to look like paired villas. (*JSC*)

Plate 120 St Anne's Villas, Norland Estate, in the Tudor-Gothic style. (*JSC*)

EAST SIDE

42　43　　　　44　　　　45　46

SOUTH SIDE

47　　　48　49　　　50　51　　　52　53　　　54

SECTION
NO.54

53　　　　　　　54

10　0　10　FEET
3　0　3　METRES
Scale for elevations & section

10　0　10　20　30
3　0　3　6　9
Scale for plans & strip elevations

SECOND FLOOR

FIRST FLOOR

27'0"

29'9"

GROUND FLOOR

BASEMENT
NO.54

N

ST. JAMES'S GARDENS

14　24

13　42

ST. JAMES'S
CHURCH

9　46

8　1　54　47

Plate 121 Looking north from Sauchiehall Street, Glasgow, to Charles Wilson's Free Church College, an Italianate building with pronounced Schinkelian overtones. The Gothic tower of Park parish church on the left is by J. T. Rochead. (*Mitchell Library, Glasgow*)

despite the existence of some survivals, for to all intents and purposes it is essentially a product of the Victorian age. Increasing commercial pressures on the city centre created a need to expand westwards, and the grand Italianate and Grecian terraces went up on an ordered town plan. Probably the most spectacular of all these developments was the area to the north of Sauchiehall Street, rising to the hill dominated by the old Free Church College (*Plate 121*). This part of Glasgow, Woodlands Hill, was commenced in the 1830s, with terraces and crescents by George Smith (1793–1877). Claremont Terrace was added by John Baird (1798–1859) in the 1840s. It was Charles Wilson (1810–1863), however, who really unified the whole design. In 1854 Wilson, with Joseph Paxton, was commissioned to lay out the park at Kelvingrove, while Wilson was asked to plan the undeveloped parts of Woodlands Hill. The centre of his scheme is Park Circus, a magnificent elliptical composition, but his crowning achievement is the Free Church College of 1856, the towers of which give form to the eminence. These towers are partially Italianate, partially Germanic, in style, and perhaps owe something to the individual designs of K. F. Schinkel and L. von Klenze (*Plate 134*). Indeed, it is the robust and

Fig 47 Plans and elevations of houses in St James's Gardens designed by John Barnett. (*Drawing by F. A. Evans reproduced by kind permission of the General Editor,* Survey of London)

193

powerful character of much of Glasgow's building that recall to mind the best of Berlin or Munich.

Further from the centre a spectacular group of terraces was laid out along Great Western Road. The plans to develop the Kelvinside area appear to have originated in the 1830s when the owners, Matthew Montgomerie and John Park Fleming, decided to transform the gently rolling countryside. They commissioned Decimus Burton (1800–81) to draw up a plan for the estate in 1840 (*Fig 48*). Burton proposed only a few terraces, and planned the estate with villas set in large gardens, recalling his plans for the Calverley Estate, Tunbridge Wells, and layouts for the Ladbroke and St John's Wood areas. The Feuing Plan of Burton was the agreed framework for future development for many years, but little of the building work was realised, although a vignette on the Burton plan shows Windsor (now Kirklee) Terrace of 1845 designed by Charles Wilson. James Salmon (1805–88) produced another Feu Plan in the 1850s, by which time some terraces were being erected, including Grosvenor Terrace (1855) and Kew Terrace (1849), both by J. T. Rochead (1814–78): Salmon's plan shows a large circus at 'Belvoir Park' which recalls Shaw's and Allason's designs in London.

As with many Victorian speculative developments progress was slow, and Belhaven Terrace, by James Thomson (1835–1905), followed between 1866 and 1874. It is apparent that the final Feuing Plan of Grosvenor (*Plate 122*), Kew, Belhaven and Windsor Terraces, with the Botanic Gardens, was probably the work of Charles Wilson.[15] The magnificent Great Western Terrace by Alexander 'Greek' Thomson (1817–75) was built in 1867–9: the contribution of this architect to Glasgow's built fabric was extremely important. Thomson was greatly influenced by the works of Schinkel in Berlin, and it is known that Thomson had a set of Schinkel's published designs in his office.

Thomson's Moray Place, Strathbungo, of 1859, is perhaps his most remarkable achievement in terrace-house architecture (*Plate 123*): the end pavilions have pediments, and the continuous row of square mullions between the pavilions derives from Schinkel's *Schauspielhaus* in Berlin. Schinkel, in turn, probably developed this theme from a combination of the square column of the Choragic Monument of Thrasyllus (which had been published in 1787) and from the simplicity of Egyptian temples like that at Syene with peripteral square columns (published in Volume 1 of the celebrated *Description de l'Égypte . . .* from 1809). Schinkel's influence can also be detected in Thomson's designs for Walmer Crescent (1857) and Queen's Park Terrace (1857–9), the latter having the new feature of canted bays at the *piano nobile* level. Thomson's villas at 25 Mansionhouse Road, 202 Nithsdale Road, Craig Ailey, Greenbank in Bothwell, Tor House, High Craigmore

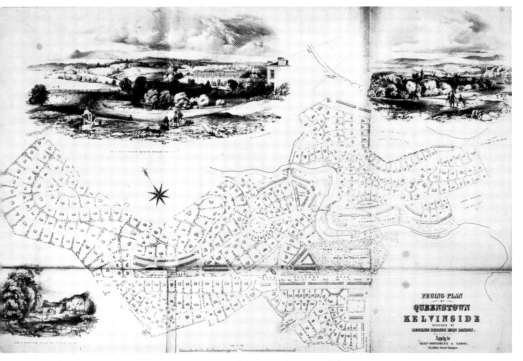

Fig 48 Feuing Plan for Kelvinside, Glasgow, designed for Montgomerie and Fleming by Decimus Burton. A vignette of Charles Wilson's Windsor (now Kirklee) Terrace can be seen top left. (*William Cowie*)

and Arran View, Airdrie, all show the influence of Schinkel's interest in Italian vernacular architecture mixed with his Graeco-Egyptian ranges of square mullions: Craig Ailey has *Rundbogenstil* motifs that show affinities with Schinkel's buildings at Potsdam.

The nature of machine-cut stone and the legacy of Thomson clearly influenced the design of Glasgow tenements for many decades. These blocks, usually of four storeys, contain spacious apartments with large living-rooms, and so have affinities with Continental patterns. Excellent tenements in Hyndland and Partick show the influence of Thomson (and Schinkel) and the beginnings of an almost style-less architecture based on the logic of cut stone and the densest use of land near the city centre (*Plate 124*).

A Summing-Up
Until the 1870s the landed aristocracy and gentry retained a strong position in terms of social structure. Much erosion of power had occurred as a result of legislation of the 1830s, but the various Gladstonian land-enactments of the 1870s (aimed at appeasing Irish

195

Plate 122 Grosvenor Terrace, Glasgow, by J. T. Rochead, of 1855. (*Mitchell Library, Glasgow*)
Plate 123 Moray Place, Strathbungo, Glasgow, by Alexander 'Greek' Thomson. Note the continuous run of square mullions derived from Schinkel's *Schauspielhaus* in Berlin. (*Mitchell Library, Glasgow*)

Plate 124 A typical tenement block in Hyndland, Glasgow. (*JSC*)

Nationalism by destroying the landed interests) pointed to the direction in which the wind was blowing.[16] Quite clearly the Acts of 1832 were only the beginning, heralding a major shift of power from the old landed families to any group with political or industrial muscle.

The splendid country houses of the eighteenth century had been an expression of political and social power, and were often stylistically close to the Palladian ideals of Lord Burlington and his circle: Palladianism and aristocratic oligarchies were closely connected. Newly enriched entrepreneurs of the Victorian period sought status in the acquisition of country seats that would be distinctively un-Palladian in style. As Palladian, Greek and Roman styles fell from favour so the Italianate and other styles gained: nineteenth-century country houses were as varied stylistically as were the backgrounds of their builders. The Italianate style, of course, had been used by Barry for the Reform Club, and it was favoured in Whig circles. Barry employed it at Trentham Hall in Staffordshire of 1834–49, at Bridgewater House in London of 1846–51, and at Cliveden House in Buckinghamshire of 1850–51. Osborne House on the Isle of Wight of 1845–48, by Thomas Cubitt and Prince Albert, set the seal of respectability on the Italianate style: countless houses, banks, and other buildings employing an Italianate style were erected over the next thirty years.

However, Gothic and Elizabethan modes were also popular styles for country houses. Scarisbrick Hall in Lancashire, by Pugin, was created between 1837 and 1845, and included a great hall that was to become a feature of many Victorian houses. Lismore Castle, overlooking the River Blackwater in County Waterford, is a romantic, castellated, asymmetrical pile, remodelled by Crace, Pugin and Paxton in the 1840s and '50s, while Salvin's Peckforton has already been commented upon. Dunrobin Castle in Sutherland by Barry and Leslie, Balmoral Castle by

197

Prince Albert and William Smith, and Belfast Castle by Lanyon and Lynn were all variations on a Franco-Scottish 'Baronial' castle style, which must be seen as a regional variation of the Gothic Revival. Elizabethan or late-Tudor Revival in country houses can be found in Harlaxton Manor in Lincolnshire, Highclere Castle in Hampshire, Mentmore Towers in Buckinghamshire and elsewhere.

High-Victorian Gothic is represented in a number of houses, including Kelham Hall in Nottinghamshire, Elvetham Hall in Hampshire, and, perhaps the grandest of them all, Eaton Hall in Cheshire by Alfred Waterhouse of 1870–83 for the Duke of Westminster, an extraordinary and ambitious pile with a clock-tower not unlike that of Manchester Town Hall.

There were oddities too, as mentioned above, like G.-H. Destailleur's Waddesdon Manor in Buckinghamshire of 1874–89, and J.-F.-A. Pellechet's Bowes Museum in County Durham of 1869–71, both in an elaborate French Renaissance château style. Grosvenor Gardens and Grosvenor Place on the Westminster Estates at Victoria employed Renaissance themes straight from France, complete with tall crested roofs and the most elaborate of façades. French Renaissance architecture was also employed in the spectacular terraces of Lancaster Gate of 1866. French medieval castle themes are found at Castell Coch and Cardiff Castle, both by William Burges, and both heavily influenced by Viollet-le-Duc.

From the 1870s (a time of acute agricultural depression) it was obvious that power was shifting to the middle class. In fact, middle-class houses set in gardens became fashionable in large numbers after 1870, although precedents had been established in the late eighteenth century and especially by Nash, Repton and others. The Picturesque villa and vernacular styles had been popularised in the 1820s, and Loudon's publications made images of such villas more familiar than Papworth's *Rural Residences* of 1818 and other pattern-books could ever hope to do. The Goths, led by Pugin and later Ruskin, deplored the use of stucco and even the employment of mass-produced ornament in favour of brick, stone, asymmetrical compositions that grew from the plans, and a more severe, less frivolous Picturesque manner that gradually merged with a strictly moral attitude to 'natural' materials, colour and free composition. Butterfield's vicarages, domestic buildings by Street and many other schemes of the 1850s used polychrome brickwork and Gothic fenestration, but by the end of that decade simpler brickwork and sash-windows became more usual, as at Webb's Red House for William Morris. The free composition of the Red House (so often misinterpreted as a prelude to the so-called 'modern movement') is firmly of the Gothic Revival, and, although

198

polychrome brick, Gothic fenestration, and buttresses began to be eschewed, the Domestic Revival grew out of the Gothic Revival, and a continuous thread can be traced all the way through the Arts-and-Crafts work of the next decades.

Asymmetrical plans, elaborate silhouettes, sash-windows, segmental heads to openings, and a growing influence for vernacular architecture of the late-medieval, sixteenth, seventeenth and early-eighteenth centuries recurred in domestic work. Webb, Devey, Shaw and Nesfield were among the first to explore these themes, as at Betteshanger (Devey) in Kent, Clouds (Webb) at East Knoyle in Wiltshire, Standen (Webb) near East Grinstead in Sussex, and Leys Wood (Shaw) at Groombridge in Sussex. The sash-window theme led to a return to early eighteenth and late seventeenth century revivals (loosely known as the 'Queen-Anne' style) as at Kinmel (Nesfield) in Denbighshire, while the seventeenth century vernacular revival led to a revival of interest in mullioned and transomed windows as at Cragside (Shaw) in Northumberland. The mullioned window associated with the seventeenth century led C. F. A. Voysey to a type of long low house with strong overhanging eaves, but he turned away from the brickwork established by the High-Victorian Goths to a rendered treatment with exposed dressings, and he re-introduced the banished buttress. He, like many of his contemporaries, also re-introduced the mullioned bay (as at Kirby Hall in Northamptonshire and revived at Voysey's houses by Lake Windermere). Later still, Lutyens was to mingle aspects of the Domestic Revival with a revival of Classicism itself.

North-European Renaissance town houses like those of Cadogan Square and Collingham Gardens introduced further ideas into middle-class domestic architecture, but the dominant motifs for the next few generations were to be those of the Picturesque vernacular revival of Bedford Park, Port Sunlight and Bournville, leading not only to the municipal housing estate types of the inter-war period, but to the favoured style of the speculative builder of the same time, variously categorised as 'by-pass variegated', 'stockbrokers' Tudor', or 'Metroland cottage'. Clearly the Sublime was far removed from all that.

A few words are needed about the terrace-house of the Victorian age, although Stefan Muthesius, in his *English Terraced House* of 1982 has covered the subject in detail. Most housing in the Victorian period was provided by private enterprise for rent, and that applied to urban housing for most classes of society. In other words, the developer or entrepreneur was obliged to make an assumption about demand and taste and hope he had got it right. Sometimes he was fortunate and his judgment was correct, but very often he was not, as the story of the Ladbroke and Norland Estates proves.

While building construction was traditional and responded to local availability of materials, building components improved to an enormous extent in the Victorian period. Sash-windows came into general use, divided into panes with fine glazing-bars (later to be ripped out as plate-glass became cheaply available from the 1840s), while cast-iron railings, grates and window-sill ornaments were cheap and plentiful. Marble fireplace-surrounds (often supplied from Italy) were widely available and cheap (reflecting the strength of the currency), but later in the century slate fireplace-surrounds became common. From the 1870s glazing-bars came back into fashion in sash-windows, while the Domestic Revival encouraged the re-introduction of casement-windows, often with lead cames. The 'Queen-Anne' style sometimes made use of small top sashes with glazing bars and long bottom sashes with large sheets of plate glass.

Early in the Victorian period terrace-houses followed a late-Georgian pattern, but stucco facings to simulate masonry were common, especially in areas where brick was used. In Newcastle-upon-Tyne and Glasgow, where good stone was available, stucco was not regarded as necessary, but in Cheltenham, Hove and London the stucco façade was *de rigueur*. From the 1850s a certain vagueness in stylistic matters seems to have prevailed, as many of the London estates developed with large semi-detached houses, and the debasing of stylistic purity became usual. In architectural circles the anguished longing to depart from stylistic niceties of historicism was a perennial theme, yet those circles seemed not to notice the almost style-less trends in mid- and late-Victorian speculative housing. Builders became more indiscriminate in their eclecticism, and often interpreted style in the loosest way. Bow-windows, usually in the form of canted bays, became popular, Gothic foliage was mingled with Classical mouldings, and a general coarsening of detail and proportion prevailed.

Gothic influences abound in the villas of North Oxford and certain terraces in the same city (as at 114–138 and 149–164 Kingston Road), while York, and other towns and cities can boast Gothic houses influenced by the High-Victorian Gothic movement. The majority of houses built in Queen Victoria's reign, however, are difficult to categorise in any style at all. There are many houses, on the other hand, that fall into stylistic categories, that display Gothic polychrome brickwork or Italianate detail, while many more still show a bewildering range of stylistic elements to the world. What is clear is that in seventy-odd years not only was there an amazing amount of domestic building, but also a vast range of styles and types. The Victorians provided a huge variety of choice at reasonable cost, and considering the risks, this makes their achievements all the more awesome.[17]

6 NEW MATERIALS AND NEW CHALLENGES

**Introduction; The Development of Structures of Iron and Glass;
The Crystal Palace; Railway Termini; Other Iron Structures;
An Afterword on New Materials**

> . . . function
> Is smother'd in surmise, and nothing is
> But what is not
>
> William Shakespeare, *Macbeth* I iii 130

Introduction

Most Victorian buildings (such as churches and houses) had precedents in plenty, but the period also saw the development of many new building-types (such as railway-stations, immense structures to house exhibitions, hospitals constructed on lines that took into account new discoveries in the spread of infection and disease, prisons that responded to new rational and humane standards, pumping stations, covered markets, swimming-baths and many others) for which there were no immediate antecedents. A need for large areas of covered space and the evolution of new building technologies happily combined to produce some extraordinary architecture.

Of all building materials to be developed during the Victorian period, iron and glass stand out for the possibilities of expression, adaptability, and ease of erection they offered. Both had been known since Antiquity, but during the Victorian Age huge advances in the industrial processes of making them not only rendered iron and glass readily available on a scale unknown before, but also at very cheap rates. Furthermore, the invention and development of techniques whereby iron and glass could be used together created new structural possibilities that the Victorians were not slow to exploit at a time of massive urban expansion.

From the last quarter of the eighteenth century cast iron for structural and decorative purposes was produced on an ever-increasing scale, and used for columns, beams, window-frames, balustrades, balcony railings and the like. Mass-produced cast-iron components such as Classical columns and even whole stairs were used by Nash in several of his buildings. The material was also used for features such as Gothic window-tracery, nave arcading, and even roof trusses in a

201

number of churches, although it is strong in compression (and therefore excellent for columns) but weak in tension (and therefore liable to fracture if overloaded as beams, as was the unfortunate case with the Tay Bridge).

Examples of the use of structural cast iron were the Church of Ireland Cathedral at St Macartan at Enniskillen in County Fermanagh of 1841 by William Farrell, Rickman's church of St George at Everton, and James Brown's Renfield Street Church in Glasgow of 1849. Huge improvements in the production of cast iron were heralded at Coalbrookdale in Shropshire (the celebrated Iron Bridge, the first structure of its kind ever, demonstrated the possibilities), but wrought iron (which is much stronger in tension) was not available in quantity and cheaply enough for building purposes until the Regency period. Cast-iron panels were used as roof-coverings for Barry's Palace of Westminster, and wrought iron began to be used extensively, notably in girder form, as for the main roof-ribs of the Crystal Palace and for the mighty train-shed of St Pancras station of the 1860s. The Darby works in Shropshire were behind the development of structural cast-iron elements, while William Fairbairn (1789–1874), author of *On the Application of Cast and Wrought Iron to Building* of 1854, was the most influential promoter of wrought iron. In 1855 Bessemer perfected a process of making steel in quantity, and this even tougher, cheaper material (ideal in tension) began to be used in structures.

The Development of Structures of Iron and Glass
Buildings using glazed panels set in frames had been used to protect plants from the worst of the weather, and there are examples going back to the seventeenth century of orangeries and conservatories that consist of brick, stone or timber buildings with large glazed windows. However, the construction and arrangement of greenhouses (with hollow hot walls, stoves, and roofs and curtain-walls [of glass and wood or iron bars] uninterrupted by heavy walls of masonry) developed during the nineteenth century partly as a result of demand caused by the importation of large numbers of exotic plants from abroad, and partly because of developments in technology. In 1812 John Claudius Loudon published his *Observations on Laying out Farms in the Scotch Style* . . . which contained information on the design of greenhouses, and in 1816 he invented an iron glazing-bar that made curved glazing possible. This consisted of a ridge-and-furrow structure with wrought-iron sash-bars which could be bent into curved shapes. Prototypes of Loudon's invention were displayed at the Horticultural Society in the same year. In 1817 his *Remarks on the Construction of Hothouses* was

published, and in the following year his *Sketches of Curvilinear Hothouses* and *A Comparative View of the Common and Curvilinear Modes of Roofing Hothouses* also appeared. He erected a glass-house in the grounds of his house at Porchester Terrace in Bayswater which incorporated his sash-bar, but he sold his rights to his invention to W. and D. Bailey of Holborn in 1818. One of the first iron-and-glass detached conservatories was the 'dome' erected for Mrs Beaumont at Bretton Hall in Yorkshire in 1827 and designed by D. Bailey. This was constructed entirely of cast and wrought iron: all the vertical supports were cast, and all the sash-bars making up the ribs of the roof were of wrought iron.[1] This was the Bailey who had bought Loudon's rights, and it is quite clear that both the curved wrought-iron bars and a ridge-and-furrow type of construction used by Paxton at Chatsworth and the Crystal Palace derive from Loudon's inventions.

Glass-houses made of curved iron frames were proposed by G. S. Mackenzie in 1815 and followed up by T. A. Knight at Downton Castle in Herefordshire. During the 1830s important innovations included a new method of glass manufacture which enabled sheets up to six feet long to be available. The improvements in the processes by which large sheets of glass could be made, combined with the availability of cast- and wrought-iron components, ensured that large free-standing glass-houses could be built in numbers. Reductions in taxation on glass also helped to popularise such structures.

The first iron-and-glass conservatory of heroic proportions with architectural qualities was the 'Great Stove' at Chatsworth of 1836–40, designed by Joseph Paxton and Decimus Burton. This consisted of an arched 'nave' some seventy feet wide carried on slender cast-iron columns, with 'aisles' of half arches: the glazed roof-structure was of the ridge-and-furrow type. While the Great Stove was being completed, the Marquess of Donegall laid the foundation stone of the Belfast Palm House in 1839, an elegant structure designed by Charles Lanyon (*Plate 125*). The iron frames were made by the contractor, Richard Turner of Dublin, the Dublin firm of Walker was responsible for the glazing, and the tall central elongated dome was by Charles D. Young & Co of Edinburgh.[2] The two wings of the Belfast Palm House are the first known examples of Turner's work in conservatory design, and he may have been helped by his brother Thomas, the architect, with whom he later submitted an unsuccessful design for the Crystal Palace.

Turner collaborated with Decimus Burton for the design and construction of the Winter Garden at Regent's Park, commissioned in 1840, but not begun until 1845. This structure was similar to Turner's various conservatories in Ireland, and indeed seems to have been designed mostly by him.[3] Burton originally proposed a wooden frame for the Winter Garden, but Turner produced a scheme based entirely on a structure of iron with glass panels. This Winter Garden had many details in common with Turner's work in Dublin and Belfast. Burton and Turner then collaborated on their greatest work, the Palm House at Kew Gardens which was erected in 1844–8 and provided a spectacular demonstration of the possibilities of large structures of iron and glass (*Plate 126*). The precise division of responsibility in the building of the Palm House at Kew has been argued by scholars, and the rôle of Burton appears to have been, very properly, as architect, the designer of the form and style, while Turner's knowledge of detailing, prefabrication techniques and engineering enabled the elegant structure to be realised. The genesis of the Kew Gardens design can be found in the Chatsworth and Belfast examples (although neither Belfast nor Kew has the ridge-and-furrow construction of Chatsworth), while similar structures to the Palm Houses at Belfast and Kew by the firm of Richard Turner were erected in Ireland at Portlaoise, Glasnevin and Killikee. Contemporary critics praised Turner's achievements, especially the execution of the designs for Kew. Most of the works at Kew had been carried out by Irish labour, a point noted in the pages of *The Builder*, so it seems that Irish expertise played a very important part in the development of glasshouses.

The Crystal Palace

Shortly afterwards London acquired two important buildings with exposed iron structures: these were the Coal Exchange of 1847–9 (a beautiful and elegant circular space defined within a cast-iron galleried construction supporting a glazed roof) by James Bunstone Bunning, Architect to the City of London (*Plate 127*); and the great reading-room of the British Museum of 1854–7 designed by Sydney Smirke.

Plate 125 Belfast Palm House of 1839 by Turner and Lanyon. (*JSC*)

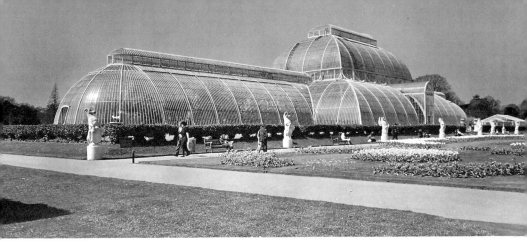

Plate 126 The Palm House at Kew Gardens of 1844–8. (*AFK*)

However, the largest, most celebrated, and remembered Victorian building of iron-and-glass construction was, of course, the Crystal Palace to house the Great Exhibition of 1851.

A building committee had been formed in 1850, and private finance was sought. An international competition was held to find an appropriate design: Turner's entry was a remarkable piece of work, based on his scheme for Lime Street Station roof in Liverpool, completed that year. This was the first railway-station roof to be constructed as a single span, and it was designed by Turner in collaboration with Joseph Locke and William Fairbairn.[4] The single span and absence of columns permitted certain changes to the layout of platforms and tracks to be made much more easily (and more flexibly), removed awkward obstructions in the platforms, and reduced the unlikely but dreadful possibility of a rogue engine careering into a column and bringing the whole structure down on the station. Lime Street roof was over a hundred and fifty feet wide, and consisted of principal trusses in the form of sickle-girders. Turner's Crystal Palace design consisted of a huge space, but this time it was nearly two thousand feet long and four hundred feet broad, with transepts and a large glass dome over the crossing. The ends of the nave aisles and transepts were to be closed with tracery of iron in the shape of a fan. This was an excellent example of Turner's work without the controlling hand of a great architect (his collaborator was his brother Thomas), and the result was something like a cross between a railway terminus and a cathedral, with a palm-house perched on top. The scale, too, was enormous.

None of the designs submitted to the body charged with housing the 1851 Exhibition was approved, so the committee (which included several distinguished architects and engineers, including Wyatt, Jones, Wild and Brunel) produced its own version which, like the work of many committees, lacked clarity and simplicity. While Turner's proposal did not possess the elegance and control of the final realised building for the Great Exhibition, it was a more practicable idea than the committee's mongrel *Rundbogenstil* aisled and transepted nave with large dome. The latter scheme also had much 'architecture' in the form of heavy brickwork supporting the iron-and-glass structure, while Turner's design (which shared joint first prize with Horeau's plans) was all iron and glass, and involved little 'architecture' of brick or masonry: it could also be prefabricated in its entirety.

Joseph Paxton came up with an idea for an iron-and-glass structure in June 1850, and soon had drawn up more detailed plans: his design as published in July.[5] Nine days later Paxton's scheme was accepted, and the contractors Fox and Henderson tendered to build it. It was actually Charles Fox (1810–74) who calculated the design solutions for the Crystal Palace, and he and his firm made the working drawings. Aware of the measures necessary to ensure safety in a novel structure intended to receive many people attending the huge exhibition, and aware also of the lack of precedent for his work, Fox was determined to avoid any possibility of error. As each drawing left his board, it was translated into ironwork by Henderson. As the calculations proceeded,

Plate 127 The Coal Exchange, London, by J. B. Bunning, of 1847–9. (*AFK*)

so mock-ups were made, and empirical experiments were carried out to prove the strength of members. Once the design was found to be more than adequate, building began.

Perhaps one of the most fascinating aspects of the Crystal Palace, apart from the amazing story of its rapid conception and realisation, is its ultra-simplicity. The stability of the joints between the columns and the beams was of paramount importance in a building where the methods tried in railway-terminus construction did not apply. The Palace was a framed building, made of repetitive units, fully glazed, which took the glass-house concept one stage further, and indeed made future innovation possible. It was, in truth, as William Makepeace Thackeray wrote:

> A palace as for fairy prince,
> A rare pavilion, such as man
> Saw never since mankind began,
>   And built and glazed!

Thackeray marvelled at the speed with which the Palace was built:

> As though 'twere by a wizard's rod
> A blazing arch of lucid glass
> Leaps like a fountain from the grass
> To meet the sun![6]

The efficient organisation that enabled the Crystal Palace to be erected so quickly involved the co-ordination of the manufacture of components in many locations, and in only nine months the Crystal Palace was finished: the Great Exhibition was declared open by the Queen in May 1851.[7]

Paxton's building united expertise that had evolved in the production of glass-houses and railway-stations, and, as at Chatsworth, he used his ridge-and-furrow system of glazing on the arched transept. The structure was carried on hollow cast-iron columns which doubled as rainwater pipes: these columns were braced by cast-iron spacers, while the structure spanning the nave and aisles was of wrought iron. The Palace was enclosed by a system of standardised repetitive units consisting of an arched panel over which was a rectangular panel with a roundel in the middle. Cladding was of glass and timber, while the arched principals of the transepts were also of wood.

The Crystal Palace as built attracted much admiration, not least because of the interior colour-scheme of Owen Jones (1806–89) who used blue for the concave parts of the structure, red on the soffits of the girders and behind the gallery balustrades, and yellow on the diagonal faces of columns and on projecting parts. The Palace, of course, was dismantled and re-erected to a variation of the design (*Plates 128 and 129*) with three transepts at Sydenham where it remained until it burned down in 1936. At the new site Paxton designed elaborate gardens with fountains.[8]

The Crystal Palace became the precedent for a great number of large temporary exhibition buildings erected during the course of the century and involving mass-produced factory-made components.[9] However, the Crystal Palace was not regarded as real architecture by several critics and practitioners. Pugin called it a glass 'horror' and 'monster', Morris said it was 'wonderfully ugly',[10] but Loudon (although he died eight years before the Palace was built), was perceptive as always, and had written that accepted notions of proportion would have to be jettisoned in the future, for architects would have to adapt their designs to the new materials and methods rather than the materials and methods to their architecture.[11] Loudon, indeed, had illustrated a large glass-house with domes as early as 1827,[12] and even saw the possibilities of enclosing entire cities with iron-and-glass structures in order to preserve buildings and to control the environment, thus anticipating many twentieth-century gurus by more than a hundred years. The Crystal Palace had an aesthetic rooted in repetition of mass-produced units such as the arched façade elements, the columns, the trusses and other standardised elements, but its unusual and most important qualities lay in its lightness, its eschewing of massive brickwork or masonry 'architecture', and its visible structure that was not hidden at all, but painted as if to draw attention to it.

Needless to say, many critics, such as some in *The Ecclesiologist*, regarded the Crystal Palace as good engineering but not as architecture,[13] while Ruskin, although conceding that it was possible that a new system of aesthetics associated with iron construction would develop, could not acknowledge that the Crystal Palace was architecture at all because 'architecture' to him meant form, and form could not be made with translucent glass as a dominant material. Ruskin saw that 'noble forms' could be made of metal (such as coins, medals, bronze sculpture, statuary and the like), but he could not acknowledge that tubular bridges, engineering, or the ridge-and-furrow glazing plus 'ordinary algebra' of the Crystal Palace were art, architecture or expressions of humanity and of genius.[14] The problem was that the Palace in Hyde Park was quite clearly a garden structure, a hot-house on a large scale,[15] storing practical knowledge and techniques in the immense range of foreign and local products on show, which were therefore equated with exotic plants in the minds of some observers. Yet, oddly, the Palace had a nave, aisles and a vaulted transept, and within the insistent rhythms of the repetitive structure were exhibits, arranged in a way

Plate 128 The Crystal Palace as re-erected at Sydenham. (V&A)

Plate 129 Interior of the Crystal Palace at Sydenham. (RCHME No BB69/1077B. B. E. C. Haworth-Loomes)

not unreminiscent of chapels, each with its altar: the Palace was thus associated by some with a great cathedral, but a cathedral of commerce.

The Ecclesiologist, however, was not all hostility, and even went so far as to describe the Palace as 'magical', 'intoxicating' and 'effective': it also, and very significantly, praised the 'truthfulness' and 'reality of construction'.[16] Beresford Hope claimed that the Crystal Palace was an offshoot of the Gothic Revival, while in the expression of structure and attitudes to colour it is not all that estranged from High-Victorian Gothic. In fact *The Ecclesiologist* recognised that the Palace was one of the first buildings in which polychrome was used to express structure, and in this respect the Palace was some eight years in advance of the consecration of Butterfield's All Saints', Margaret Street.[17] Paxton's great building was far more than that, however, for its vastness and its repetitive elements suggest the Sublime qualities of Neoclassicism (an allusion accentuated by the many repetitions of the semicircular arches of the façades).

Railway Termini
Several railway termini were influenced by the precedent of the Crystal Palace. King's Cross Station of 1851–2 by Lewis Cubitt (1799–1883) has two arched sheds carried on a brick structure (*Plate 130*): originally the arched principals were of laminated timber, but these were replaced in 1869–70 with steel held in place by Cubitt's original cast-iron supports. The brick façade expresses the shapes of the sheds behind, for Cubitt created two huge lunettes with a rather small Italianate clock-tower between them (*Plate 131*). This design is probably influenced by Duquesney's Gare de l'Est in Paris of 1847–52 (which has a large lunette in the centre of the façade), but more especially by the two lunettes and central clock-tower of Lenoir's Montparnasse Station of 1850–52. Cubitt noted that at King's Cross he desired to achieve fitness for purpose and the expression of that purpose.[18]

Paddington Station of 1852–4 by Isambard Kingdom Brunel and Matthew Digby Wyatt (1820–77) has three arched roofs carried on wrought-iron principals which rest on girders carried on columns. Wyatt's scheme introduced a Moresque note, and the decorative scheme is much more elaborate than the straightforward structural geometry of King's Cross. Wyatt himself had noted that the use of iron

Plate 130 Train Shed at King's Cross Station, London, in 1895. (*GLPL No 70/10400. 27.315KIN*)
Plate 131 Exterior of King's Cross Station in *c* 1865. (*GLPL No 58/3911. 27.314 KIN*)

would systematise a scale of form and proportion, and that engineering and architecture would draw together towards a future 'consummation', so that it would be difficult to ascertain where civil engineering ended and architecture began. Such a consummation is difficult to decipher at Paddington for, as a contemporary commentator wrote, Wyatt's designs were conceived on the principle of avoiding precedent rather than on the qualities of the material.[19] New techniques and traditional methods were seen to come together as in the medieval cathedrals, and indeed railway termini were seen by many as the true cathedrals of the nineteenth century.[20]

The greatest of all railway terminus sheds in Britain is undoubtedly at St Pancras (*Plate 132*) for the Midland Railway (1863–5), with a span of nearly two hundred and fifty feet, designed by William Henry Barlow (1812–1902) – who worked on design details for the Crystal Palace – and Rowland Mason Ordish (1824–86). These huge lattice-girders form a vast pointed vault spanning a huge space within which trains, people, cabs and luggage could be moved with ease and protected from the weather. The principals are formed of compound

Plate 132 St Pancras Station, train shed, *c* 1895. (*GLPL No 81/120/6269-1 27.317 StPan*)

curves and meet at an apex over a hundred feet above the tracks: they spring from masonry and brickwork in a completely integrated manner. Scaffolding for this immense shed and the prefabrication of the ironwork were designed by J. G. N. Alleyne (1820–1912), the manager of the Butterley Company, while masonry and brickwork were constructed by Waring Brothers.[21]

Other large stations in which iron and glass were used with success and architectural verve included Central Station at York by William Peachy and Thomas Prosser of 1871–2, Newcastle Central by John Dobson of 1846–65 (both constructed on curved plans to spectacular effect), Liverpool Street in London by Edward Wilson of the 1870s (extremely elegant with its cast-iron detailing on a complex arrangement of naves, aisles and intersections), and the massive Manchester Central of 1876–9 by Sir John Fowler (1817–98), a building comparable to St Pancras train shed for its enormous volume and simple form. Both Charing Cross (1862–4) and Cannon Street (1863–6) Stations in London by E. M. Barry had kept segmental curved roofs spanning between massive walls: Cannon Street, with its massive bridge and monumental towers, was especially successful as a composition.

Other Iron Structures

Cast-iron building components, details, ornaments and even whole structures became widely (and cheaply) available, but nothing quite like the Crystal Palace was to recur. The material began to be associated with utilitarianism, temporary structures and cheapness. Iron-framed buildings clad in corrugated iron were erected in some quantity during the 1850s. One example was the temporary Museum of Science and Art at South Kensington (known as the Brompton Boilers) of 1855–6: this was designed by William Dredge and built by Charles D. Young & Co of Edinburgh in association with Sir William Cubitt (*Plate 133*). It consisted of three segmental roofs covering a rectangular space, the whole exterior of which was clad in green-and-white striped corrugated iron.[22] The 'Boilers' were removed to Bethnal Green where, in 1873, the iron structure was clad in a robust brick exterior to designs by J. W. Wild. Young & Co, like Hemming of Bristol, made entire buildings, including iron churches, for export. Prefabricated iron churches, complete with Gothic arcaded nave, triforium and clerestory, lean-to aisles, rood-screen and details were proposed. An interesting example was designed by R. C. Carpenter, adapted by William Slater (1819–72) (Carpenter's pupil and successor), and published by The Ecclesiological Society in *Instrumenta Ecclesiastica* of 1856: here was Victorian industrialised building developed to a fine art, and, although the exterior was to be clad in corrugated iron, other proposals were

213

Plate 133 The 'Brompton Boilers' of 1855–6, clad in striped corrugated iron. Photograph of the 1850s. (*V&A Library Collection x.601, No 33966*)

that the panels between the iron frame should be of marble.[23] Beresford Hope also proposed iron for the ribs of roofs and ceilings of cathedrals, the panels to be of hard glazed faience or porcelain. The search for hard, coloured, durable materials that led to the architectural treatment of All Saints', Margaret Street, seemed to find in iron and glass ideal solutions.[24] George L. Hersey has pointed out the similarity between Slater's iron church and F. A. Skidmore's iron-and-glass covered court at the University Museum, Oxford, of 1856–9, and indeed Skidmore had proposed the marble panels for the iron church.[25] Henry Acland, one of the personalities behind the formation of the museum, advocated a combination of Gothic art and railway materials,[26] and indeed the extraordinary cast- and wrought-iron structure at Oxford fits snugly within an arcaded two-storey cloister in the Italian Gothic style (*Plate 14*).

Almost universal execration heaped upon the Brompton Boilers did not encourage many further experiments in exposed iron structures, although Sheerness Naval Dockyard by G. T. Greene of 1858 employed a four-storey iron frame with bands of low windows and infill panels of corrugated iron, but then it was an industrial building and therefore not subjected to the same criticism. Captain Fowke's building (about which scarcely a good word has been said this century) for the London Exhibition of the Works of All Nations of 1862 (*Plates 134–6*) had a prefabricated metal-and-glass structure that was elegant, logical and architectonic (arguably even more so than Paxton's Crystal Palace), having two glass domes and clerestoried naves, but the exterior was clad with brick façades in a *Rundbogenstil* manner, felt to be more dignified following the *debâcle* of the Brompton Boilers.[27] Fowke's Royal Scottish Museum in Edinburgh of 1861 also has a most elegant, light, and logical galleried, arched and this time top-lit interior, but the masonry exterior is again in a round-arched Lombardic Renaissance style.[28]

James Silk Buckingham (1786–1855) was an early enthusiast for cast-iron construction, and mentioned work by 'Mr Laycock of Liverpool' and a pamphlet by Alexander Gordon in his *National Evils and Practical Remedies with the Plan of a Model Town* of 1849,[29] which included in the ideas for 'Victoria' (the proposed model town) designs for structures of iron and glass. Cast-iron façades of considerable elegance were built at 36 Jamaica Street in Glasgow (*Plate 137*) in 1855–6 to designs by John Baird (1798–1859), who had used an exposed iron frame in the hammerbeam roof of the Argyle Arcade in that city as early as 1827.[30] At Jamaica Street the patentee and ironfounder was R. McConnel. There were several other cast-iron fronted buildings in Glasgow.[31] In London, E. M. Barry's Floral Hall of 1858–60 had a cast-iron structure and a façade conceived more as 'architecture' than in the spirit of the Crystal Palace. Like Gardner's store in Glasgow there is a reference to a design derived from earlier non-ferrous buildings: it is a deliberate attempt to dress the building up to make the cast-iron façade acceptable, although the arches clearly derive from the Paxton prototype in both examples. During the 1860s Peter Ellis (1804–84) designed Oriel Chambers in Liverpool (1864), a stone-faced building with oriel windows constructed of extremely light and slender cast-iron frames (*Plate 138*). Ellis's other office block, at 16 Cook Street (1866), also has large amounts of plate glass in iron frames, while the rear of the building had very thin iron mullions and much glazing, similar to the so-called 'curtain walling' of the 1950s.

Kits of parts provided scope for elaborate designs using cast iron: shop-fronts were often of this material. These kits could provide anything from a *pissoir* to an exportable church, but the ingenuity of design enabled elaborate structures to be fitted into difficult sites, as at

Plate 134 Exhibition Building of 1862 at South Kensington. Western Annexe in March 1862. (*V&A Neg No HH2168. Library Collection 93,62701*)

Plate 135 Exhibition Building of 1862 in Exhibition Road, South Kensington. Photograph of 5 May 1862. (*V&A Neg No HH2169 Library Collection 92, 67242*)

Plate 136 Exhibition Building of 1862. Nave as completed. (*V&A Library Collection 41225*)
Plate 137 36 Jamaica Street, Glasgow. Gardener's Warehouse. (*RCAHMS A 62019*)

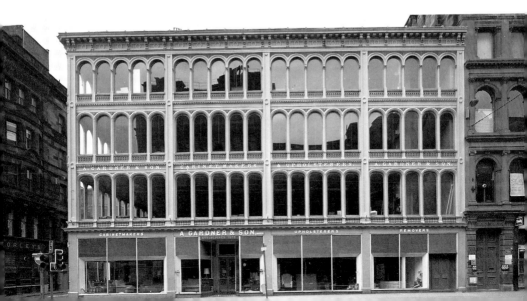

the Barton Arcade, Deansgate, Manchester (*Plate 139*). Cool in summer and protected in the winter, arcades were planned with shops in the ground floor, while often galleries on the upper floors would lead to offices. At the Barton Arcade the detail, all mass-produced, is wonderfully put together: the building, with two glass domes, was designed by Corbett, Raby & Sawyer in the early 1870s using parts cast at Macfarlane's Saracen Foundry in Glasgow.

A combination of masonry, brickwork, iron and glass, as at the University Museum, Oxford, several railway stations and many shopping arcades and market-halls, was found in many buildings of the Victorian Age. Fowler's Covent Garden Market of 1828–30 acquired its iron-and-glass coverings to its avenues later (and these are reminiscent of King's Cross Station in the beautifully stylish and logical treatment of the structure): the 'Fruit Halls' set within the Fowler building are built of semicircular iron ribs on cast-iron columns, and the usual tie-bars are dispensed with. Elaborate covered markets were built in numbers: occasionally structures are mixtures of cast iron and timber, as at Smithfield Poultry and Meat Market of 1866–7 by Sir Horace Jones (1819–87) (an elegant building with cast-iron columns and arcades, but with a timber roof), the same architect's Leadenhall Market of 1881 (on a cruciform plan of glass-roofed arcades with decorative iron façades), and the shed for the Leeds Public Baths by Henry Walker, a clerestoried nave with galleried aisles, all of timber carried on cast-iron columns. Timber had been used in some of the early railway sheds, but as it soon deteriorated it was superseded by iron.

At Kelham Hall and in St Pancras Station Hotel (1865–74) Scott used exposed iron which is treated with great élan and distinction, especially in the stairs. Scott himself saw that metal structures might lead to many new architectural developments, and indeed his work at the Midland Grand Hotel, St Pancras, points the way forward, anticipating certain Continental experiments, such as those of Horta, by more than a generation.[32] E. Bassett Keeling used iron for the nave piers of his 'acrobatic' Gothic churches of St Mark, Notting Hill (1863), St George, Campden Hill (1865), and St Paul, Anerley Road (1866), and a harsh polychrome scheme of decoration. Keeling's Strand Music Hall of 1864 (*see Frontispiece and Fig 49*) gave every faction, Gothic, Classic, conservative or progressive, common ground in that all joined to condemn it as appalling: the building, which even the explorer Sir Richard Burton found remarkable, had cast-iron columns with wrought-iron capitals, cast-iron brackets supporting the heavy cornice, an extraordinary ceiling of coloured glass set in the zinc frames of panels, and glass prisms set in the soffits of the hollow ribs (*Fig 49*). The Strand Music Hall was a veritable Aladdin's cave of entertainment architecture and

Plate 138 Oriel Chambers, Liverpool
of 1864. *(JSC)*
Plate 139 Barton Arcade, Manchester.
(JSC)

of Victorian innovation.[33] Iron was used increasingly in Victorian
buildings, but, with the fall from favour of Keeling and others, and the
universal dislike of buildings like the Brompton Boilers, was often
disguised or cased in: however, the use of exposed iron in architecture
by Victorian designers remains extremely interesting.

An Afterword on New Materials

The development of structures using iron and glass has been outlined
above. Air pollution was a conspicuous evil of Victorian Britain, and
materials such as stucco introduced by Nash and others were ill-
adapted to the corrosive effects of the London atmosphere. Early
nineteenth-century fashion for stucco had been anticipated by John
Gwynn in 1766 who felt that a mere brick face on a 'publick edifice'
made a mean appearance. Although stucco had been used in ancient
times, in England stuccoed buildings were the exception until the mid-
eighteenth century. Coade Stone was a successful attempt to provide a
durable material rather like stone, but it, like terracotta, had to be
manufactured and then brought to the building site. Stucco was, of
course, an *in situ* material, and was admirably suited to the enrichment

219

of unified terraces popularised by Wyatt, Nash and the Adam Brothers. By the 1850s 'Parker's Roman Cement' was the most widely used variety of stucco, and was specified by many architects working during the first half of the century. Roman Cement was a brown-grey colour, and was often left in its natural state. Early-Victorian stucco was not painted gleaming cream and white as we see it today, but was intended to look like stone, with simulated 'masonry' joints, and was reasonably satisfactory when air pollution was not as severe as it became in mid-Victorian times. It was cheap, could be repaired easily, and could be moulded as grandly as desired. Stucco was reasonably elastic, and moved, so it was relatively stable, but, if water got behind it, deterioration and spalling were rapid. Minute cracks could also harbour dirt, vegetation and moisture, causing patches of stucco to become detached.

As the number of coal fires increased, the railways came, smashing their ways through the urban fabric, gas-light became ubiquitous, and coal-fired power came into general use, then rapid deterioration of buildings was to be expected. Stone also suffered, but where stucco was used (as the Italianate style decreed if stone were too expensive) oil paint had to be applied to preserve it, an expensive, continuous and hardly satisfactory state of affairs. Even where stucco was used sparingly, as in architraves and door-cases of brick façades, problems of maintenance became acute. It is perhaps difficult for young people today to imagine what

Fig 49 Sectional View of the Strand Music Hall, London, by E. Bassett Keeling. (Building News, *1864*)

Victorian cities were like when the frequent acidic fogs fouled faces, clothes, lungs and buildings. Atmospheric pollution was destructive, and conditions in some centres were almost intolerable. The blackened fabric of Leeds, Manchester and Liverpool was astounding and memorable (the writer can recall his first impressions of Liverpool on a dark, dank, and foggy morning in 1948 when porters of stunted growth, like *Nibelungen*, coughed their ways along the platforms of Lime Street Station: it was a fascinating, yet horrible vision of a Sublime Inferno unknown to recent generations). In buildings, concern for proper ventilation in an age of gas-light was voiced by many commentators, and early attempts to provide adequate air changes were made in hospitals, prisons and workers' hostels. Even Evangelical clergymen often suffered from headaches on Mondays following Sundays spent in overcrowded, badly ventilated preaching-houses.[34]

Butterfield, Street and other High-Victorian Goths attempted to solve the problem of ecclesiastical fabric becoming dulled and dirty by introducing glazed tiles, hard brickwork, structural polychromy and polished granites and marbles. Public houses were fitted out with marble, tiles, plate-glass, mirrors, polished granite and other hard-wearing materials for easy cleaning. Glazed bricks, faience, terracotta and other building materials were developed and used where cleanable and decorative surfaces were required. Glazed bricks were also useful in light-wells to reflect light, while their employment in public lavatories, corridors, and other instances where ease of cleaning and resistance to heavy use was essential, was widespread.

In his essay entitled 'Of Colour in the Architecture of Cities',[35] Halsey Ricardo (1854–1928) noted that the revolt against the grey stucco-fronted houses 'was in part due to the same feeling that followed on the Gothic Revival – a desire to avoid anything that might savour of dishonesty in construction'. He believed that the red buildings of brick were erected as a reaction against the monotony and colourlessness of so many streets. Just as elaborate unified façades of stucco were a revolt against the long drab stock-brick fronts of Georgian London, so the hard red-brick façades of the 'Queen-Anne' manner were, Ricardo felt, a revolt against the imitation stone of stucco fronts. Yet brick façades would only work if they were very hard and impervious to atmospheric pollution. Ricardo demanded a further development to yet more impervious hard materials: red brick and terracotta were both subject to discoloration, while the structural polychromy of banded stone grew dim and perished (the popular mixture of Bath Stone and Red Mansfield was particularly unfortunate as the limestone and sandstone reacted against each other chemically as well as being easy prey to acids in the filthy atmosphere). He advocated that buildings should be

221

constructed of materials with glazed surfaces to resist the depredations of the atmosphere found in the average industrial town.[36]

Ricardo argued that the use of coloured materials would supply the equivalents of the shadows and half-tones provided by cornices, pilasters and mouldings. In this he was anticipating the designs of Otto Wagner in Vienna, who used coloured tiles set in the same planes as walls and piers to *suggest* capitals, friezes and cornices. At Melbury Road in Kensington and at Addison Road nearby he used hard, impervious materials to clothe the façades. He recognised and accepted the impurities and dirt in the atmosphere, so he used salt-glazed ware (fire-clay vitrified at high temperatures) as proof against the disintegrating forces of the London air. Inside, halls, passages, staircases and bathrooms had walls covered with tiles and floors laid with marble.[37]

Industrial mass-production helped to create Victorian architecture, not least in the availability of hard facing materials such as that provided for Waterhouse's Natural History Museum in Kensington. Cast-iron railings, lamp-post standards, rain-water goods, balcony railings, boot-scrapers, gratings, man-hole and coal-hole covers, ventilators, crestings, ornament and entire buildings, such as *pissoirs*, were made cheaply and in plenty. Hard-glazed ware, polished granites and plate-glass all added richness to Victorian fabric. Today, we can enjoy the cleaned stencilled patterns on the metalwork, and the hard Italian Gothic arcading of the University Museum in Oxford, the ironwork, brickwork and masonry of the Midland Station at St Pancras, and the superlative detailing of Holborn Viaduct as it spans Farringdon Street. St Pancras Station Hotel looks marvellous when seen across the rooftops from the heights above Clerkenwell, but to imagine it raw, red and new, rising above the muddy streets with horse-drawn vehicles everywhere, requires an effort of our imaginations. We can see Wormwood Scrubs today, but it requires an equivalent jump of our imaginations to see convict labour burning the bricks, constructing the buildings and working to plans drawn up by the soldier Du Cane.[38] If we could be transported back to the London of the 1860s and 1870s we would be astonished by the sheer amount of building activity, shocked by the din, dirt and dust, amazed by the coarse clothes, sickened by the stenches, and appalled by the faces grown old before their time, with toothless mouths and filthy skins and hair. In the yellowish fog of a rainy morning or evening in a great Victorian city, we would experience the Sublime terror of urbanisation. Astonishment, awe and uneasiness would still affect us: the immigrant from the olive groves of Italy, from the villages of Poland and Russia, from quiet rural England, or from the green hills of Ireland must have felt emotions the intensity of which we can only try to imagine. It must have been aweful.

7 TRAFFIC RELIEF, REFORM AND HYGIENE

Introduction; Schemes for Traffic Relief and Improving of Communications; Urban Hygiene; Steel Bridges; Institutional Buildings

The Holborn Valley Viaduct ranks second to no work which the Metropolis can boast as the production of the present century
The Architect 1 (1869) 176

The buildings are planned on what is now well known as the pavilion principle, so that each block of buildings is, as far as is compatible with facility of communication and administration, isolated from other portions of the building
On the St Charles Hospital in *The Builder* (19 March 1881), 354–5

Introduction
During the 1860s building activity was immense, not least in London, with its new railways, roads and buildings: it is staggering to consider the sheer amount of demolition, new work, noise, scaffolding, mud and dirt that must have been evident.

Traffic-jams are not a contemporary phenomenon: Victorian cities suffered from them, as old photographs make clear, and they were phenomenal jams, too. Measures to relieve these produced architectural and engineering solutions that were often immensely destructive, but which not infrequently were of considerable quality.

Schemes for Traffic Relief and Improving of Communications
Various schemes to improve traffic were mooted, including one for 'Metropolitan Traffic Relief', an early-Victorian idea for placing all heavy horse-drawn transport in underground roads, constructed on a cut-and-cover system, leaving the surface free for buses and pedestrians.

James Clephan, architect (who was in practice in London during the 1830s), collaborated with William Curtis, engineer, in a design for a public-transport railway system carried on cast-iron arcading above pavement level, shopping being provided under the railway (*Plate 140*). This extraordinary proposal did not involve steam-driven engines, but rather a vacuum-suction principle or one based on compressed air carried in tubes: electric power would have been

Plate 140 A system of tracked public transport designed by James Clephan, architect, and William Curtis, engineer. (*RIBA British Architectural Library*)

equally feasible had it been developed at that time. Brunel had promoted a railway powered by vacuum, but the difficulties of constructing a vacuum tube using materials available then, such as leather, proved too great to overcome. The Clephan-Curtis design was a remarkable piece of integrated architecture, planning and transport, although problems of vibration and noise would have been difficult to resolve. Other forms of continuously powered tracked systems in which chains or hawsers were attached to the trains and driven on a centrally placed steam-engine were also proposed, and were feasible.

The first London underground railway was constructed over a period of three years, and was opened in 1863. It began at Paddington and terminated at Moorgate, and most of its stations were open to the sky except for Baker Street and Gower Street, which were completely underground, with roofs of arched brickwork immediately below the streets. The construction of the retaining walls consists of piers ten feet apart between which are vertical arches to resist the thrust of the earth behind. The tops of these piers are connected by arches, and thus it was possible not only to resist the pressure of the earth on either side of the excavated area, but also to carry the structures overhead. This railway was constructed on the cut-and-cover basis (*Plate 141*): later on, the 'tube' system got over the problems of fitting a new transport route within a built-up-city by simply burrowing away far below ground.[1]

The success of London's Metropolitan Railway created such an influx of bills for the proposed formation of railways that almost half of the built fabric of London would have been demolished had the plans been implemented. A committee of the two Houses of Parliament was set up to examine the whole of the railway system and to rationalise the layout to maximum benefit. The admirable results formed the nucleus of London's underground railway.

Frederick Marrable (1818–72) designed a prototype for one of the most ambitious viaducts of all (and as it turns out one of the most destructive in terms of the numbers of old properties that lay in its path): this was Holborn Viaduct in the City of London. Marrable's 'Proposed High Level Road and Viaduct from St Sepulchre's Church to Hatton Garden' had a series of shops with elegant fronts set in the arches under the viaduct, and streets were spanned by cast-iron bridges. This scheme for traffic relief was designed in conjunction with

Plate 141 King's Cross in London: the station on the Metropolitan Line under construction. (*GLPL No 63/1347 27.315Kin*)

moves to develop large unified façades in the manner of Nash to front desirable residences with shops at the level of the viaduct. In May 1863 Holborn Viaduct was commenced on site to designs by the chief engineer to the Commissioners of Sewers for the City of London, William Haywood (1821–94). Haywood became chief engineer in 1846 and held the post for forty-nine years during which he was responsible for an immense number of works including the design, layout and building of the City of London Cemetery at Little Ilford, Holborn Viaduct, the introduction of asphalt for the roads in the City from 1869, and many schemes for drainage. Holborn Viaduct was not just a raised road: two lateral arched passages on either side supported the pavements, while the main carriageway lay between these. The vaulted passages were divided into storeys. First was a space for cellars of the adjoining buildings, then against these was at the top a subway in which were laid the gas-, water- and telegraph-pipes; then a passage, and below this a vaulted chamber at the bottom of which was a main sewer. Ventilation of the underground passages was cunningly provided within the pedestals of the cast-iron lamp-posts. A large tunnel and a subway for pneumatic dispatch tubes were also incorporated.[2] Architectural details of Holborn Viaduct are handled superbly well, especially where cast-iron arches meet granite columns above exquisite gilded metal capitals that begin to herald Art-Nouveau forms (*Plate 142*). Even earlier, at Blackfriars Railway Bridge of 1862–4 designed by Joseph Cubitt and F. T. Turner for the London, Chatham and Dover Railway, the pier capitals were pronouncedly Art-Nouveau in character, deriving from late Gothic-Revival designs (*Plate 143*).

Urban Hygiene

In the 1850s Haywood had collaborated with G. B. Forster, chief engineer to the Metropolitan Commissioners of Sewers, in schemes to divert sewage from the River Thames, and later he worked with Bazalgette on the improvement of the sewerage system. Sir Joseph William Bazalgette (1819–91) created a great system that solved the problem of sewage collection and disposal in London. He designed a layout of sewers leading east, intercepted by a secondary system of sewers laid on both banks of the river, eventually discharging into settlement tanks at the northern and southern outfalls from which the effluent could be pumped out after high water. Bazalgette's scheme was enormous in its conception, and involved the construction of one thousand five hundred miles of street sewers,[3] eighty-two miles of main intercepting sewers, the erection of pumping-stations, and the construction of the Thames Embankment. At the Doulton factory at Lambeth stoneware pipes were manufactured which were both strong and impervious, while the use of Portland cement to bond the brickwork in the sewers was another innovation introduced by Bazalgette: the tests carried out during the construction of the sewers from 1859 to 1866 enabled cement manufacturers to improve their products.[4]

Two of Bazalgette's pumping-stations deserve special mention: those at Crossness and Abbey Mills, the former because of the vast beams of the engines, and the latter because of the architectural detail. The style chosen for Abbey Mills was said to be Medieval with Byzantine and Norman features, while the buildings had 'an amount of decoration in carved stone to doorways and other parts, that may be deemed great . . .'[5] James Watt & Co provided the engines which were placed symmetrically within marvellous interiors of polychrome brickwork. The various galleries and levels were carried on robust iron columns with Byzantinesque capitals (*Plate 144*). Light filtered down from the central octagonal cupola, illuminating cast-iron detail. Even the floors of the cat-walks were composed of beautifully crisp cast repetitive geometrical patterns, and the balustrades were exquisite examples of robust High-Victorian design. Balusters were simply bolted on to beams, and support-castings were bolted to the balusters and handrails.

Plate 142 Details of Holborn Viaduct. (*JSC*)
Plate 143 Details of Blackfriars Railway Bridge. (*JSC*)

The functional aspects of the lace-like cast-iron floors should not be overlooked, for they were designed with perforations to save weight, and the patterns helped to give a sure grip to the soles of shoes, but, apart from these considerations, the iron floors were aesthetically attractive. Naturalistic patterns of door-hinges not only helped to support the heavy doors, but also gave added strength to the wooden panels. Abbey Mills Pumping Station had an ecclesiastical quality about it, and the Byzantine cupola suggested that the building was an Orthodox church. This is not a bizarre association, for the cleaning up of great cities, the improving of public health, the saving of life, and the potty-training of urban man had a moral as well as a practical side, so something of the magnificence of a religious building could be detected in many such pumping-stations.

Bazalgette was also involved in the construction of the Thames Embankment (originally proposed by Sir Christopher Wren), which became imperative when the noxious effluvia of the mud-flats exposed at low tide made business in Parliament difficult. The building of the Embankment narrowed the river and ensured that most of the flats would be covered, but the structure held within it the Metropolitan District Railway, linking Westminster with the City, a subway for services, a low-level sewer, and supported a new carriageway. It must be remembered that specially designed steam-engines operated on the

Plate 144 Interior of Abbey Mills Pumping Station. (*JSC*)

Metropolitan Railway fuelled with coke to avoid the production of too much sulphur, while the engines had means by which steam was condensed in the tanks on either side of the boiler, thus enabling the engines to 'hold their breath' when underground, although suitable ventilation was provided. Lighting of carriages was by gas carried in india-rubber bags on the roofs, and the lighting was so bright that it was regarded as a great improvement on the 'semi-obscurity of ordinary oil-lighted railway carriages'.[6]

Steel Bridges

The limitations of early-Victorian engineering were already apparent in 1847 when Robert Stephenson's Dee Bridge collapsed under a train: the trussed cast-iron girders were too brittle to withstand the considerable stresses caused by vibration. The development of steel, as previously noted, was a result of the work of Bessemer and of the Siemens Brothers, but Britain lagged behind Europe in its use. The engineer Barlow noted that steel had been used for structural purposes in the United States, but its similar employment in Britain was 'obstructed by some deficiency in our own arrangements and by the absence of suitable regulations from the Board of Trade . . .' As with many reforms in Britain it needed a disaster to change things: like cholera in the 1830s and '40s, which had been responsible for reforms in sewerage and the provision of drinking-water, as well as for solving some of the problems of disposing of the dead, wind-pressure was to effect great changes in engineering regulations and calculation. The disaster which gave impetus to the encouragement of the use of steel in building had its origins in the competition for passenger traffic to Scotland. Two great railways were built: the difficulties of the western route to Glasgow were considerable, but once Shap had been negotiated the country was relatively easy; the east-coast companies had a clear run from London to Yorkshire, but the Rivers Tyne, Forth and Tay offered only miserably slow ferry connections, so in order to improve matters, bridges were proposed. The Tyne was bridged in 1849, and Sublimely too, but it was not until the 1870s that Thomas Bouch was commissioned to bridge the Tay and the Forth. He chose a structure of wrought-iron lattice-girders supported on cast-iron piers standing on brick-and-stone bases for the Tay bridge. The enormous feat was completed in 1878. On the last Sunday of 1879, however, the Edinburgh express plunged into the river during a storm with considerable loss of life, and at the ensuing enquiry it was found that the bridge had been badly designed, badly constructed, and badly maintained, and that its downfall was due to inherent defects in the structure. Sir Thomas Bouch was indicted as mainly to blame, and work on his plans for the Forth Bridge was at once stopped. The defects appear to have been mainly due to a gross underestimation of the maximum wind-pressure likely to bear on the bridge, a miscalculation that appears to have been due to the advice of the Astronomer Royal who had stated the wind-pressure was unlikely to exceed ten pounds per square foot. Bouch was ruined and took his own life. W. H. Barlow rebuilt the Tay bridge on new piers of massive solidity compared with Bouch's filigree piers, transferring Bouch's girders to the new piers, but strengthening them with wrought-iron and steel decking. Sir John Fowler and Benjamin Baker then submitted a design for the Forth bridge: the enormous spans needed and the heights at Queensferry posed problems to the engineers which they solved with a novel and breathtaking design. Baker decided to use steel in the construction, and the superior technology of the 1880s enabled enormous plates of steel to be produced from the rolling mills. The contractors, Messrs Tancred Arrol, had special plant installed at Queensferry, and slowly the huge tubes that formed the main members of the structure grew out from the piers. The principle of the cantilever was fully explored in this incomparable work of Victorian engineering, and Fowler remarked that he did not believe in astronomy as a safe guard to practical engineering. The bridge was completed in 1890.

At once the newly-knighted Baker was assailed by criticism, for the bridge was condemned as a supreme specimen of all ugliness. Baker replied that if the bridge were to be judged from the same standpoint as a chimney ornament the exercise would be ludicrous: it was impossible to pronounce authoritatively on the beauty of an object without knowing what it was used for and how it worked. William Morris believed that every technical improvement was bringing about more and more ugliness, and he could never accept that there would ever be a true architecture of iron, for every improvement in machinery brought about more 'ugliness'.

At Tower Bridge, designed by Sir Horace Jones and Sir John W. Barry (built 1886–94), the Victorian problem of aesthetic and functional considerations is demonstrated with dramatic effect: the response to the Tower of London produced two steel towers clad in masonry to look like late-medieval work, but those masonry towers *appeared* to carry the ends of the chains of the suspension elements. H. Heathcote Statham (1839–1924), editor of *The Builder* from 1884 to 1910, and author of *A History of Architecture* first published in 1912, denounced Tower Bridge as a sham, declaring that either the bridge should have been all steel or that the masonry towers should have been massive and truly monumental structures carrying the footbridges and the suspension chains.

Institutional Buildings

The Poor Law Reforms of the 1830s and the formation of workhouses were essentially utilitarian in origin, and by the time Queen Victoria had been on the Throne for a decade, various measures relating to sewerage, workhouses, burial of the dead, housing, asylums, prisons, hospitals and other aspects of urban life were in force.

Prisons, asylums, hospitals, workhouses, military barracks and the like require similar architectural and planning consideration: all these building types suggest a degree of segregation from the rest of society. Prisons incarcerated those who had fallen foul of the law, and the criminals were segregrated from the public both as a punishment and to protect the public from the criminal; hospitals, especially those with infectious diseases, needed to be set aside both for the benefit of the public and the patients; barracks contain troops who must be segregated from civilians to maintain discipline and avoid trouble; asylums were sited out of town so that the mentally ill would benefit from country air and would not be objects of spectacle as in the eighteenth century; while workhouses also needed to house large numbers of people in spacious buildings.

The plans of Victorian institutional buildings tend to be logical and orderly, and the structures are sited in what was once open country. Blocks arrayed in a pattern radiating from some central point, or grouped in rows, are commonest, and derive from schemes devised in the eighteenth century. Workhouses separated men, women and children, and housed the workless poor who were supposed to be employed usefully. In the early years of Victoria's reign the workhouses were often built in a late-Tudor style, although sometimes early-seventeenth-century gabled styles were preferred. Attention was paid to heating and lighting in these establishments, and adequate ventilation was essential, as was the provision of bath-houses. At the same period separate institutions for lunatics were established.

To go to hospital before about 1860 was a dangerous adventure, for poor ventilation, light and hygiene made the chances of becoming infected very high indeed. The scientific study of infection really began in the eighteenth century, and was reflected in proposals for hospitals, first in France. J. R. Tenon, in his *Mémoires sur les hôpiteaux de Paris*, published in 1788, suggested that the pavilion type of design was most suitable for hospitals, and quoted the Royal Naval Hospital near Plymouth as an ideal type of plan (this hospital was also specifically mentioned by the prison reformer Howard). The pavilion plan of hospital was developed which allowed plenty of light and air to penetrate each building: wards were reduced to thirty-bed size, while washing and WC facilities were provided for each ward.

Perhaps the finest of all pavilion hospitals was the new St Thomas's, built between Westminster Bridge and Lambeth Palace between 1868 and 1871. Some nine acres of land known as Stangate Bank were purchased, and the existing tenements, wharves and boathouses were demolished. The foreshore was reclaimed, and this accounted for about half the site. The hospital was built as eight four-storey pavilions linked by corridors (*Plate 149*), the central six buildings being for patients, that next to Westminster Bridge being allocated to officers of the hospital, and the block to the south containing the medical school, museum and lecture-room. The whole structure was fire-resistant, the floors of each storey being laid on iron girders protected by concrete. Floor finishes of oak ensured a good appearance and hard-wearing qualities, while the walls of each ward were coated with Parian cement. Heating was augmented by a warm-water system, and natural ventilation was encouraged by open fires. A contemporary opinion of the hospital was that the plan was perfect and that in spite of the cost (nearly half a million pounds then) it was cheap for the good it would effect. 'As an addition to the great public edifices of the metropolis, it certainly will not be surpassed in appearance . . .'[7]

The architect for St Thomas's Hospital was Henry Currey (1820–1900), a competent designer in the Italianate manner favoured for certain public buildings at the time. The plan is adapted from that of French precedents, and was certainly influenced by the advice and opinions of Florence Nightingale. Associated with this great scheme was the construction of the Albert Embankment under the direction of Bazalgette.

One architect specialising in hospital design was Henry Saxon Snell (1830–1904), who practised with his sons H. Saxon Snell and A. Saxon Snell in London. Their St Charles Hospital (*Fig 50*) in north Kensington, begun in 1879 for the Poor Law Board of Guardians, consisted of a block of buildings situated at the entrance and containing

Plate 145 St Thomas's Hospital, London. Henry Currey was the architect. (*RIBA British Architectural Library*)

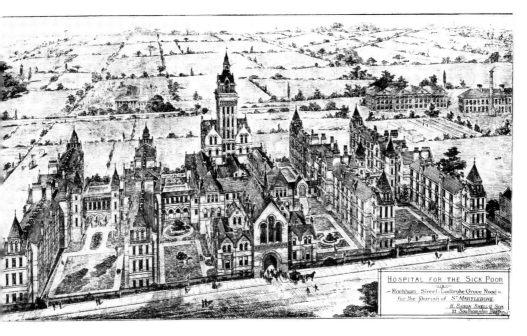

Fig 50 Hospital for the Sick Poor in Rackham Street, Ladbroke Grove Road, for the Parish of St Marylebone, by H. Saxon Snell and Son, architects. (*From* The Builder, *25 June 1881*)

the residences of the medical officer, matron and assistant medical officer, while over the arched carriageway was a chapel. The architects provided a description of the buildings, later published by Batsford, in which much was made of the function of the hospital, including the efficiency of air-changes, the system of ventilation and the heating. The latter was by open fires which heated coils of pipes containing water which then circulated. Humidity was also controlled so that air would not be too dry, a great advance for the time.[8]

The system of pavilions which Saxon Snell devised had a central administration block flanked by two double-ward blocks parallel to each other and to the central block, so that there were five buildings in all, linked by light cast-iron galleries and canopied ways. The architects' 'Thermhydric' system allowed for upright flues in the external walls: inlets were provided for fresh air, which was warmed as it entered, and air was also admitted directly through the walls into skirting-boxes between the beds. The flues carried off the foul air and the products of gas combustion used for lighting. The central feature of the administration block was a massive machicolated tower containing the chimney, while at the top were the water-tanks. This tower was based on north-Italian structures of the Middle Ages.

Saxon Snell built other hospitals, all on advanced principles, and similar in style to his Kensington work. David Bryce's Royal Infirmary in Edinburgh of 1870–79 was also built on the pavilion pattern, but the style was in the medieval Scottish 'Baronial' fashion, complete with bartizans, towers with conical caps, corbie-stepped gables and a massive central tower. Also turreted, but this time based on a saltire cross plan with turrets at the ends of the arms, was Alfred Waterhouse's University College Hospital of 1897–1906, a tall building on a cramped site with four wards on each floor, the whole exterior harshly red, like the same architect's Prudential offices in Holborn.

The disgraceful conditions of the Crimean War, the example of Henry Roberts's Model Houses for the Great Exhibition, and the death-rates among troops in barracks in peacetime led to demands for new barracks based on the pavilion planning of hospitals, and several examples were built, all in a very simple, utilitarian and almost bleak manner, with no concessions to ornament, style or aesthetics.

Architecturally, prisons were much more interesting, and gave architects much stylistic, planning, grouping and functional scope. During the eighteenth century ideal designs for prisons were intended to reform the occupants morally and physically. Bentham had produced polygonal plans for prisons (the *Panopticon*) and this Benthamite utilitarian image was lampooned in Pugin's *Contrasts*. The Victorians, however, favoured regular blocks separated by courts or by open spaces, and some designs consisted of long cell-blocks radiating from a central building, as at Pentonville of 1840–42 by Sir Joshua Jebb, and Holloway of 1849–52 by J. B. Bunning. A type of cell-block was developed consisting of several storeys of cells grouped in long ranges on either side of a top-lit space (today it would be called an 'atrium'): access to the cells was by means of galleries, usually of cast iron.

The primary influence on the improvement of prison conditions was John Howard, whose *The State of Prisons in England and Wales* of 1777 was of great importance. Hygiene and straightforward logical planning were among Howard's main concerns, themes to which he returned in his *An Account of the Principal Lazarettos in Europe* in 1789. Howard's works demonstrate the similar planning requirement of prisons and hospitals, where ease of supervision, security, segregation and hygiene were of great importance. It was Howard, too, who helped to mould a climate of opinion that encouraged the notion of correcting offenders instead of punishing them.

A medieval castellated style was adopted for Reading Gaol of 1842–4 by George Gilbert Scott and W. B. Moffatt, and for Holloway (where Kentish rag and Caen stone dressings were used). Crumlin Road Gaol in Belfast of 1846 by Charles Lanyon was an assured Classical design, while Weightman's Walton Gaol in Liverpool of 1848–55 was in a Norman Revival manner.

Among the most interesting of the new generation of prison designs is Wormwood Scrubs Prison, west London, of 1873–85, designed by Sir Edmund Frederick Du Cane (1830–1903). Du Cane had been an officer in the Royal Engineers, rose to the rank of major-general, and had a long and distinguished career. He was assistant superintendent of the foreign side of the Great Exhibition of 1851, and until 1856 organised convict labour in Swan River colony in Australia where he promoted public works and general improvements.

In 1863 Du Cane was appointed director of convict prisons as well as an inspector of military prisons, administered the system of penal servitude following the Prisons Act of 1865, and was responsible for the provision of extra prisons after the abolition of the punishment of Transportation in 1867. In 1869 he became Chairman of the Board of Directors of Convict Prisons, Surveyor-General of Prisons, and Inspector-General of Military Prisons. He advocated the use of convict labour for works of national utility and gave a paper on the subject in 1871: using convict labour he improved the defences of Portland, the docks at Portsmouth and Chatham, and prison accommodation.

Du Cane's great monument, as far as the present study is concerned, is Wormwood Scrubs Prison. The new site was obtained from the Ecclesiastical Commissioners, and the whole new building at Wormwood Scrubs was erected using convict labour on lines developed from Du Cane's Australian experiences. Bricks were made on site, the boundary wall was completed in 1883, and there were cells for 1,381 convicts, with a cookhouse, bakery, laundry, workshops, chapel, infirmary and baths. Cell blocks were built parallel to each other, orientated north-south, and each block contained 351 cells. The blocks were linked by covered ways. Du Cane's scheme is remarkable for its clean, logical plans, and for the heating and ventilating system which served each cell. Staircases, vents and sanitary stacks were expressed in the building, and the completed prison combined that direct

Plate 146 South-east view of Wormwood Scrubs Prison showing the boundary wall and cell block. (*Papers of the late Mr A. W. Pullan*)

integrity familiar from early warehouse and industrial buildings with an Italian Romanesque concession to some fenestration and other features including the towers. Du Cane supervised the building of Wormwood Scrubs himself, charging a guinea a day, pointing out that by employing convict labour and personally supervising construction, he was avoiding architects' and surveyors' fees, and therefore saving public money. His methods caused unease in certain quarters, and he got into hot water for expressing his ideas in print in 1894: he was attacked as an autocrat in *The Daily Chronicle*,[9] but there is no doubt that his achievements and methods deserve respect and study. Du Cane also inaugurated the registration of criminals, suggested the development of composite portraiture of criminals, and encouraged the use of Sir Francis Galton's finger-print system for the identification of suspects. He was an *uomo universale* of his day, with wide interests including archaeology, architecture, literature and painting. Du Cane's model plan for Wormwood Scrubs influenced the design of prisons for many generations afterwards (*Figs 51 and 52 and Plate 146*).

Fig 51 Plan of Wormwood Scrubs Prison. (*Papers of the late Mr A. W. Pullan*)
Fig 52 Section and Plan of Cell Building at Wormwood Scrubs Prison.
(*Papers of the late Mr A. W. Pullan*)

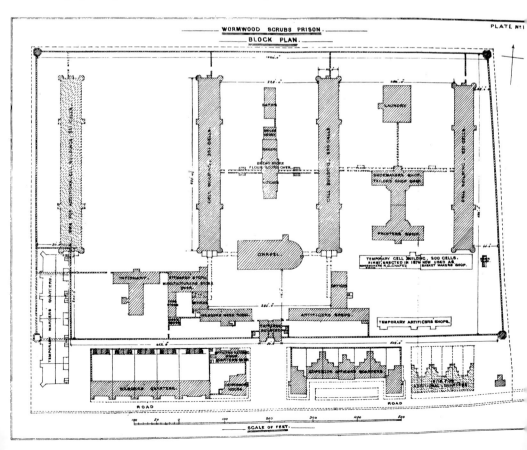

PORTION OF A CELL BUILDING

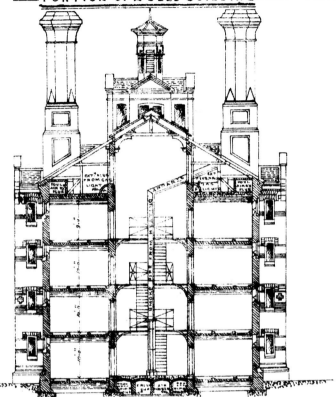

SECTION A.B.

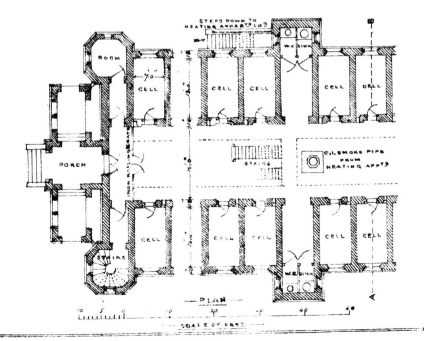

PLAN

SCALE OF FEET

8 BUILDINGS FOR LEISURE

Introduction; Gin-Palaces and the Transformation of the Urban Public House; Clubs, Hotels and Restaurants; Theatres; Conclusion

We may observe here, that the fitting up of public house bars in London forms almost a distinct trade; and that the expense incurred in this way by the owners of public houses is almost incredible, every one vying with his neighbour in convenient arrangement, general display, rich carving, brass-work, finely veined mahogany, and ornamental painting

J. C. Loudon: *An Encyclopaedia of Cottage, Farm and Villa Architecture* (Longman, London, 1834) Section 1444

Introduction

At the end of the seventeenth century the popular consumption of beers, ales, porters and wines was challenged by a new and menacing intoxicant. When William of Orange and Queen Mary arrived from the Netherlands, their Court brought *jenever* or *geneva* with them as a fashionable alcoholic drink. This was nothing to do with the capital of Calvinism, but was from the Dutch *genever* or *jenever*, referring to the juice of juniper berries used to flavour a white ardent spirit distilled from grain or malt. In the shortened form, gin, the term denotes a spirit of British manufacture in imitation of the Dutch spirit, and flavoured not with juniper but with some substitute. By the time Hogarth produced his famous and savage images depicting the evil effects of drinking 'Blue Ruin' contrasted with the wholesome Englishness of 'Beer Street', the consumption of cheap gin had become a national problem.

The late 1820s and early 1830s were, once again, crucial years in the history of public houses as with much else influenced by the Evangelical Conscience, utilitarianism and major changes of attitude. A huge reduction of the duty on gin in the 1820s led to a doubling of the consumption of spirits on which duty had been paid, and coincided with a four hundred per cent rise in criminal convictions in London alone. Needless to say the drinking of spirits and the rise in crime were seen to be connected, and in 1829 the Middlesex magistrates noted and deplored the great increase in the number of gin-shops and the conversion of public houses (where working men could refresh themselves with meals and wholesome beer in the tap-rooms) into 'flaming dram-shops'.

The devastating effects of 'dram-drinking' were obvious, and alcoholism was a major scourge.[1] Thus, in 1829, were founded the first societies advocating total abstinence from spirits and moderation in other alcoholic drinks: Belfast led the way, and a Temperance Society was established in London in 1831. The problem was that the advocates of free trade were becoming more and more vociferous, and, in their campaigns, were actually encouraging the removal of economic and fiscal controls that had a regulating effect on consumption. A combination of politically motivated free traders and morally earnest anti-spirits Evangelicals was somewhat irresistible so, in an attempt to wean people off gin, duty on beer was abolished in 1830, and any householder able to pay a small fee was enabled to obtain a licence to sell beer. Freed from the control of the licensing justices nearly forty thousand beer-shops opened within a few years.

Gin-Palaces and the Transformation of the Urban Public House

Establishments licensed to sell alcoholic drinks of all sorts were rapidly embellished to make them smarter and more attractive than the common public house: fronts acquired pilasters, entablatures, plate glass and costly gas fittings, while interiors sported spirit barrels, counters, mirrors and ornament. Drink was dispensed by young women dressed in finery, chosen for their attractive appearance. The difficulty was, of course, that the owners of taverns and modest shop-like public houses saw the beer-shops as threats to business, so they started to renovate their premises and to make them 'gaudy, gold-beplastered temples', as Cruikshank the cartoonist called them. These 'gin-palaces' were therefore the result of legislation aimed to lessen the attractions of gin-drinking; they were not the cause of the gin-drinking epidemic. Stephen Geary is credited by some with the design of the first gin-palace, but the site was not identified. It seems likely that the prototypical gin-palace was Thompson and Fearon's establishment (apparently designed by J. B. Papworth) which was opposite St Andrew's, Holborn, near the corner of Holborn Hill and Ely Place. The gin-palace (94 Holborn Hill)[2] had a front of four pilasters carrying crossettes and a cornice with an iron balcony over which was a plain and dignified façade: between the pilasters were modest plate-glass windows. Another early gin-palace was Weller's in Old Street which appears to have had a rather more ornate front, but still with four pilasters carrying an elaborate entablature. Thompson and Fearon's was demolished when Holborn Viaduct was constructed, but a drawing of it survives.[3]

The fashion for bright new public houses began to catch on. In 1835 Charles Dickens noted that:

> the epidemic began to display itself among the linen-drapers and haberdashers. The primary symptoms were an inordinate love of plate-glass, and a passion for gas-lights and gilding. The disease gradually progressed, and at last attained a fearful height. Quiet dusty old shops in different parts of town, were pulled down; spacious premises with stuccoed fronts and gold letters, were erected instead . . .[4]

He tells us that the 'disease' burnt out among the chemists, then the hosiers, and seemed to abate:

> when it burst forth with tenfold violence among the publicans, and keepers of 'wine-vaults'. From that moment it has spread among them with unprecedented rapidity, exhibiting a concatenation of all the previous symptoms; onward it has rushed to every part of town, knocking down all the old public houses, and depositing splendid mansions, stone balustrades, rosewood fittings, immense lamps, and illuminated clocks, at the corner of every street.[5]

Dickens, with his keen sense of contrast, was able to compare the drabness of the poorer quarters of London with the splendours and attractions of the new gin-palaces:

> You turn the corner. What a change! All is light and brilliancy. The hum of many voices issues from that splendid gin-shop which forms the commencement of the two streets opposite; and the gay building with the fantastically ornamented parapet, the illuminated clock, the plate-glass windows surrounded by stucco rosettes, and its profusion of gas-lights in richly-gilt burners, is perfectly dazzling when contrasted with the darkness and dirt we have just left. The interior is even gayer than the exterior. A bar of French-polished mahogany, elegantly carved, extends the whole width of the place; and there are two side-aisles of great casks, painted green and gold, enclosed within a light brass rail, and bearing such inscriptions, as 'Old Tom, 549;' 'Young Tom, 360;' 'Samson, 1421' − the figures agreeing, we presume, with 'gallons,' understand. Beyond the bar is a lofty and spacious saloon, full of the same enticing vessels, with a gallery running round it, equally well furnished.[6]

Descriptions of gin-palace interiors such as that reproduced above are augmented by drawings and engravings which help us to have an idea of what they were really like, although we have to be aware that George Cruikshank was exaggerating in order to make his point, especially after he took the temperance road (*Fig 53*). Cruikshank, however, suggested the appearance of a gin-shop in its early stages before it became completely palatial. The moral tone is clear, and the devastating effects of gin-drinking are depicted: the paths to the workhouse, madhouse, gaol and gibbet. There are advertisements displaying the attractions at Drury Lane, including *The Road to Ruin* while members are wanted 'to complete a Burial Society'. Of particular interest is the décor shown by Cruikshank within the 'gin-shops': casks have become coffins containing 'Old Tom', 'Blue Ruin', 'Gin and Bitters', and 'Deady's Cordial', while the bar is little more than a shop counter, and the floor is unhygienically wooden. The beginnings of some display are, however, in evidence: the 'marbled' timber pilasters with debased Corinthian capitals, the bunches of grapes in swags, and the ornate candelabrum (*Fig 54*).

Cruikshank, like others, was tending to contrast the gin-shops with the older more modest public houses they were replacing. These early

Fig 53 George Cruikshank's illustration of the interior of a 'splendid gin-shop' as described by Dickens in *Sketches by Boz*. Note the bar, the sub-Egyptian detail of the column, the huge casks and the gas-lamp.

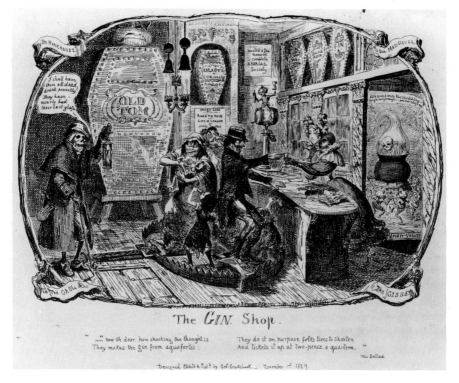

The *GIN* Shop.

"... now Oh dear, how shocking the thought is
They makes the gin from aquaforlis:

They do it on purpose folks lives to shorten
And tickets it up at two-pence a quartern."

New Ballad

Designed, Etched & Pub.d by Geo. Cruikshank — November 1.st 1829.

Fig 54 The Gin Shop designed and etched by George Cruikshank, 1829. The moral tone is clear, and the dangers of gin-drinking made plain. (*Guildhall Library, City of London*)

public houses looked very much like ordinary houses, and accommodation on the ground floor would include a public parlour, a tap-room, a bar, a kitchen and the publican's private room. Tap-rooms were furnished with tables, fixed benches or settles and a fireplace, while the parlour would have chairs, a grander fireplace and perhaps some pictures. A bar was not a bar in the modern sense, but was an office, strategically placed so that customers would be seen as they entered or left the premises. Larger public houses of the better type had 'coffee rooms' which were divided into compartments with timber partitions, each stall containing a table and benches with hat-racks over the partitions. A good example of this type of room survives at Simpson's off Cornhill in London. Drink and food were brought by staff to the customer. Counters seem to have been introduced when draught or bottled drink began to be served to customers calling as though to a shop, and gradually the bar began to dispense drink to all parts of the establishment across counters, probably to help to control security. This was a very great change, and soon the bar-counter became a feature of the gin-palace, with ornate gantries, spirit dispensers and beer-engines.

242

Later, in the series *The Drunkard's Children* (*Plate 147*), Cruikshank recorded features from typical gin-palaces of the 1830s and '40s: while the effects of the gin habit are clearly shown in terms of degradation, poverty, disease and madness, the drawing is of great architectural interest. The double doors contain etched glass, and gaslight illuminates the plate-glass window. A large advertisement in florid lettering, probably etched into the plate-glass of a mirror, offers the supply of wines and spirits to families. Huge casks carried on a stand contain 'Cream of the Valley' and 'The Celebrated Double Gin'. The only capital visible is a free invention on the grape motif, and owes little to Classical precedent. The bar is no longer a shop-counter, but is a fully developed public-house bar-counter, in a form that remained relatively unchanged until recent times. Illumination is bright, and is by gas.

Huge sums of money were expended on gilded columns, mahogany fronts, silvered bar-engines, mirrors and carvings of all description. The blaze of gaslight within and without a gin-palace must have been a welcome sight to the inhabitants of the dismal half-world of the unsavoury back streets. Gin-palaces provided an illusory refuge from dirt, failure, squalor, cold and hunger, and gave warmth, brightness, glamour and company. The lushness of the décor and the exotic flash of silvered mirrors reflecting the gaslight gave the poor a fleeting illusion of finery that was never to be theirs. An investment in good hardwearing materials soon paid off, as people deserted the gloomy,

Plate 147 The Drunkard's Children by Cruikshank, showing a typical gin-palace interior of the early-Victorian period. (*Guildhall Library, City of London*)

sordid pubs for the splendid emporia where alcohol was served by barmaids dressed up for effect. It was important to suggest the richness of the interiors in the architectural treatment of the façades: indeed, the great hanging gaslights outside Victorian urban pubs identified them, and were derived from the early gin-palaces or gin-temples of the 1830s (*Plate 148*).

As new techniques and materials were developed, wooden floors, 'marbled' columns and pilasters, and timber-topped bar-counters were superseded by tiled floors, cast-iron columns, glazed tiles for walls, and marble or even granite bar-tops. More durable and easily cleaned, these hard, robust materials gave a new richness to the public house, and, as plate-glass and mirrors became larger and more ornate, ever more elaboration of décor was possible. Even better from the commercial point of view was the fact that redecoration at frequent intervals was no longer necessary. Sir Benjamin Ward Richardson (1828–96), physician and sanitary reformer, proposed in his model town of Hygeia that many new materials should be employed, such as glazed fireclay, glazed bricks, and *Lincrusta* and *Anaglypta* embossed papers in order to improve hygiene because of their impervious surfaces. It is interesting that Richardson, one of the first physicians to warn against the powerful effects of alcohol from a scientific point of view, should have proposed materials that were used with enormous success by designers of public-house interiors. Embossed papers, sealed and varnished or painted with gloss paints, were the almost universal coverings for ceilings and dados, and were decorative, hardwearing and easily cleaned.

Public houses had rooms which were also used for meetings, and this appears to have been a usual feature for the next few generations. Gradually, however, the upper classes and professional people began to desert pubs for clubs, and publicans introduced musical and other entertainments to attract customers: this was the origin of the music-hall. Just as eighteenth-century publicans had developed pleasure-gardens and 'spas',[7] so certain publicans in the Victorian period exploited grounds, displays of statuary, musical performances, fountains, gaslight, painted panoramas, stage-sets and variety 'turns' to attract trade. One of the largest, earliest and grandest of these establishments was the celebrated Eagle Tavern of 1839–40 in Shepherdess Walk just off the City Road, and celebrated in the famous song. The building itself was a large Classical structure with a Giant Composite Order of pilasters and engaged columns linking the first and second floors: the interior was embellished with marble fireplaces and the whole of the woodwork was grained.

The success of The Eagle prompted the building of many imposing taverns that were often run up before houses were built, so they stood alone, waiting for their customers. *The Builder* of 1854 describes imposing pubs standing alone and complete in some numbers in areas such as Camden Town and Kentish Town, glittering in their sham splendour. The reason for this extraordinary outbreak of building of large and showy pubs was that after the passing of the Act removing beer-houses from the control of magistrates, the authorities gave up limiting numbers of fully licensed houses which, nevertheless, re-mained under the control of the licensing authorities. Beer-houses, on the other hand, could multiply with ease, but the grander establish-ments, able to sell all types of drink, could be subject to official supervision. From 1869 beer-houses were placed under the control of the magistrates as well.

Corner sites began to be sought for public houses, where they often

Plate 148 The Angel Tavern, Crutched Friars, at the corner of Vine Street. The marbled pilasters and large lamp were developed from gin-palaces. (*Guildhall Library, City of London*)

act as 'book-ends' for whole ranges of terrace-houses, but very well-mannered pub-fronts, like that of the Norland Arms of 1850 by Robert Clements, also were built. By the 1850s the corner-site pubs were developing with an outer façade largely of plate glass subdivided by means of pilasters and engaged columns, plans based on a series of segmental wedges subdivided by wooden screens, and a curved or polygonal bar-counter with a 'gantry' standing in the centre with barrels, glasses and bottles. This plan allowed for several rooms with various degrees of comfort, and permitted some privacy yet enabled the publican and his staff to keep an eye on the customers. This type of plan evolved into the late-Victorian and Edwardian horseshoe-shaped corner pub, with a series of timber partitions (often enriched with etched- or stained-glass panels), and ever more elaborate display stands, or gantries, behind the bar. In the case of long bars, be they curved or straight, screens were provided which divided the length of the bar-counter, and broke it up into more friendly and private sections. 'Snob-screens' were also provided at the bar counter containing panels which swivelled on vertical axes, and these protected the users of the saloon or private bars from the gaze of the vulgar using the 'public', while the orders could be given to barmen without being observed from other bars. These swivelling screens survived in The Lamb, Lamb's Conduit Street, London, in 1989.

While some public houses had rooms for entertainment, these were often unprepossessing places. Grander establishments like The Eagle were the begetters of the Song and Supper Rooms which provided food, drink, and entertainment for persons out on the spree: the interiors of such places were often very ornate, but they were a curious hybrid that developed from the grander taverns. Gradually pubs and music-halls became separated, and although musical entertainment was provided in such places as the Grand Hotel and Brasserie de l'Europe, Leicester Square (and indeed in the 'Palm Courts' of many hotels until well into the twentieth century), pubs, music-halls, and restaurants began to develop along distinct lines of their own.

Public-house exteriors were often very elaborate as a form of advertisement, but, while they sometimes conformed to currently fashionable architectural tastes, they were usually more flamboyant and larger than life, as it were. There are not all that many Gothic pubs (understandably perhaps, as the association with the sacred would put off those in search of more profane pleasures), and a robust if over-elaborate Classicism seems to have been favoured. The Citadel in Belfast had some coarse Gothic screens, but generally these were rarities. The late-Victorian period saw numerous pubs in free eclectic styles, but the striped and turreted manner of Shaw's Scotland Yard

246

seems to have inspired many designers of public houses, probably because of the possibilities of elaborate upper-works on the façades.

The Crown Liquor Saloon in Belfast is an extraordinary survival, although it is rather late in date (supposedly the 1880s), but, like much architecture in Ireland, often reflects tastes and styles of earlier epochs. Before it became The Crown, this celebrated building was the Ulster Railway Hotel, dating from 1839–40: the stucco-faced first and second storeys, with the Giant Order of Corinthian pilasters, the shafts of which are incised with sub-Greek-Revival decoration, the entablature and the architraves (with crossettes) around the first-floor windows, date from this period (*Plate 149*). The ground storey acquired its frontage of coloured, glazed and moulded tiles (by Craven Dunnill) with distyle *in antis* porch, painted and fired glass, and gilt and lettered fascia in 1898 when the bases of the pilasters were curtailed. Inside, the startling richness of lettered advertisements, mirrors, a tiled long bar with a granite top, painted, etched and fired glass panels, and fine woods, combine in one of the most marvellous creations of this building type (*Plate 150*). The entrance-doors had splendidly robust pull-handles, push-bars, and engraved plates, while the painted and fired glass was as fine as anywhere could be found. Woodwork was grained or varnished for its hard-wearing qualities, and all fittings were designed to stand up to use. The designer of The Crown was supposed to have been a Mr Flanagan, or Flannigan, the son of the proprietor, but, like a lot of popular beliefs, this is incorrect. The architects were E. and J. Byrne, a local firm, who carried out their design in two stages. The extraordinarily detailed interior, with the boxes (or snugs) along the long frontage that were elaborately decorated with painted glass panels, carvings, tiles and mirrors, was commenced in 1885. The floor was a masterpiece of the tilers' art, while the ceiling, bar-counter (with vertical screens), gantry and mirrors combined in a splendid expression of High-Victorian pub design that is unique.[8]

In the last years of Victoria's reign pubs began to respond to Arts-and-Crafts influences, to the 'Queen-Anne' style, and to other themes. The predominant style of the Victorian pub, however, was a robust, elaborate and even coarse interpretation of Classical and early-Renaissance themes: what is amazing is the extraordinary richness and variety found in this architecture, always exuberant, interesting, and even perhaps distinguished at times.

Clubs, Hotels and Restaurants

Moulded, coloured and glazed fireclay was used in quantities during the 1880s and '90s for restaurants, public houses and public rooms. Examples of the uses of this material were the interior of the Auction

Plate 149 Exterior of the Crown Liquor Saloon, Belfast. (*JSC*)

Plate 150 Interior of the Crown, Belfast. (*JSC*)

Mart Restaurant (*Fig 55*) in the basement of the Somers Clark Gothic building at the corner of Tokenhouse Yard and Lothbury, London, by E. Bassett Keeling[9] (who used 'Glazed Burmantofts Faience' made by Wilcock & Co of Leeds), and the interior of the National Liberal Club, Whitehall Court, of 1885–8 by Alfred Waterhouse.

The latter building was a comparative latecomer to the magnificent series of gentlemen's clubs which seem to have evolved from a long tradition of convivial meeting-places for persons of similar interests, be they political or professional. Clubs provided libraries, sitting-rooms, dining facilities, recreation rooms and wine-cellars, and were often of considerable architectural magnificence. The United Service Club in Waterloo Place in London superseded an earlier building of 1817 by Smirke (on another site), and was designed by Nash in 1827 after the destruction of Carlton House. The building was remodelled by Decimus Burton in 1842: Burton had built the Athenaeum opposite in 1828–30, and those three buildings by Smirke, Nash and Burton set the models for later Clubs. Barry's Reform and Travellers' Clubs in Pall Mall of 1837–41 and 1829–32 respectively, in Roman and Florentine

Fig 55 The Auction Mart Restaurant, Tokenhouse Yard, Lothebury, London, with wall surfaces decorated with glazed Burmantofts Faience by Wilcock & Co, Leeds. Enoch Bassett Keeling, architect. (*Lithograph of Print by James Akerman*)

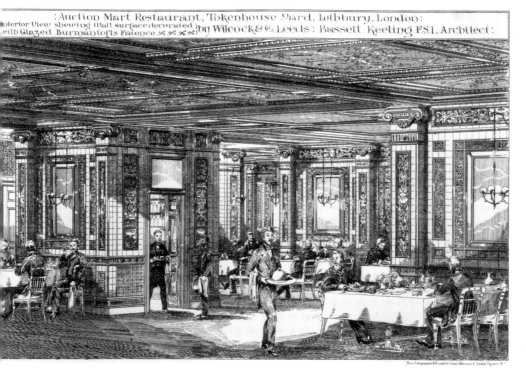

Renaissance styles, set the fashion for Italianate architecture, and provided models of magnificence that were very much more refined than anything the public houses and gin-palaces could offer less august strata of society. Whereas the Athenaeum, in spite of its nod towards the Greek Revival, is essentially within the Palladian tradition, the Reform Club, with its enormous astylar façades and huge *cornicione* is based on Italian *palazzi*, especially the Farnese in Rome (*Plate 44*).

Later clubs tended to follow London precedent, like Barry's Athenaeum in Princess Street, Manchester of 1837, another *palazzo* of stone, or Yeoville Thomason's Union Club in Birmingham of 1869. Oddly enough, in Belfast Lanyon remodelled Sir Robert Taylor's Assembly Rooms in the *palazzo* style for the Belfast Bank (*Plate 43*), but chose a lush Brighton-Regency and North-Kensington stucco bow-fronted style for the Ulster Club of 1863. The later Reform Club in Belfast of 1883 by Maxwell and Duke of Manchester is in a free eclectic Classical style, very different from Edward Salomons's Venetian Gothic Manchester Reform Club of 1870. Robert Edis's Constitutional Club in London's Northumberland Avenue of 1884 introduced North European Renaissance gables while, as has been noted previously, Waterhouse's National Liberal Club of 1885–7 employed so many styles that it was said to reflect all the varieties of opinion within the party (*Plate 85*).

The railways, as Donald J. Olsen has pointed out,[10] destroyed the old coaching inns and created the prototypes of the modern hotel. This phenomenon began in the 1850s, with each railway company building and managing hotels associated with its main stations as an important part of its operations.[11] These railway hotels were not only places where excellent standards of overnight accommodation could be had, but they also provided sitting-rooms, smoking-rooms, drawing-rooms and restaurants which were specifically designed to cater for those persons who had deserted the public houses, and who demanded higher, more luxurious standards. Hotels provided bathrooms, plenty of lavatories and other facilities. The first of the metropolitan railway hotels was the Great Western at Paddington (*Plate 151*) of 1851–3 which screened the train sheds previously described. The hotel was designed by P. C. Hardwick (1820–90), and included suites of rooms, small bedrooms and all facilities: its success prompted the building of other railway hotels, including the Grosvenor of 1860–62 beside the terminus of the Brighton line (now Victoria Station), designed by James Knowles Senior (1806–84) and Junior (1831–1908) (a vast seven-storey pile in the French Renaissance style of the Second Empire mixed judiciously with some Italianate round-arched elements), the Charing Cross Hotel of the 1860s by E. M. Barry (another enormous Frenchified building with a roofline derived from Renaissance châteaux), and the

Plate 151 Great Western Hotel, Paddington. (*RCHME No BB47/878*)

even grander four-hundred-bed Midland Grand at St Pancras of 1868-74 by George Gilbert Scott in the polychrome Gothic style (with interiors of the greatest richness and some extraordinarily forward-looking exposed ironwork) (*Plate 25*). John Giles's Langham Hotel in Portland Place was one of the first to employ hydraulic lifts. In the provinces the enormous Grand Hotel at Scarborough of 1863–7 by Cuthbert Brodrick with a spectacularly memorable skyline deserves mention (*Plate 152*), as does C. Trubshaw's glorious free-Renaissance-style Midland Hotel in Manchester of 1898. Bassett Keeling's designs for the Brighton Club and Norfolk Hotel Company Ltd of 1864 (*Fig 56*) is an interesting variant, with its festive iron balconies and

accommodation including a club, music room, restaurant and hotel facilities.

Railway hotels, of course, set standards for other private hotels, which quickly overtook them in the provision of luxurious (and decorous) accommodation. Victorian grand hotels catered for provincial visitors and tourists and gave the middle classes inexpensive alternatives to clubland:[12] even more forward-looking, they provided women with dining-rooms and drawing-rooms where they could resort without any problems. The Hotel Cecil on London's Embankment was one of the most luxurious of the new monster hotels, and had a reputation for excellent service and comfort.

Large restaurants serving good food at reasonable prices were not usual in London before the middle of the nineteenth century. 'Dining rooms' were usually small, dingy places, with snugs or stalls, but the advent of railway hotels and railway 'refreshment rooms' effected a revolution in the provision, scale and quality of restaurants. Messrs Spiers and Pond operated a number of new, cheap and excellent restaurants including The Gaiety in The Strand, which opened in 1869. The Criterion at Piccadilly Circus of 1875 by Thomas Verity (1837–91) was regarded as a fine example of its type, and included various dining-rooms, a large restaurant, grill-room, buffet, smoking-room and a grand hall: the whole complex was associated with a theatre. Public dining-rooms and restaurant facilities developed, and these, with the hotels, offered a marvellous range of sumptuous interiors serving reasonably priced menus: the fact that these were available to women helped their success, while the contrast with the grim old dining-rooms for businessmen could not have been more marked. In Leicester Square Baker's Grand Hotel and Brasserie de l'Europe of 1899 offered French and German fare, music, and ample English menus as well, served in elaborate schemes of interior decoration with many faience finishes and a dazzling array of electric light-fittings, the whole designed by Walter Emden.

In the 1850s, then, the upper and middle classes were starting to abandon the pub for clubs and hotels. Pubs responded by providing grander interiors with various rooms with separate entrances segregated from each other. The rise of the club, hotel and restaurant reflected a growing demand for higher standards, better food and hygiene, and greater variety. Only an enormous increase in national

Plate 152 Grand Hotel, Scarborough, by Cuthbert Brodrick. (*RCHME No BB81/8203*)
Plate 56 The Brighton Club, by E. Bassett Keeling. (Building News, *12 February 1864*)

wealth could have made this transformation possible, and it is clear that by the end of Victoria's reign Britain could offer hotels and restaurants to compare favourably with many elsewhere in the world.

Theatres

If Continental standards had played some part in improving hotels and restaurants, the case of theatres was somewhat different. To start with, the patronage of theatres was not civic, not Royal, and certainly not State, as it was in so many Continental countries, and theatres were provided entirely by private enterprise, and usually not given prominence in civil design terms. The development of entertainment associated with public houses, supper-rooms and other establishments led to the curious concept of music-halls, variety shows and the like. In the 1840s a distinction was made between theatres which put on plays and did not serve alcohol, and those which had licences and featured musical and variety shows. Purpose-built music-halls appeared from the mid-century: they had platforms for performances and halls furnished with rows of tables, but they were curiously hybrid forms of supper-rooms, public houses and places of amusement. Bassett Keeling's extraordinary Strand Music Hall (*Frontispiece and Fig 49*) of 1862–4 has already been mentioned as the most remarkable example of this building type, with its amazing ceiling and detailing.

Strict systems of licences for theatres, and the ambivalent position with which this building type was regarded, led to the design of theatres that were relatively modest compared with those of Continental Europe. Among the grander theatres were the Royal Opera House, Covent Garden, of 1857 by E. M. Barry, a Classical building with a hexastyle Corinthian portico at *piano nobile* level on the Bow Street frontage; the Criterion of 1870–74 by Verity with a free Renaissance façade and elaborate high roof which completely dwarfed the remains of Nash's Piccadilly Circus; G. H. Holloway and T. E. Collcutt's very elaborate English Opera House in Cambridge Circus of 1889 with its striped Northern Renaissance façade (*Plate 153*); and the extraordinary concoctions of Frank Matcham (1854–1920) such as the Belfast Grand Opera House of 1895 (*Plate 154*) and the Empire at Hackney of 1900, both weirdly festive in a somewhat vulgarly overblown manner that incorporates debased motifs from many sources. Interiors were usually very elaborate, owing much to a ripe Baroque style that had much in

Plate 153 Palace Theatre, Cambridge Circus, London, once the English Opera House, of 1889, by T. E. Collcutt. (*RCHME No BB88/4349*)

Plate 154 The Grand Opera House, Belfast, of 1894–5, by Frank Matcham. (*JSC*)

common with some of the more spectacular public houses, while Matcham, in the Belfast Opera House, mingled Baroque architecture derived from eighteenth-century Continental theatres with Indian elements, including the extraordinary elephant heads between the boxes on either side of the proscenium.

In addition to theatres were the great halls designed for public meetings and musical performances of the more serious sort. The largest was the Royal Albert Hall of 1867–71 by H. Y. D. Scott, based on a design by Captain Francis Fowke, a huge elliptical amphitheatre (*Plate 58*) with an exterior of red brick and cream-coloured terracotta very much in the 'South Kensington style' adopted for the original parts of the Victoria and Albert Museum and the 1862 Exhibition buildings. Other purpose-built halls were the Free Trade Hall in Manchester by Edward Walters of 1853 in the Italian Renaissance style of the sixteenth century; the incomparable Neoclassical St George's Hall in Liverpool by Elmes and Cockerell of 1841–56 (*Plates 30 and 31*); the hall of Brodrick's Town Hall in Leeds of 1853–8; the St Andrew's Halls in Glasgow by James Sellars of 1873; and the Ulster Hall in a provincial Italianate manner of 1860 by W. J. Barre.

Conclusion

Victorian architecture associated with leisure and entertainment is amazingly diverse in style. As use of the traditional public house ceased to be fashionable among all classes, and demand for higher standards increased as national wealth grew, so clubs, hotels, restaurants, music-halls and the smaller 'variety' theatres and concert-halls evolved. Elaborate early-Victorian public houses, with their gardens, entertainments and the like had in turn evolved from eighteenth-century London spas, especially those at Bagnigge and Sadler's Wells, and even the distinctly rough 'London Spaw' in Clerkenwell. A certain festive vulgarity present in the public houses influenced by gin-palace designs spread to music-halls and theatres, a trait particularly true of the newly developing seaside resorts like Brighton and Blackpool. The exotic element present in the Brighton Pavilion seems to recur in theatre designs, notably those by Matcham, where Oriental motifs (like Belfast's elephants) abound. Lushly oriental themes also were found in such places as the smoking-room of the Hotel Cecil on the Embankment, which had much *Lincrusta*, embossed leather, and glazed faience-faced columns in the Indian taste.[13]

Seaside structures often employed cast-iron motifs for decorative purposes such as balconies, cresting and canopies, while several iron piers were erected for entertainment as well as transportation purposes. Brighton's chain pier of 1823 designed by Captain Samuel

Brown had four iron pylons in the Egyptian style carrying the suspension chains,[14] and that resort had two other piers carried on cast-iron uprights on which platforms support iron-framed pleasure-buildings of a raffish eastern appearance influenced by the Pavilion. Clevedon had an elegant pier (*Plate 155*) constructed by Hamilton's Windsor Iron-Works Company of Liverpool and designed by John William Grover and Richard Ward using quantities of 'Barlow' rails abandoned by Brunel for the South Wales Railway.[15] Other seaside piers were not so long and had very elaborate superstructures. Different resort structures which were used for many purposes were often constructed of iron and glass cased in frontages of masonry or brick, and frequently decorated with lively patterns and panels of glazed tiles. Harrogate, Margate and many other resorts could boast multi-purpose buildings associated with leisure activities: many of these structures employed iron-and-glass techniques, were embellished with tiles and faience, iron crestings and ornament, and laid out on a lavish scale. The impact of palm-houses, the Crystal Palace and similar structures was widely felt, and influenced much architecture intended for leisure purposes, including that associated with hotels, resorts, spas and the like.

Plate 155 Clevedon Pier. (*JSC*)

9 THE ARCHITECTURE AND LANDSCAPES ASSOCIATED WITH THE DISPOSAL OF THE DEAD

**Introduction; The Position in Britain and Elsewhere;
The Movement to Establish Cemeteries; The British Cemeteries,
First Phase; The British Cemeteries, Second Phase;
The Landscape Design of Later Cemeteries;
Arbroath Mortuary Chapel; Epilogue**

A garden cemetery and monumental decoration, are not only beneficial to public morals, to the improvement of manners, but are likewise calculated to extend virtuous and generous feelings. (They) afford the most convincing tokens of a nation's progress in civilization and the arts . . . The tomb has, in fact, been the great chronicler of taste throughout the world
John Strang (1795–1863), *Necropolis Glasguensis* (1831)

Churchyards and cemeteries are scenes not only calculated to improve the morals and the taste, and by their botanical riches to cultivate the intellect, but they serve as *historical records*
John Claudius Loudon (1783–1843),
On the Laying Out, Planting, and Managing of Cemeteries
(1843)

Introduction
In Antiquity the dead were disposed of outside cities, far from the living, where they would be appeased with offerings of various kinds, for they were feared, and dead bodies were regarded with disgust. Even with the advent of Christianity the dead were not at first buried within towns, but, as the veneration given to relics grew in favour, the custom of burying the dead near the remains of holy men and women became respectable, in spite of attempts by the ecclesiastical authorities to prohibit the practice. During the medieval period burial in churches, in close proximity to altars, became desirable for those who could obtain such concessions, while burial in churchyards (which were regarded as part of the churches), was usual, often involving interment in communal ditches and the storage in charnel-houses of bones displaced by more recent burials. The dead, in fact, were abandoned to the Church, and in time society became indifferent to the precise locations where bodies were laid. Only the great, rich and holy were

accorded marked permanent graves with effigies, monuments and inscriptions. Familiarity with the sight of bones in the charnels and churchyards created a climate in which society was no longer afraid of the dead who lay in close proximity to the living.

A somewhat blasé and unsentimental attitude to the dead prevailed until well into the eighteenth century, for the dead were disposed of in unpleasant ditches in overcrowded churchyards or in dank smelly crypts where no tender thoughts could be entertained. Gradually, during the Enlightenment and the Romantic period perception changed. Blair's *The Grave* alerted society to the horrors of eighteenth-century crypts and graveyards, while Goethe's *Elective Affinities* created visions of the beautiful mausoleum in which the 'dear remains' would lie for ever. Romantic poets and writers, such as Scott, Shelley, Goethe and Gray, helped to create a new vision of a peaceful burial-place, while painters like Caspar David Friedrich, Caspar Wolf and many others explored themes concerned with cemeteries, graves and death.

From the Enlightenment grew the movement that helped to create the spacious landscaped cemetery, while a concern for the sensibilities of the common man, together with a desire to provide permanent, pleasant, hygienic and beautiful burial-places, gave rise to the great metropolitan *necropoleis* that are a familiar feature of most cities. This new sensibility rejected the traditional indifference as to the fate of the body, and a new tenderness evolved that was to produce a popular and almost universal attitude to death in the nineteenth century.[1] The pilgrimage to the tomb and the respect for the cemetery both survived well into our own time, until death again became the great unmentionable subject: once more, fear of the dead has become prevalent. However, medical and sociological opinion is swinging round to the view that death should be discussed and ritualised for therapeutic reasons, and growing awareness of the great importance of cemeteries in the histories of landscape and architecture is starting to become apparent: it is not before time.[2]

The Position in Britain and Elsewhere

Until the nineteenth century cemeteries in the British Isles were rare, although burial or entombment of the whole body was universal. Most bodies were disposed of by being laid in lead coffins in church crypts or in brick-lined shafts under the floors of churches, or were interred in wooden coffins in the burial-grounds that were attached to churches. Sometimes the landed gentry could afford to bury their dead in large mausolea (roofed tombs built above ground to house the dead), and there were also some examples of elaborate mausolea erected in churchyards for the same purpose.[3] While many rural churchyards were sufficient for parish needs, growing populations in towns created considerable problems, and urban burial-grounds and crypts were severely overcrowded by the end of the eighteenth century so that additional burial-space had to be provided in a number of instances.[4]

As a revolt against the Established Church of England, various Dissenters formed burial-grounds of their own from the seventeenth century, where any Dissenter could be interred without payment of a fee to the incumbent of a parish.[5] In Scotland, where Calvinism had triumphed in the reform of the Church of Scotland as a body organised on Presbyterian lines, new burial-grounds were established, remote from the living, not only for hygienic reasons, but also to discourage the prayers for the dead that were such a feature of the old religion: in 1581 the Reformed Church of Scotland forbade burial in churches.

The need to form new, spacious, hygienic cemeteries set apart from churches and from the living was recognised in eighteenth-century Belfast where advanced radical ideas were rife. In 1774 the Earl of Donegall gave land on which the Belfast Charitable Institution was to be built, together with land for a new 'Burying-Ground'. The New Clifton Burying Ground was enclosed with high stone walls, laid out with paths, and opened in 1797: a further section was added in 1819, and the whole contains several fine mausolea and monuments.[6]

The Movement to Establish Cemeteries

The earliest modern European cemeteries unattached to churches, laid out on spacious lines, ornamented with permanent mausolea and tombs (not possible in the overcrowded obnoxious churchyards), and large and remote enough not to be a danger to the living, were formed in India. The English and other Europeans established cemeteries near Surat in the seventeenth century that were designed on regular lines with walls and paths, and embellished with tombs of considerable architectural grandeur: they were inspired not only by the cemeteries of Classical Antiquity, but also by the stupendous mausolea of Moghul India.

So spectacular were these cemeteries and tombs to European eyes it is not surprising that John Vanbrugh (1664–1726) recorded his impressions of the English cemetery at Surat in a sketch that survives in the Bodleian Library, Oxford.[7] Surat cemetery was the prototype for one of the finest of all British cemeteries, the South Park Street Cemetery in Calcutta, which was founded in 1767: it quickly acquired formal classical mausolea,[8] splendid monuments with domes, colonnades, porticoes, obelisks, pyramids, cubes and every conceivable variety of tomb (some of which were based on designs by Chambers and others) arranged along formal tree-lined avenues.[9]

Many Parisian parishes had obtained new burial-grounds in the seventeenth century, not adjacent to the church buildings, but not far away either, and so it was also in London, Berlin, Vienna and other cities. Thus, in the two centuries before the Victorian period began, the links between the church and the burial-grounds in many countries were becoming weakened by physical separation of church building and burial-ground, even in countries where Roman Catholicism was pre-eminent: almost by stealth, a secularisation of burial was taking place.

In 1804 Père-Lachaise, the first great landscaped necropolis of modern Europe, was laid out to designs by Alexandre-Théodore Brongniart (1739–1813). Set on a hill to the east of Paris, Père-Lachaise cemetery soon became ornamented with house-tombs, Classical monuments, *stelai* and humbler memorials. The translation of bodies of several celebrated personages to this great cemetery was part of a cult of the dead that grew in post-Revolutionary France, and soon became an essential element in the Romantic period. By the second decade of the nineteenth century Père-Lachaise had become the admired model for other cemeteries, although it was clearly based on the precedent set by European cemeteries abroad and on the English landscaped garden.

English influence on the French prototype cannot be overestimated, for the late eighteenth-century manner of landscape design introduced informal and 'natural' motifs. A monument set against trees or on a hill is as much an integral part of the so-called 'picturesque' garden as is the 'informal' winding path or the contrived 'natural' clump of trees on an eminence. Mausolea at Downhill, Co Londonderry, Cobham in Kent, Castle Howard in Yorkshire, Brocklesby in Lincolnshire, Blickling in Norfolk or William Shenstone's (1714–63) funerary urn in the grounds of The Leasowes in Worcestershire are all part of an approach to placing objects in a landscape that became an essential element of cemetery design in the nineteenth century. Such an approach had a literary background: Alexander Pope's (1688–1744) garden at Twickenham had a memorial obelisk set among groves; Thomas Gray's (1716–71) *Elegy in a Country Churchyard* celebrates a rural burial-ground in Buckinghamshire; while the Neoclassical tomb of Jean-Jacques Rousseau (1712–78) on the Isle of Poplars at Ermenonville of 1778 was a potent image. An Arcadian landscaped garden, adorned with monuments, became the ideal, with attractions that put the unsavoury urban burial-ground to shame. Père-Lachaise contains many visual allusions to The Leasowes, to Ermenonville, to the gardens at Stowe, and to other celebrated designs:[10] the new cemeteries were to contain images of Elysium and Arcady, where memorials to the dead would stand among pastoral 'natural' landscapes giving solace to the bereaved and secure resting-places for the dead. Mourners would 'see the dropping branches of a green tree' falling over the monuments, thus adding to the 'beauty and solemnity'.[11]

The British Cemeteries, First Phase

England did not develop her first non-denominational cemetery of the nineteenth century until 1821: this was at the Rosary in Norwich (a centre for Dissent since the Reformation), but it was a small ground. The next was the Low Hill Necropolis at Liverpool of 1825, a relatively minor cemetery with a fine Neoclassical entrance by John Foster Jr. A larger cemetery was created in a disused Liverpool quarry from 1825 to 1829 at a cost of £21,000 to designs by John Foster Jr (c1787– 1846): this was obviously influenced by the Parisian cemetery of Montmartre which had originally been formed in a quarry in the 1790s, and which was remodelled at the same time as St James's Cemetery in Liverpool was being constructed. The architectural style of the Liverpool cemetery was Neoclassical, with a Greek Doric temple as the mortuary chapel, vaults hollowed out of the rock, ramps, and a Sublime arched entrance. The landscape (of which hardly a trace survives) was designed by one Shepherd, who disguised the baldness of some of the naked rock by planting shrubs and trees at the base of the quarry and by creating thick clumps of foliage on the slopes near the central monument (1834) to William Huskisson, MP (1770–1830).

There was an important difference between British and French cemeteries: while the Parisian examples had been established by central authorities, St James's Cemetery in Liverpool was erected by a joint stock company that by 1830 was paying an eight per cent dividend to its shareholders, a figure that was higher than the rewards that could be expected from many other investments of the day. These first cemeteries were not attached to a church, but were open to all who could pay: part of the grounds could be (and usually was) consecrated for burial of members of the Anglican Church, while part would be left unconsecrated for use by Dissenters. When other companies attempted to set up new cemeteries, notably in London, they were encouraged by the gratifyingly large dividends being paid at Liverpool, but there was opposition from churchmen, who were concerned about loss of income from burial fees.

George Frederick Carden, a barrister, had begun his personal campaign to form public cemeteries (recorded in *The Penny Magazine* in the 1830s), and he urged the French model of Père-Lachaise on his compatriots, comparing it favourably with the hideously overcrowded burial-grounds of urban Britain. When it is remembered that the population of London increased by twenty per cent in the 1820s, and that the average number of new burials was two hundred bodies per acre in existing long-established graveyards, an idea of the revolting conditions that prevailed can be gained.[12] Carden pointed out that the new French cemeteries were 'places of resort for the neighbouring population' and that they were pleasant and delightful spots where architecture, sculpture and landscape could be studied. Into the pro-cemetery arguments crept the idea of moral uplift, education, improvement of taste and decorous recreation. As a result of Carden's campaign a cemetery was proposed for Primrose Hill (a location not dissimilar to the site of Père-Lachaise), and Thomas Willson (born *c*1780) designed a General Metropolitan Cemetery in the form of a monster pyramid to hold five million corpses.[13]

A more subdued plan, influenced by the precedent of Père-Lachaise, was favoured, and in 1830 it was decided to form a new body known as The General Cemetery Company.[14] Having rejected Willson's pyramid, the founders of the company displayed a design by Francis Goodwin (1784–1835) for a 'Grand National Cemetery' that was to consist of an enormous rectangular enclosure surrounded by colonnades with Neoclassical temples and Towers of the Winds at each corner of the colonnaded walks: all the architecture was to be in the purest Greek and Roman manner.[15] The proposal is a fine essay in itself, and it embraces both the landscape-garden and the monumental-cemetery approaches: the former was to be the theme of the British and American cemeteries, while the latter was to be adopted by southern European countries, notably Italy.[16] From 1830 a further influence on British and American cemetery design was John Claudius Loudon (1783–1843), the Editor of *The Gardener's Magazine* and compiler of many important books on aspects of architecture, design, and landscape, who was to write the most important Victorian treatise on cemeteries.[17] Loudon argued in a letter in *The Morning Advertiser*[18] that the new cemeteries ought to be big enough to serve as public parks and botanic gardens.

Not much progress was made by The General Cemetery Company until 1831 when the Hon Thomas Liddell (1800–56) presented a plan for a new cemetery he had prepared with the assistance of John Nash (1752–1835).[19] Over fifty acres of land were bought at Kensal Green, and works of drainage and enclosure were commenced. In October 1831 the first of a series of terrible cholera epidemics occurred in London and elsewhere, and, apart from the mayhem in the over-crowded churchyards, an additional impetus to establish cemeteries was provided by the belief that cholera was caused by the 'miasmas' that lingered over the malodorous burial-grounds. In July 1832 the Bill for establishing the General Cemetery of All Souls at Kensal Green received the Royal Assent, and between 1832 and 1847 Parliament gave permission for eight commercial cemetery companies to be established in the London area alone. There appear to have been plenty of people willing and able to invest in these ventures.[20]

Although Liddell had presented a plan for the new cemetery grounds, the final executed design was by John Griffith of Finsbury (1796–1888), whose name appears on the plans[21] deposited with the Westminster Sewer Commissioners in June 1832, and on the drawings of the Anglican Chapel: he became architect to the Company, and finally its chairman. The previous year, an architectural competition had been held to find suitable designs for chapels, entrance-gates and other buildings for the cemetery,[22] and in March 1832 the first prize was awarded to Henry Edward Kendall (1776–1875) for his Gothic designs that included a 'Proposed Picturesque Arrangement' (*Plate 156*) of the grounds with winding avenues, a chapel, a water-gate and a turreted entrance-gate with offices.[23] These were not realised, however, for Sir John Dean Paul (1802–68), the chairman of the company, felt that Gothic was not a style his own robust Evangelical views could tolerate, so Griffith was obliged to draw up designs for buildings in a chaste Greek Revival style with which no taint of Popery or Ritualism could be associated. It seems that support for Kendall had

Plate 156 Proposed Picturesque Arrangement of the General Cemetery of All Souls at Kensal Green, showing Kendall's buildings. (*Lithograph by Thomas Allom, printed by C. F. Hullmandel*)

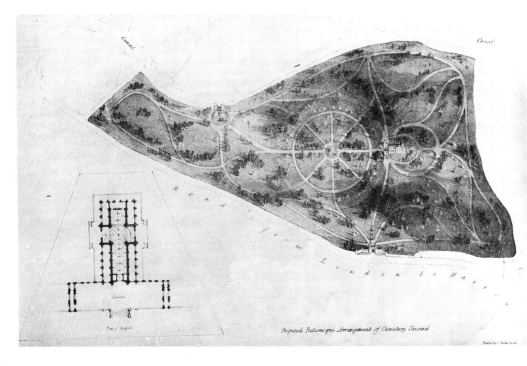

been led by two important personalities who were also key figures in the company: these were Carden, the registrar, and Augustus Charles Pugin (1769–1832), the father of A. W. N. Pugin, both of whom were Goths. Unfortunately for the Gothic faction Pugin died in December 1832, and Carden was sacked as registrar in June, so the Goths were routed and the Greek-Revival faction was victorious. A perspective of the Kensal Green Cemetery (*Plate 157*), attributed to Thomas Allom (1804–72), who had been a pupil of Francis Goodwin, demonstrates the connection between the design of early Victorian cemeteries and the English landscape tradition, with trees shading individual tombs, and an avenue of trees leading the eye to the Anglican chapel, as at Père-Lachaise. The cemetery had two chapels (the Nonconformist one completed in 1834 in an Ionic style, and the Anglican completed in June 1837 in a severe Greek Doric style, both designed by Griffith, and both built by William Chadwick of Southwark) (*Fig 57*).

Soon Kensal Green Cemetery, which had acquired hundreds of trees even before the chapels were built, was further beautified with flowers and evergreens, and by 1843 presented a 'smiling countenance' to the world. According to descriptions in *The Gardeners' Chronicle* of 1848 the landscape design in Kensal Green was by Richard Forrest, who had been Head Gardener at Syon Park, who later designed the Manchester

Plate 157 Perspective of Kensal Green Cemetery attributed to Thomas Allom (but probably by John Griffith) showing the Greek-Revival Anglican Chapel and a first version of the entrance-gate, both buildings by Griffith. (*The London Museum. Print kindly provided by Mr Andrew Wyld*)

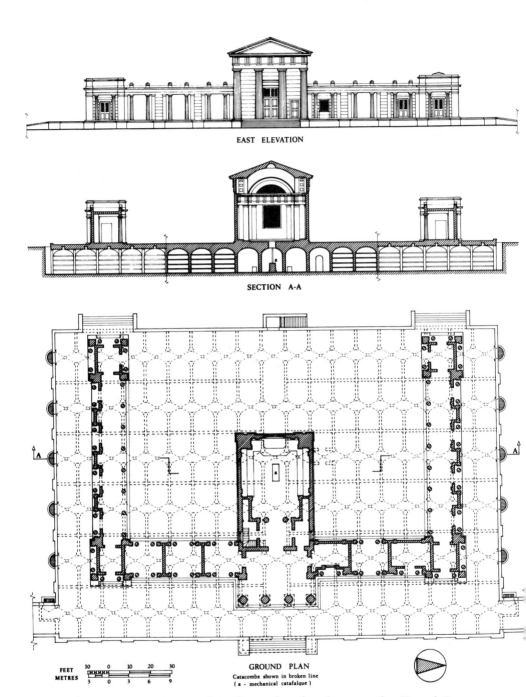

EAST ELEVATION

SECTION A-A

FEET
METRES

GROUND PLAN
Catacombs shown in broken line
(a - mechanical catafalque)

Fig 58 The Greek-Revival Anglican chapel and catacombs, Kensal Green Cemetery, of 1837, by John Griffith. Drawing by John J. Sambrook. (*Reproduced by kind permission of the General Editor,* Survey of London)

266

Zoological Gardens, and whose skills were greatly respected by J. C. Loudon. The contractor for the planting was William Ronalds of Brentford, nurseryman, who later published a significant work on fruit. Thus it was that within the cemetery's 'sacred precinct' the visitor could enjoy the 'floral charms' and the view of the 'extensive and pleasing scenery'.[24] By 1843 Loudon was writing that a cemetery, properly laid out, designed, ornamented with tombs, planted with trees, shrubs and herbaceous plants all named, and the whole properly kept, might become a school of instruction in architecture, sculpture, landscape-gardening, arboriculture, botany, and in those important parts of general gardening, neatness, order and high-keeping.[25] Even by 1839 the original shares of The General Cemetery Company had doubled in value, and the status of the cemetery as a fashionable place of burial was further improved when Princess Sophia (1777–1848) and her brother Augustus Frederick, Duke of Sussex (1773–1843), both children of King George III, were buried there rather than at Windsor. Both Royal tombs stand before the Anglican chapel: the Princess is commemorated by a singularly beautiful *quattrocento* sarcophagus designed by Professor Ludwig Grüner of Dresden, and carved by Signori Bardi of Carrara (*Plate 158*).

At Kensal Green the whole range of Victorian taste is displayed in the tombs. The earliest monuments, as would be expected, are

Plate 158 The tomb of Princess Sophia, designed by Professor Ludwig Grüner, with the Anglican chapel behind, at Kensal Green Cemetery. (*JSC*)

Neoclassical: among them can be mentioned the Graeco-Egyptian mausoleum of Andrew Ducrow, equestrian and circus-owner (1793–1842), erected in 1837 to designs by John Cusworth and modestly proclaiming that it was erected by genius for the reception of its own remains. Ducrow's mausoleum was denounced in *The Builder*[26] as an example of 'ponderous coxcombry', which was only to be expected after Pugin and others had successfully demolished the reputation of the Egyptian style (*Fig 58*). In spite of some extraordinary examples of tombs by distinguished designers, including those of St John Long (1834 by Robert Sievier, a member of the board of the company), the Hankey family (1838 by Basevi), General Foster Walker (1866 by Edward Blore),[27] Captain Charles Ricketts (1867 by William Burges), Lady Pulteney (1849 by C. R. Cockerell),[28] and the Molyneux family (1864 by John Gibson) (*Plate 159*), *The Builder* described the cemetery as a '*rendezvous* of dreary inanities'.[29] Nevertheless, the styles as revealed in the tombs, monuments, and mausolea of Kensal Green Cemetery demonstrate the changing phases of taste in architecture with admirable clarity, and the memorials have the advantage of being dated, for the most part. Here are Égyptiennerie, severe Greek temples, Gothic chapels, polychrome Venetian-Gothic pile-ups, sinister caryatids, obelisks, sarcophagi, tomb-chests and canopied tombs (like that of William Mulready [1786–1863]).

At Glasgow Necropolis, the most Sublime of all the cemeteries in Britain, and certainly the most splendidly sited, the dominant architectural style is Neoclassical, as would be expected in a city that was then dominated by Presbyterianism. The Necropolis was established by the Merchants' House of Glasgow in 1831, and it contains a magnificent array of Victorian tombs (*Plate 160*). York Public Cemetery, designed by James Pigott Pritchett (1789–1868), was established in 1836, and acquired a pretty Greek-Revival chapel and attractively planted grounds. The Newcastle General Cemetery Company laid out Jesmond Old Cemetery at Newcastle-upon-Tyne to designs by John Dobson (1787–1865): it has severe Schinkelesque buildings that contain the chapels and offices and act as a propylaeum for the cemetery.[30] Loudon thoroughly approved of Dobson's designs (*Plate 161*), for the cemetery entrance could 'never be mistaken either for an entrance to a public park or to a country residence'.[31] The planting of both these cemeteries is varied, and is considerably influenced by Loudon's writings in *The Gardener's Magazine* in which he advocated dark evergreens, such as hollies, mixed with deciduous trees. It was Loudon who was to invent the 'cemetery style' of planting that prevailed for much of Victoria's reign.

As exemplars and as financial successes the northern British

Fig 58 Pugin's lampoon of an Entrance Gateway for a New Cemetery in the Egyptian style from his *An Apology for the Revival of Christian Architecture in England*. 'The entrance gateway is usually selected for the grand display of the company's enterprise and taste . . .' It is a 'cement caricature of the entrance to an Egyptian temple, 2½ inches to the foot' . . . while 'to prevent any mistake, some such words as "New Economical Compressed Grave Cemetery Company" are inscribed in *Grecian* capitals along the frieze . . .'

Plate 159 Molyneux Mausoleum at Kensal Green of 1864 by John Gibson. It is in the Italian Gothic Revival style. On the right is the Neoclassical memorial of the Collett family. (*RIBA British Architectural Library*)

Plate 160 The Glasgow Necropolis showing the range of Classical monuments. (*Photograph by Francis Frith & Co*)

Plate 161 Anglican chapel (left) and Dissenters' chapel offices at the entrance to Jesmond Old Cemetery, Newcastle-upon-Tyne, in a Schinkelesque style of 1836–8 by John Dobson. (*JSC*)

cemeteries and the huge and successful Cemetery of All Souls at Kensal Green encouraged a climate of opinion in which several other important *necropoleis* were laid out. The South Metropolitan at Norwood, South London, was consecrated in 1837: the architect was William (Sir William from 1869) Tite (1798–1873), who designed both the grounds and the buildings. The style for the Anglican and Nonconformist chapels, catacombs and entrance was Tudor Gothic Revival, demonstrating the inexorable shift in taste that was starting to reject Classicism. The cemetery looked rather like a Gothic Revival country house with outbuildings set in an informal park, with clumps of trees placed in a manner Loudon called the 'Pleasure-Ground Style' (*Plate 162*). Indeed, Loudon was so critical of the landscaping that he designed a variation (*Plate 163*) of Tite's perspective showing his own ideas for planting with evergreens, including cypresses as an allusion to the 'cemeteries of the ancients'.[32] From the 1830s British cemeteries acquired a characteristic collection of willows, Irish yews, cypresses and hollies, but trees of the weeping variety went out of fashion (in spite of their allegorical associations with mourning) because they

Plate 162 The South Metropolitan cemetery at Norwood, by (Sir) William Tite, showing the Gothic-Revival chapels (with catacombs) in the Third-Pointed style. Note the Third-Pointed (Perpendicular) entrance gate with Gothic-Revival lodge. The grounds are laid out in the 'Pleasure Ground' style of a landscaped park. (*Lithograph by Day and Haghe*)

needed a lot of water and suggested badly drained grounds: they were therefore regarded, by Loudon especially, as unsuitable for cemeteries. As a leader of taste in planting, Loudon also began to advocate the banishment of deciduous trees from cemeteries as they not only shaded the ground but shed their leaves in autumn, thus making the ground permanently damp and difficult to maintain.[33] To Loudon it was important to arrange the planting so that the whole of the cemetery and its buildings could not be seen at once on entering the gates. He was opposed to the planting of belts and clumps of trees because they were unnecessary for shelter or shade, and because they impeded the passage of fresh currents of air and prevented the drying influence of the sun.

> By scattering the trees and shrubs singly, graves may be everywhere formed among them; and, by placing trees continuously along the roads and walks, shade is afforded to those who are on them, and a foreground is established to the cemetery beyond. But the plantations in most of the London cemeteries appear to have been made without the guidance of any leading

Plate 163 The South Metropolitan cemetery at Norwood, planted in the 'Cemetery Style' designed by J. C. Loudon. A design dating from the 1840s showing Loudon's preference for evergreens. (*Lithograph by Day and Haghe*)

principle. In one we have a thick belt round the margin, occupying one of the finest situations which any cemetery affords for border graves; in another we have scarcely any trees along the walks, while we have a number grouped together along the centre of the compartments, where they lose much of their effect; in another we have clumps scattered throughout the grounds without any connexion among themselves, or with anything around, destroying all breadth of effect, and producing neither character nor expression.[34]

The success of the capital's first two cemeteries encouraged the London Cemetery Company to establish new cemeteries, and an Act of Parliament[35] enabled the company to start operations. The designs of the Cemetery of St James at Highgate were prepared by Stephen Geary (1797–1854), who appointed David Ramsay as landscape-gardener in order to embellish the grounds. Ramsay and Geary began to transform the southern slopes of Highgate Hill by means of winding paths and lush planting. They retained an ancient Cedar of Lebanon around which Geary constructed a circular group of burial-chambers in the Egyptian Revival style known as the Cedar of Lebanon catacombs.[36] Shortly afterwards, around 1839, James Bunstone Bunning (1802–63) took over from Geary as executive architect, and designed the Egyptian Avenue with its great portal and long range of catacombs that line the path to the circular group by Geary around the Cedar of Lebanon. These Egyptian-Revival buildings are among the most extraordinary of all necropolitan architecture, for they suggest the awe, terror and finality of death in the *architecture parlante* (architecture expressive of its function) tradition of the French Neoclassicists (*Plate 164*). Here architecture and landscape-design are conceived in a perfect balance: the varied planting and serpentine walks convey an impression that the cemetery is bigger than it actually is, while the Egyptian style arouses associations with death. Yet such a strangely uncouth and unscholarly variety of Egyptian architecture, constructed of stucco-faced brickwork, could not convey permanence because of its materials, and had curious connections with showmanship such as the Egyptian Halls in Piccadilly and the circus-owner Ducrow's tomb at Kensal Green. Pugin was to denounce the 'grossest absurdities' of the 'cement caricatures of an entrance to an Egyptian temple, 2½ inches to the foot' being perpetrated by the new cemetery companies which he describes as the 'new Economical Compressed Grave Cemetery Company'[37] (*Fig 59*).

At St James's Cemetery, Highgate, landscape and architecture are cunningly merged. Although the chapels (combined in one building) were described as an example of 'Undertakers' Gothic',[38] and as 'neatly

273

constructed'[39] somewhat earlier, the 'subterraneous depositaries, with the beautifully diversified grounds, . . . lately improved under the judicious management of Mr J. B. Bunning, the architect to the company'[40] always struck visitors as a 'pleasing and ornamental addition to the hamlet'.[41] Commentators were to note the 'irregularity of the ground',[42] the 'winding paths leading through avenues of cool shrubbery and marble monuments',[43] the 'groups of majestic trees casting broad shadows below', and the 'dazzling' effect of the 'varied hues of beautiful flowers'.[44] In fact, the effect of the flowers would have been somewhat gaudy to our eyes, for the Victorians, and especially the early Victorians, liked strong, even violent, clashes of colour in their planting. The Egyptian style of the catacombs always attracted comment: the 'solemn association of the architectural style' in which the 'well-constructed vaults' were built rendered it 'singularly appropriate'.[45] Justyne mentioned the 'massive portals', the 'echo' of footsteps that intruded on the 'awful silence' of the 'cold, stony death-place'.[46] The 'boldness', 'heaviness' and 'death-like grandeur' of the architecture, and the 'ponderous iron doors' of the vault-compartments made it clear that Highgate Cemetery fell firmly into the Sublime category, and its extraordinary and somewhat spooky atmosphere struck chords in commentators. The man at the helm of the board of the company responsible for the development of the cemetery until it reached perfection in the 1870s was Sir Benjamin Hawes (1797–1862), sometime MP for Kinsale in Co Cork, Whig, Corn-Law Repealer, supporter of the Penny Post, and husband of Sophia Macnamara, daughter of Sir Marc Isambard Brunel (1769–1849). Further embellishments were made to the cemetery after Hawes's death with the erection of a Neoclassical range of catacombs to designs by Thomas Porter on the outer circumference of the path around Geary's original Cedar of Lebanon catacombs,[47] and the building of the huge mausoleum (with stepped Halicarnassus-like roof and Diocletian windows) of Julius Beer (1836–80) designed by John Oldrid Scott (1842–1913).

In 1840 the second of the London Cemetery Company's grounds, on a hill near Peckham, was consecrated as the Cemetery of All Saints, Nunhead. This time Bunning was entirely responsible for the layout,[48] and, as at Highgate, he chose serpentine walks, except for the straight main avenue leading to the Anglican chapel from the entrance gates. Loudon was very critical of the London Cemetery Company's practice of using winding paths yet dividing the grounds into 'imaginary squares' for purposes of numbering and locating burial-spaces because:

it does not admit of walking among them on a continuous path; it affords a very unsatisfactory mode of registration, since it depends

Plate 164 The entrance to the Egyptian Avenue at Highgate Cemetery by J. B. Bunning, 1840. (*JSC*)

> on the accuracy of the mapping of the graves in the map book; it renders it next to impossible for relations of the deceased to find out the grave without the aid of some person connected with the cemetery, unless the grave has a monument; it prevents an efficient system of grass paths from being formed; and it totally prevents the establishment of a permanent system of surface drainage by having the drains under the paths.[49]

He observed that the London cemeteries were already acquiring an appearance of confusion because of the random placing of graves and monuments in which there was 'no obvious principle of order or arrangement' except that the most elaborate tombs were sited along the 'margins of the walks': he saw that the time was fast approaching when, as at Père-Lachaise, some monuments could only be reached by scrambling between others.[50] He was also critical of Bunning's twin Neoclassical entrance-lodges because they attracted attention as separate objects and destroyed the dominant accent which ought to be on the gates.[51] The gate-piers by Bunning were also severely

Neoclassical in manner, of Portland Stone, with enrichments on the dies in the form of cast inverted torches (allegories of the extinguishing of life) and on the attics in the form of serpents eating their tails (allegories of eternity). These, with the distinguished Schinkelesque lodges, provided an uneasy frame to the main avenue centred on the clumsy Second-Pointed Gothic Anglican chapel by Thomas Little (1802–59), who won the contract for the construction of the chapels in 1844. The ragstone walls of the chapels were typical of the Gothic Revival at that time, even in London, and demonstrated why the Ecclesiologists and Butterfield sought a more sensible, functional, and urban material with All Saints', Margaret Street.

Loudon would not have approved of the Sheffield General Cemetery either, which was also on a hill, and which was more like a landscaped park incorporating gently rising ground planted with deciduous trees. The consecrated part was designed in 1836 by William Flockton (1804–64), and the Greek Doric chapel and unconsecrated grounds by Samuel Worth (1779–1870) in the same year.[52]

Geary and Ramsay were also involved in the early history of the West of London and Westminster Cemetery at Brompton,[53] consecrated in 1840. As with other cemeteries, a competition was held to find an architect for the buildings, and this was duly won by Benjamin Baud (1807–75) in 1838: Geary ceased to be involved by early 1839 and Baud took over as architect, working with Ramsay until the latter was also removed.[54] Baud's scheme was grand indeed (*Plate 165*) and included three chapels (one for Anglicans, one for Dissenters, and one for Roman Catholics): the whole layout was axial, with regimented trees and shrubs, a triumphal arch for the lodges and entrance, and long

Plate 165 Panorama of the West of London and Westminster Cemetery of 1840. Benjamin Baud, architect. The polygonal chapel is that of the Anglicans, and the circus of arcaded galleries contains the Roman Catholic and Nonconformist chapels. Note the very long ranges of catacombs. (*Royal Borough of Kensington and Chelsea Public Libraries L/79 c.47*)

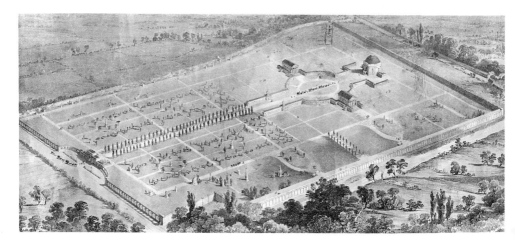

ranges of catacombs with arcaded galleries over them. The provision of such an amount of catacomb accommodation was very surprising, for by 1840 opinion was starting to turn against the placing of bodies on shelves or in vaults on grounds of hygiene and expense: Loudon himself was particularly critical of catacomb 'burial'. In the architectural design, therefore, especially the provision of so many catacomb spaces, lay the origins of financial collapse, for it involved a huge capital investment that could not be justified by the projected income from interment.

The City of London and Tower Hamlets Cemetery, Mile End Road, was laid out to designs by Thomas Henry Wyatt (1807–80) and David Brandon (1813–97), and consecrated in 1841. It had two Perpendicular Gothic chapels, and a lodge and gate in the same style which was much admired by Loudon. The landscape had varied planting, including evergreens, and there were two fine cedars near the entrance. Abney Park Cemetery, Stoke Newington, was designed by Professor William Hosking (1800–61) and laid out between 1839 and 1843. It had a somewhat gimcrack Gothic chapel, but architecturally the most interesting buildings were the Egyptianising entrance-gates and lodges designed by Joseph Bonomi Jr (1796–1878).

Unusually, no part of Abney Park Cemetery was consecrated, and consequently it became an important place of burial for Dissenters. Apart from the Egyptian-Revival lodges, Abney Park is of great interest as an example of the Loudonian idea of making a cemetery double as an arboretum, with all the plants clearly labelled for the education of the public. The landscape was planted by George Loddiges (1784–1846), a remarkable nurseryman, who made Abney Park 'the most ornamented cemetery in the neighbourhood of London, as far as respects plants', and who created the 'complete arboretum' in which there were 'all the hardy kinds of rhododendrons, azaleas, and roses in Messrs Loddiges's collection' as well as 'dahlias, geraniums, fuchsias, verbenas, petunias, etc'. The Victorian cemetery was to be the means by which history, chronology, biography, arboriculture, horticulture, art, design and sculpture were to be brought to the general public. By its 'botanical riches' it would 'cultivate the intellect', while the monuments would improve morals and taste while serving as historical records. Cemeteries like Abney Park, then, were educational, morally uplifting and civilising. Yet the overall effect of the planting must have been startlingly loud.[55]

The British Cemeteries, Second Phase
By 1850 informed opinion in Britain was veering away from the support of joint-stock cemetery companies, not only because death

began to be regarded as an unfit subject for commercial speculation, but also because the cemeteries already established were often on badly drained soil and were near the rapidly expanding city suburbs. Faced with scandalous revelations[56] of overcrowded burial-grounds and church vaults, the government moved towards prohibition of intramural interment, the closure of foul graveyards and crypts, and nationalisation of existing commercial cemeteries by means of the Metropolitan Interments Act of 1850.[57] The General Board of Health was given powers to be the agent for the laying out of new cemeteries and for the purchase of those already established. As a corollary, vast new cemeteries were to be established on well-drained land far from centres of population, and these were to be served by funeral boats, barges and trains. In the event, only one cemetery, the financially disastrous West of London and Westminster Cemetery at Brompton, was acquired.

As early as 1842 *The Westminster Review* had noted that many of the new main railway lines passed near land suitable for interment, and G. A. Walker (1807–84), one of the heroes of the campaign to establish hygienic cemeteries, took up the theme in his *Practical Suggestions for the Establishment of Metropolitan Cemeteries* in 1849. Walker proposed Woking Common as an ideal site for a new cemetery because of its well-drained subsoil, ease of access from London, and proximity to a main railway line. A company was formed, two thousand acres were purchased from the Earl of Onslow, and negotiations began with the London and South Western Railway Company regarding the conveyance of funerals cheaply and quickly to the new site only twenty-four miles from London. A private Act of Parliament (to which the L & SWR Company was party) to enable the scheme to proceed received the Royal Assent in 1852 (the year in which the Metropolitan Interments Act was repealed and replaced by legislation[58] obliging local authorities to establish cemeteries), and the London Necropolis and National Mausoleum Company was duly incorporated. Soon five hundred acres were enclosed for use as a cemetery and existing vegetation was augmented by a subtle scheme of landscaping: heathers, rhododendrons, silver birches, copper beeches, Wellingtonias and cypresses were planted in profusion to an overall scheme by William Tite, not uninfluenced by Loudon's writings.

A private railway terminus was constructed near Waterloo Station to designs by Tite and Sir William Cubitt (1785–1861) and the branch siding at Brookwood itself, with embankments and planting, was built to plans by Tite and Joseph Cubitt (1811–72). Two temporary stations at Brookwood were built by Messrs Lucas to designs by Sydney Smirke (1798–1877), who succeeded Tite as architect to the company.

Britain's largest cemetery, served by rail from London, was in business following consecration in 1854. Until the funeral train was destroyed by a bomb in 1941, and the terminus near Waterloo was also damaged, thousands of bodies were transported from London to Brookwood: after the war it was decided to discontinue funerals by train. A new necropolis terminus was built in 1889, and new office buildings were opened in Westminster Bridge Road in 1902. The first part of the funeral service took place in the terminus, then mourners entered reserved carriages: coffins were transported in a special hearse-van. *The Builder*[59] reported that funerals at Brookwood were only about a quarter the cost of those in the older London cemeteries. So successful was the venture that funeral trains were also established to link Belle Isle near King's Cross with the Great Northern Cemetery at Southgate between 1861 and 1867, but they were never as fashionable as the Brookwood example. The most spectacular version of this idea was in Australia, at Rookwood Cemetery, Flemington, near Sydney, where rail-borne funerals departed from Regents' Street, Redfern, to Haslam's Creek at Rookwood from 1867 to 1939. Both Sydney stations, in a wonderful spiky Gothic style (*Plate 166*) reminiscent of E. Bassett Keeling at his best, were built to designs by James J. Barnet

Plate 166 Mortuary station at Redfern, Sydney, Australia, by J. J. Barnet, of 1867. (*Public Transport Commission of New South Wales*)

(1827–1904), who later described his buildings as 'Gothic architecture adapted to a novel purpose'.[60]

Following agitation against intramural interment and the change of climate in which commercial ventures were to be discouraged, many public cemeteries were established, one of the first and finest being the City of London Cemetery at Little Ilford, opened in 1856. It was designed by William Haywood (1821–94), chief engineer to the Commissioners of Sewers of the City of London, a position he held for forty-nine years during which he carried out an enormous number of improvements in the metropolis, including Holborn Viaduct (1863–9). Haywood's plan for the cemetery was very clear, logical, and beautifully contrived with several axes converting on *rond-points* in two of which the chapels were sited: the Anglican chapel is in the *Flamboyant* manner with a graceful spire, while the Dissenters' chapel was more First Pointed; the lodge had a pretty Burgundian tower; and the catacombs, set in a valley the shape of a Roman circus, were of a rudimentary Gothic style. The cemetery grounds contained marvellous planting (including rhododendrons, azaleas, and many trees and shrubs), clearly influenced by J. C. Loudon. At Little Ilford the contents of many crypts, vaults, and city churchyards were re-interred and commemorated with monuments several of which were designed by Haywood.

Following the various enactments relating to burial reform, many hundreds of consecrated graveyards were closed from the 1850s, and there was even an hysterical campaign by those determined to pursue

Plate 167 Decorated Gothic chapels in the cemetery at Oakham by Bellamy and Hardy of Lincoln. (*JSC*)

the efforts against intramural interment to close and clear the Royal vaults at Windsor and Westminster. As the century grew older many more graveyards were closed by Orders in Council and by other means, including the Disused Burial Grounds Act[61] of 1884, the Metropolitan Board of Works (Various Powers) Act[62] of 1885, and the Open Spaces Act[63] of 1887 which allowed for the conversion of graveyards into parks. In this latter respect the Metropolitan Gardens Association was very active from its foundation in 1882.[64]

Thomas Little designed the public cemetery for the parish of Paddington in 1855: a formal axial path leads to the two chapels (in the Gothic style), and the grounds are regularly laid out with a series of concentric avenues joined by paths radiating from the chapel complex in the central *rond-point*. From the 1850s two Gothic-Revival chapels linked by means of a belfry over a covered porch became usual in English public cemeteries: a typical example is the pretty design in Second-Pointed (or Decorated Gothic) at Oakham Cemetery in Rutland by Bellamy and Hardy of Lincoln, completed in 1860 (*Plate 167*).

The Landscape Design of Later Cemeteries

After the 1850s most British cemeteries were established by local authorities, although there were still to be some private burial-grounds. In terms of style Abney Park, with its extraordinary arboretum and flower-gardens, was the great forerunner of the later Victorian municipal cemeteries, not least in its non-denominational character and its emphasis away from catacomb 'burial'.

Loudon's influence on cemetery design[65] became more apparent in the late 1830s and '40s, although he was interested in cemeteries at the very beginning, but from the 1850s his championing of stylistic variety, notably evergreens, became very important, and indeed Loudon's functional, hygienic and utilitarian approach seems to have had its greatest influence during the 1850s, '60s and early '70s (in spite of the fact that the more utilitarian notions were going out of fashion by 1875). Just as Ruskin's writings, especially the *Seven Lamps* and *The Stones of Venice*, to a certain extent appeared at exactly the right time, confirming certain trends in taste that were already occurring, so Loudon, with his immense industry and magpie methods in collating notions of the time, not only was part of a move in taste, but also helped to create that taste. His recommendations of lists of trees and shrubs suitable for planting in cemeteries seems to include all of those planted at Abney Park by George Loddiges.[66]

Loudon is particularly important in the history of cemetery design because of his arguments that cemeteries should have a distinct character unlike that of a public park or a pleasure-ground. He was also concerned with ideas of suggestion, and recommended evergreens, dark-leaved trees and fastigiate trees found in Classical or other cemeteries. His approval of Dobson's entrance to Jesmond cemetery was given because it could not be mistaken for an entrance to anything other than a cemetery. Loudon wanted to create a 'Cemetery Style' that would be clearly defined in landscape, planting, and architecture: there should be no mistaking the purposes of landscape, of a place with a certain planting scheme, or of buildings. He opposed the planting of flowers at all in cemeteries, feeling they were inappropriate and inimical to his intention of creating a sense of quiet and repose: if flowers *had* to be planted, Loudon recommended laying them in beds the shape of coffins, but only where graves were to be dug, in order to give the flower-beds a 'distinctive character' appropriate to a cemetery. Most of the London cemeteries had floral displays, and there was a rosarium established at Abney Park by Loddiges containing over a thousand cultivars that must have looked as garish as the display of flowers outside a modern crematorium during a funeral. What Loudon wished to avoid was the lack of an overall plan for planting flowers, trees or shrubs: individual grave-owners selecting their own schemes caused visual mayhem. The fact that individuals also created visual chaos by erecting monuments that added new terrors to death seems to have struck Loudon as less important than the effects of individually-planted flower-beds, any suggestion of dampness by the choice of weeping willows, or cemeteries that did not look like cemeteries. And, most importantly, he regarded dark-foliaged evergreens, with narrow conical heads and a great height in proportion to the breadth, as more Sublime than spreading forms because they were classically and popularly associated with places of sepulture.[67]

The designers who came after Loudon did indeed create a distinct cemetery character by means of planting, layout and built fabric, and in the making of landscapes they were aided by the import of American redwoods and other trees, as at Brookwood Cemetery, where flower-beds were insignificant, although further outbreaks of floral enthusiasm recurred in the 1870s when Loudon's 'cemetery style' was felt to be too severe.

The great cemeteries described above are not only important in any consideration of improvements in urban hygiene and in the campaign to utilise urban man, but also as places where style in architecture and in landscape design can be demonstrated in its various phases. The original layout of Kensal Green cemetery as proposed by Kendall, and in which there is evidence there was an influence of Nash through Kendall and Liddell, shows certain affinities with Nash's schemes for Regent's Park, which was certainly an important factor in the preparation of early layouts for the Ladbroke Estate by Thomas Allason in 1820s. Another 'circus' plan for the Eyre estates at St John's Wood had been exhibited at the Royal Academy in 1802–3, so the idea of huge circular avenues lined with detached or semi-detached villas in their own landscaped gardens was current in the years leading up to the formation of the first great metropolitan cemeteries. The circle recurs in the Cedar of Lebanon catacombs at Highgate by Geary, and there are certain parallels with both Nash's designs for Broad Walk and Brongniart's axial approach to Père-Lachaise that are echoed at Kensal Green, Nunhead and, especially, at Brompton.

The design of cemetery layouts and architecture, therefore, must be seen with the design of estate layout prevalent at the time. It is interesting in this respect to consider the revival of floral show in cemeteries thanks to the influence of Sir Joseph Paxton's (1801–65) displays in gardens following his layout for the cemetery at Cheylesmore, Coventry, of 1844–7. This cemetery was built with an Italianate lodge, and two chapels (one Norman, one Greek Ionic *in antis*, reflecting the growing eclecticism of the Victorian period). Paxton built a bastioned terrace at Cheylesmore that was to be the model for some of his later formal garden features, as at Sydenham after 1853, and he reintroduced colour in the form of flower-beds of which Loudon would not have approved. In the event, a revival of the riot of strong colour Loddiges used at Abney Park occurred after Paxton's 1850s gardens, and appears to have been common in the 1870s (where it was employed at Maidstone Cemetery by John Davis), and at Belfast City Cemetery (laid out to designs by William Gay of Bradford in 1866–9).

Floral planting of individual graves was widely debated in the 1870s, and wholesale planting in large beds became popular, surviving in diluted form in Scotland until almost this day. In this respect it is worth noting that Stirling Cemetery was designed by a gardener, William Drummond, who created one of the most stunning *necropoleis* in a land where the cemeteries are among the most noble on earth. They also retain a hint of their Victorian planting, especially in the Dean at Edinburgh, laid out by David Cousin (1809–78) from 1845, and at Arbroath, of which more anon. By the time of the death of Queen Victoria some cemeteries were staffed by many gardeners, and thousands of bedding-plants were raised on site each year (Highgate had twenty-eight gardeners and produced 300,000 bedding plants in 1906).[68]

Arbroath Mortuary Chapel
There are some extraordinary Victorian buildings in Britain, but none can surpass in strangeness the mortuary chapel that stands in the

cemetery of the little east-coast town of Arbroath in Scotland. Patrick Allan-Frazer, the distinguished painter and designer, built the Arbroath chapel to his own plans as a philanthropic gesture in the best traditions of the Victorian period, as a centrepiece to the recently formed cemetery in Arbroath.

Work began in 1875, and only the best materials and workmanship were used in its construction. The stone chosen was the red local sandstone, and a particularly hard batch was selected that has stood the test of time. The design is a marvel: it is a richly bizarre composition with a pronounced vertical emphasis owing much to traditional Scottish and even Gallic precedent, but given an exotic quality by the richness and sheer exuberance of the many architectural features (*Plate 168*). Bartizans, turrets, corbels, balconies, canopied niches, machicolations, knobbly crockets on stumpy finials, and a silhouette of extraordinary vitality combine in an ensemble of confident synthesis worthy of the most accomplished architectural virtuosi of the age. Viewed from either the side or the front, the building's wildly busy superstructure presents an ever-changing relationship of vertical elements as the visitor walks around it. If the exterior is a tour-de-force of sheer invention, the interior is also that, as well as a repository of some of the most delicate and original carving to be found in any Victorian building. The sculpture was by John Hutchison and his pupils and was executed over a number of years to embellish Patrick Allan-Frazer's architectural scheme.

Epilogue

A study of cemetery design reveals much about the history of taste, social history and style in gardening: Strang was quite serious when he drew attention to the importance of garden cemeteries and monumental decoration in widening the horizons of those who beheld them. In the garden cemetery the uninstructed could learn about varieties of trees and shrubs, could study the creations of the sculptor, and could improve their sensibilities by becoming familiar with the iconography and architecture of death, with symbolism, and with inscriptions and admonitory homilies. These aspects of the cemetery movement are almost forgotten today: perhaps it is time they were remembered.

The Victorian cemetery was created as a response to a problem, and is as important in the history of urban hygiene as other reforms that have received greater attention: it is also significant in the histories of landscape design and of architectural taste, and is not a separate subject in the context of a consideration of Victorian urban fabric. Victorian cemeteries are full of character: they have found their places in the landscape and have their own distinctive note, with their pines,

Plate 168 The mortuary chapel at Arbroath by Patrick Allan-Frazer, begun in 1875. A free eclectic mixture of Scottish and Continental medieval elements. (*JSC*)

redwoods, and cedars darkly towering amid the paler deciduous trees. They are oases of peace within the turmoil of so much of urban existence, and they convey a gentle melancholy, reminding us that death is the only certainly in life. As Robert Louis Stevenson put it, there is a 'certain frame of mind to which a cemetery is, if not an antidote, at least an alleviation. If you are in a fit of the blues, go nowhere else.'[69]

10 A CONCLUSION

Introduction; The Monument; Civic Buildings; Commercial Buildings; Epilogue

Only today, with architectural horizons stretching to irredeemable monotony, does the Victorian city, by the very nature of its complexity, once again strike the imagination
Sir John Summerson, 'London, the Artifact', *The Victorian City*
(Routledge & Kegan Paul, London, 1973) 1, 328.

Introduction
Sir John Summerson's remark at the end of his perceptive essay in *The Victorian City*[1] is illuminating, because appreciation of the Victorian achievement as the twentieth century draws to its close has tended to increase, partly as a reaction against the dreariness of so much non-architecture that has blighted whole cities since the end of the Second World War. There is thus a curious parallel with the reaction against Georgian architecture, perceived by the Victorians to be dull and monotonous. Victorian architecture, with all its richness of expression, developed not least because the architecture, and especially the domestic architecture, of Georgian England was so deadpan, flat, unemphatic and reticent: what remains of the Victorian legacy of buildings can also be seen today as rather more entertaining, interesting and even grand compared with the joyless, badly designed, poorly made, and architecturally illiterate structures of more recent times.

The Monument
Perhaps one of the most interesting features of the Victorian Age in terms of its buildings is the great change in commemoration and celebration that occurred during the nineteenth century. Kings, prelates and princes had been commemorated by monuments in past ages, and the range was extended to include artists, writers and others from the Age of Humanism. In the eighteenth century the Temple of British Worthies at Stowe had commemorated princes, statesmen, scientists, an architect, a philosopher, poets, adventurers and a Member of Parliament: two of those celebrated were still alive when the temple was built. National heroes might be commemorated by tall structures

286

(Nelson at London, Dublin and Edinburgh; Wellington at Dublin), but the common man was not commemorated to any significant extent until the nineteenth century. A change of sensibility that developed with the Evangelical Conscience, concern for the underdog, increase in political representation and organised labour led to the universal desire for individual memorials in the new cemeteries (where there was sufficient room and a permanence of burial-rights unknown in the overcrowded churchyards). By the end of the nineteenth century commemoration of private soldiers in churches and cathedrals was becoming common, and led to the naming of great numbers of individuals on memorials to the dead of the South African, First and Second World Wars. The dead of earlier campaigns (such as the Battle of Waterloo of 1815) were buried in pits with no individual commemoration for the ordinary soldier: the war cemeteries of Flanders Field developed after 1914–18 would have been unthinkable in the early nineteenth century, just as the village, town and parish memorials to the named dead of the First World War were a modern phenomenon that grew from Victorian attitudes to the individual. The American Civil War seems to have been the first war in which proper cemeteries for all ranks were laid out, and the Franco-Prussian War of 1870–71 produced a similar concern for the dead of both sides. By the time of the First World War soldiers were no longer 'professionals', in the sense that armies became huge and were largely composed of conscripts: individually marked graves were therefore felt to be desirable.

Monuments to local worthies, clergymen, politicians and heroes were erected in numbers during the Victorian period: London, Belfast, Manchester, Liverpool, and many provincial towns and cities acquired civic memorials, usually in the form of statues on pedestals, to representatives of professions and classes who would not have been so honoured in earlier times.

Civic Buildings
In another sense the great civic buildings of Victorian Britain are also monuments, for they celebrate a new political structure that grew after 1832. The development of municipal government and enterprise was mirrored in the monumental public architecture of so many cities which grew to eminence in the Victorian era. Repeal of various enactments enabled Nonconformists and Roman Catholics to partici-pate in government, and the influence of Dissent was particularly marked in the north and in the midlands. Architectural grandeur in town halls, exchanges and other public buildings reflected a new civic pride, competition among towns, and the shift of power from the old

landowning Tory aristocracy to the Nonconformist commercial classes. It is not surprising to find so many municipal buildings that responded to the new political changes and to the growth in public participation in affairs. Most Victorian town halls had a large room or hall (decorated with considerable architectural pretension) which was used for meetings, musical performances, civic functions and the like. They also contained offices, suites, council chambers, and occasionally courts and exchanges as well.

In the eighteenth century the grandest buildings were usually the fine Palladian palaces of the great aristocratic families and the large town houses of the same class. After 1832 the first of the major national and public monuments was associated with a wider franchise, with government, and with a shift in political power: the Palace of Westminster, with its celebrated Gothic silhouette and world-famous clock-tower containing the huge bell known as Big Ben was extremely important as a model and as a milestone in the acceptance of the Gothic Revival. Dixon and Muthesius,[2] perspicacious as ever, have pointed out most interestingly that the clock-tower or turret that was a feature of so many town halls and civic buildings seems to have derived from the Palace of Westminster clock-tower, and can be seen as symbolising the new post-1832 franchise.[3] Manchester's Town Hall by Alfred Water-house is perhaps the grandest of the Gothic Revival municipal buildings, but it is late, dating from 1868, and boasts a stupendous clock-tower with spire.

An association of High Anglicanism and Roman Catholicism with Gothic Revival through Pugin and the Ecclesiologists led to the adoption of Classicism in many towns where Nonconformity was dominant. (The great number of Dissenters' places of worship in pleasing Classical styles bears testimony to this point, while the extraordinary Free Presbyterian churches by Alexander Thomson in Glasgow mix Greek, Egyptian and Neoclassical themes in a marvel-lously inventive manner [Plate 169]). Birmingham acquired its town hall by Hansom based on the temple of Castor and Pollux in Rome from 1832, Manchester its Italian-Renaissance (after Sansovino) Free Trade Hall by Walters of 1853, and Liverpool its Neoclassical St George's Hall (with interior influenced by Roman Imperial Baths) of 1841–56 by Elmes and Cockerell. With Leeds Town Hall of 1853–8 by Brodrick the dominant architectural theme moves away from Neoclassicism to a mixture of the Italianate manner of Barry, the civic and commercial Classicism of Brongniart (at the Paris Bourse of 1808–26) and of Tite (at London's Royal Exchange of 1838–44), and a variation of Baroque flourish in the gigantic clock-tower (Plate 32). The interior of the great hall of Leeds Town Hall shows a pronounced Roman influence, but

Brodrick's other civic masterpiece in Leeds, the Corn Exchange of 1861–3, an elliptical building consisting of two storeys of arcaded offices around a large space roofed (*Plate 170*) with iron and glass, is probably based on the Halle du Blé in Paris of 1763–8 by Lecamus de Mézières with its iron-and-glass dome of 1803–13 by Bélanger.[4] The design of the Halle du Blé probably also influenced J. B. Bunning in his Coal Exchange in London of 1846–9. Halifax Town Hall merged a Gothic composition with free Renaissance eclecticism, but William Hill's Bolton Town Hall of 1866–73 and the same architect's Guildhall at Portsmouth seem to return to Neoclassical principles.

Even more overtly Neoclassical and clearly influenced by Continental and Scottish buildings, is the Harris Library and Museum in Preston of 1882–93 by James Hibbert (*Plate 171*), a design that appears to owe not a little to Schinkel's *Schauspielhaus* in Berlin. Yet another clock-tower appears at the extraordinary Sheffield Town Hall of 1890–7 in a free eclectic Renaissance style (*Plate 80*), but by the time Colchester's Moot Hall by Belcher of 1898–1902 and Brumwell Thomas's Belfast City Hall of 1897–1906 were being built the favoured style was grandly Baroque (*Plate 100*).

Plate 169 'Greek' Thomson's Queen's Park Free Presbyterian Church, Glasgow, of 1867. An eclectic mixture of Graeco-Egyptian motifs, a dash of Schinkel's architecture (Berlin *Schauspielhaus*) and a touch of Orientalism. (*Mitchell Library, Glasgow*)

Plate 170 Interior of the Corn Exchange, Leeds. (*JSC*)

Plate 171 The Harris Library and Museum, Preston, Lancashire, of 1882–93. (*AFK*)

Commercial Buildings

Exchanges have been mentioned, and in earlier chapters banks have been discussed. Banks proliferated after various enactments of the 1820s and '30s, and the buildings were often in a Classical style, either firmly Roman or Italianate, based on club architecture. Good examples of the *palazzo* styles can be found at the former Manchester and Salford Bank in Mosley Street, Manchester by Walters of 1860 and the headquarters of the Belfast Bank of 1844–5 by Charles Lanyon (*Plate 43*), who was also responsible for the Belfast Bank in Londonderry of 1853, another fine Italianate building with aediculated first-floor windows. Brown's Warehouse in Manchester of 1851 by Walters was one of the grandest of the *palazzo*-based office buildings and stores, while the huge warehouse of Messrs Watt, in Portland Street, Manchester (*Plate 172*) displays a virtuoso performance in differing elevational treatments for each storey. Alexander Thomson's 'Grecian' building of 1865 at 336–56 Sauchiehall Street and his 'Egyptian Halls' of 1871–3 at 84–100 Union Street (*Plate 173*), both in Glasgow, show how Neoclassical ideas, developed from precedents by Schinkel, could be used for commercial and office buildings.

Plate 172 Watt's Warehouse (Britannia House), Portland Street, Manchester, of 1856 to designs by Travis and Magnall. Each floor is given a distinct architectural treatment, using a wide range of motifs taken from Classical, Neoclassical and Renaissance precedent. (*RCHME No BB82/729*)

Early in the Victorian period offices were found in dwellings, but from the middle of the century purpose-built office chambers were erected, and the 'office' became quite separated from the house. To give confidence to clients office buildings were often Classical, like banks and other major institutions, and the *palazzo* style was commonly found on commercial and business premises from the 1850s. An Italianate Gothic style was employed by J. W. Wild at the Northern District School of St Martin in the Fields, London of 1849–50, and this seems to have been the model for a series of commercial façades that were based on Italian secular medieval precedent: examples are the Crown Life Assurance Company offices, New Bridge Street, Blackfriars of 1856–8 by Deane and Woodward,[5] G. Somers Clarke's General Credit and Discount Company in Lothbury of 1866, the Albert Buildings in Queen Victoria Street in London by F. J. Ward of 1871, and the majestic Richardson Sons and Owden's building at 1 Donegall Square North, Belfast (*Plate 9*), by Lanyon, Lynn, and Lanyon. Even more lushly extravagant is William Leiper's Carpet Factory for Messrs Templeton at Glasgow Green of 1889, a gaudy essay in Paduan Gothic, with a façade of red terracotta and polychrome glazed brick and faience set beneath an exotic set of Guelphic crenellations (*Plate 174*). This strange building was a deliberate attempt to erect something of permanent architectural interest.[6] In 1900 Glasgow also acquired a warehouse in Tradeston Street designed by W. F. McGibbon and based on the Bargello in Florence.[7] Even earlier, in 1872, John Honeyman's furniture warehouse known as the Ca d'Oro in Gordon Street, Glasgow, employed Venetian devices in its delicate iron-and-glass façades.[8]

As the century drew to its close commercial buildings in a hard Gothic style (as at the Prudential Assurance Company, Holborn, London, by Waterhouse), free interpretations of vernacular revival, timber framing, and Continental Gothic (as in the Fothergill blocks in Nottingham), seventeenth-century Domestic Revival and 'Queen-Anne' style (as at New Zealand Chambers, Leadenhall Street, London, by Shaw), and the free eclecticism of the Doulton terracotta-fronted Harrods store in Brompton Road, London, by Stevens and Hunt of 1897–1905 give an idea of the range of styles exploited by designers. Harrods was designed to have very large plate-glass windows at ground-floor level, and these, with the development of ferrous columns (mainly

Plate 173 Nos 84–100 Union Street, Glasgow (the Egyptian Halls) by Alexander 'Greek' Thomson of 1871–3, a vigorous and inventive design using Graeco-Egyptian and Schinkelesque elements. (*RCAHMS No GW/2020*)
Plate 174 Templeton's Factory, Glasgow Green, of 1889, by William Leiper, an extraordinary essay in Paduan Gothic. (*RCAHMS No GW/4761*)

of cast iron) to support the structure above, had been common in the larger and more forward-looking shops and stores since about 1840, although the techniques were pioneered in the 1830s. The difficulty with large plate-glass windows was that the heavy masonry, brick or stucco faced elevations above the fasciae appeared to sit on glass alone, with no visible means of support, a point that was not lost on critics.

Epilogue

Not surprisingly, the sixty-four years of Queen Victoria's reign left no single architectural style in a dominant position. Yet, if any area could typify the range of Victorian architectural choice, it would probably be the museums area of South Kensington. There can be found one of the best monuments of the High-Victorian Gothic Revival in the Albert Memorial; plenty of stucco-faced terrace-houses in the Italianate style survive; ecclesiastical architecture is represented by the hard polychrome Gothic of St Augustine's, Queen's Gate, by Butterfield of 1870–76, and by the broad airy late-Gothic Holy Trinity, Prince Consort Road, of 1901 by G. F. Bodley. Domestic-Revival works by J. J. Stevenson at 8 Palace Gate and 1 Lowther Gardens, and by Norman Shaw at 18 Hyde Park Gate, Lowther Lodge, 170, 180 and 196 Queen's Gate give an excellent idea of the range of the phenomenon. A large block of flats in the 'Queen-Anne' and Northern Renaissance styles by Norman Shaw at Albert Hall Mansions shows the versatility of styles. Elaborate North European Renaissance façades by W. Flockhart at 108 and 110 Old Brompton Road show at a very small scale a style fully exploited by George and Peto elsewhere in Kensington; and the round-arched styles are gloriously represented at Waterhouse's National History Museum and in the quadrangle of the Victoria and Albert Museum. Other styles are represented by A. W. Blomfield's Royal College of Music of 1890–4 (Franco-Caledonian early Renaissance and bartizanned Baronial), the Royal College of Organists of 1874–5 by H. H. Cole and F. W. Moody (Italianate with Ipswichian seventeenth-century windows after Shaw and with *sgraffito* decoration) (*Plate 175*), the tower of the old Imperial Institute of 1887–93 by T. E. Collcutt (Sevillian Renaissance), the Huxley Building by H. Scott, Gamble, Wild and others of 1867–71 (partly *Rundbogenstil* Italianate Renaissance), and, of course, the Albert Hall itself (a grandly Roman theme dressed in a Franco-Italianate cloak).

The banks and warehouses of Belfast, Manchester, Glasgow and Edinburgh offer a stunning range of solidly worked building styles, while London, the greatest of all Victorian cities, even today, provides object-lessons in the history of Victorian architecture. The planned developments of Bedford Park, Saltaire and Port Sunlight remain to instruct, while the leafy melancholy of Victorian cemeteries can still enthral, move and sadden the visitor. Many Victorian railway stations (though often altered and maltreated) are in use today, while Victorian banks, offices and shops are still in business. Easily the greatest legacy of Victorian architecture is of the domestic type, but this has often suffered through ignorance, the vagaries of taste and insensitive alterations. Victorian architecture, Victorian fabric and Victorian artefacts are still, to a very large extent, part of the experience of the twentieth century, even so late in that century: from the vantage-point of our own time Victorian accomplishments, panache, and even brilliance are still clear, save to the most closed of minds.

Plate 175 Royal College of Organists' building, South Kensington, of 1874–5 by H. H. Cole and F. W. Moody. (Italianate with seventeenth-century-style windows derived from Sparrowe's House in Ipswich, a type often used by Norman Shaw.) The façade is covered with *sgraffito* decoration. (*JSC*)

REFERENCES

NOTES FOR CHAPTER I: THE VICTORIAN AGE
PAGES 11–26

1 *Dictionary of National Biography*
2 Lampard, Eric E. 'The Urbanising World' in Dyos, H. J. and Wolff, Michael (*Eds*) *The Victorian City. Images and Realities* (Routledge & Kegan Paul, London and Boston, 1973) 1, 3–57
3 See Curl, James Stevens. *The Life and Work of Henry Roberts (1803–76), Architect* (Phillimore, Chichester, 1983), and Briggs, Asa. *Victorian Cities* (Penguin, Harmondsworth, 1968)
4 Curl, James Stevens. *A Celebration of Death* (Constable, London and New York, 1980)
5 Curl. *Henry Roberts Op. cit, passim*
6 *Ibid*
7 *Ibid*
8 *Ibid* See also Eastlake, Charles L. *The Gothic Revival* (Leicester University Press, Leicester, 1970) *passim* and Chapter XI
9 Eastlake. *Op. cit*
10 *Ibid*
11 *Ibid* 190
12 *Ibid* 191
13 *Ibid*
14 *Ibid* 191–2
15 My italics: a 'deep chancel' in an Evangelical church would have been unthinkable
16 Kingsley, Charles. *Alton Locke. Tailor and Poet* (Thomas Nelson, London, 1908) 365–7
17 9 and 10 Victoria, c. 22
18 40 George III, c. 38
19 10 George IV, c. 7
20 3 and 4 William IV, c. 37
21 10 Victoria, c. 1
22 For a description of Schinkel's visit see Ettlinger, L. D. 'A German Architect's Visit to England in 1826', *The Architectural Review* 97 (May 1945). See also *Karl Friedrich Schinkel. Architektur Malerei Kunstgewerbe* (Catalogue of Exhibition at Charlottenburg 13 March 1981 – 13 September 1981 – Verwaltung der Staatliche Schlösser und Gärten und Nationalgalerie Berlin, and Staatliche Museen Preussischer Kulturbesitz, Berlin, 1981), *Karl Friedrich Schinkel 1781–1841* (Catalogue of Exhibition at the Altes Museum, Berlin, 23 October 1980 – 29 March 1981 – Verlag das Europäische Buch, Berlin, 1981), and *Karl Friedrich Schinkel. Sein Wirken als Architekt* (VEB Verlag für Bauwesen, Berlin, 1981)
23 For interesting development of these points see Taylor, Nicholas. 'The Awful Sublimity of the Victorian City' in Dyos and Wolff *Op. cit* 431–47. See also Crook, J. Mordaunt. *The Dilemma of Style. Architectural Ideas from the Picturesque to Post-Modern* (John Murray, London, 1987) *passim*, for a full elaboration

NOTES FOR CHAPTER 2: THE QUESTION OF STYLE I
PAGES 27–72

1 *The Builder* (1868) 582
2 Payne Knight, R. *An Analytical Inquiry into the Principles of Taste* (T. Payne and J. White, London, 1805) *passim*, but see 102
3 (1816)
4 *An Encyclopaedia of Cottage, Farm, and Villa Architecture* (Longman, Rees, Orme, Brown, Green & Longman, London, 1833) Section 2201
5 *Ibid* Sections 2201–2
6 Conner, Patrick (*Ed*). *The Inspiration of Egypt* (Brighton Borough Council, Brighton, 1983) 54–5
7 See Crook, J. Mordaunt *The Greek Revival: Neo-Classical Attitudes in British Architecture, 1760–1870* (John Murray, London, 1972) and Curl, James Stevens. *The Egyptian Revival* (George Allen & Unwin, London, 1982) for details of sources and major buildings
8 Colvin, Howard. *A Biographical Dictionary of British Architects 1600–1840* (John Murray, London, 1978) 889
9 Illustrated in Crook, J. Mordaunt. *The Dilemma of Style* (John Murray, London, 1987) 38
10 10 George IV, c. 8
11 14 and 15 Victoria, c. 60
12 Wedgwood, A. (*Ed*). *A. W. N. Pugin and the Pugin Family*

(Victoria and Albert Museum, London, 1985) 111 and *passim*
13 Crook, J. Mordaunt. *The Dilemma . . . Op. cit* 53
14 Eastlake, Charles L. *A History of the Gothic Revival* (Leicester U.P., Leicester, 1970) 242
15 Hersey, George L. *High Victorian Gothic. A Study in Associationism* (The Johns Hopkins University Press, Baltimore & London, 1972) 95
16 Webb, Benjamin. *Sketches of Continental Ecclesiology, or Church Notes in Belgium, Germany, and Italy.* (No publisher given, London, 1848) 118
17 *The Ecclesiologist* 5 (1846) 52
18 *Ibid* 12 (1851) 180–2
19 Hersey. *Op. cit* 102–3 and 117
20 *The Builder* (1857) 572–3. See also *The Architect* (1870) 142
21 See Blau, Eve. *Ruskinian Gothic. The Architecture of Deane and Woodward 1845–1861* (Princeton University Press, Princeton and London, 1982)
22 Eastlake. *Op. cit* 252
23 *Ibid* 251–2
24 Paris, edited by B. Bance
25 Crook. *Op. cit* 69
26 *The Builder* (1861) 403
27 These and other matters are discussed in J. Mordaunt Crook's *The Dilemma . . ., Op. cit, passim*

NOTES FOR CHAPTER 3: THE QUESTION OF STYLE II
PAGES 73–148

1 Crook, J. Mordaunt. *The Greek Revival: Neo-Classical Attitudes in British Architecture, 1760–1870* (John Murray, London, 1972)
2 See Bibliography
3 Curl, James Stevens. *The Life and*

Work of Henry Roberts (1803–76), Architect (Phillimore, Chichester, 1983) *passim*
4 Curl, James Stevens. *The Londonderry Plantation 1609–1914* (Phillimore,

Chichester, 1986) Chapters VI and VIII

5 See *Romantik und Restauration. Architektur in Bayern zur Zeit Ludwigs I. 1825–1848*, edited by Winfried Nerdinger (Münchner Stadtmuseum, Munich, 1987)

6 See Gomme, Andor and Walker, David. *Architecture of Glasgow* (Lund Humphries, London, 1968) 123–52

7 Sheppard, F. H. W. (*Ed*). *Survey of London* 38 *The Museums Area of South Kensington and Westminster* (The Athlone Press, University of London for the Greater London Council, London, 1975) Ch. VI and *passim*

8 *Ibid*

9 Jervis, Simon. *The Penguin Dictionary of Design and Designers* (Allen Lane, Penguin, London, 1984) 216

10 Curl, James Stevens. *A Celebration of Death* (Constable, London, 1980) 196–98

11 Curl, James Stevens. 'Acrobatic Gothic, Freely Treated. The Architecture of E. Bassett Keeling (1837–86)' *Country Life* (2 October 1986)

12 Catalogue issued by William Watt: *Art Furniture Designed by Edward W. Godwin F.S.A.* (London, 1877)

13 *The Building News* (1885) 1021–5, (1886) 378, 479 and (1887) 670–1

14 *The Builder* (1885) Pt. 1, 721

15 Corbelled turrets

16 See Gray, A. Stuart. *Edwardian Architecture. A Biographical Dictionary* (Duckworth, London, 1985) *passim*. Mr Gray's book is a useful and finely illustrated source of information on this era

NOTES FOR CHAPTER 4: PHILANTHROPIC HOUSING AND THE CONCERN FOR THE UNDERDOG: MODEL DWELLINGS AND MODEL VILLAGES PAGES 149–177

1 *D.N.B.*

2 (Longman, Rees, Orme, Brown, Green & Longman, London, 1834) Items 477–80

3 Curl, James Stevens. *The Londonderry Plantation, 1609–1914* (Phillimore, Chichester, 1986) *passim*

4 *The Labourers' Friend* New Series, 1

5 *D.N.B.* Smith also dissected the body of Jeremy Bentham who had left his corpse to Smith in order to assist the latter in his anatomical lectures

6 Paul was also Augustus J. C. Hare's maternal grandfather: Hare,

in his autobiography, refers to Paul as 'rather mad'

7 The Minutes of the SICLC held by the Peabody Trust

8 Curl, James Stevens. *The Life and Work of Henry Roberts (1803–76), Architect* (Phillimore, Chichester, 1983) 78

9 32 Henry VIII c. 42 (1540) *An Act Concernyng Barbours and Chirurgeons to be of One Companie*

10 25 George c. 37 (1752)

11 2 and 3 William IV c. 45 (1832)

12 2 and 3 William IV c. 75 (1832)

13 4 and 5 William IV c. 76 (1834)

14 These killers were known as

'burkers', after Burke and Hare who supplied the Edinburgh anatomists: the term was also applied to the London murderers Bishop and Williams. 'Burkophobia' was rampant by 1832

15 Richardson, Ruth. *Death, Dissection, and the Destitute* (Routledge & Kegan Paul, London, 1987) *passim*

16 *The Westminster Review* (1832) Vol 10, 128–48

17 Curl. *Henry Roberts . . . Op. cit* 79, quotes from Roberts's *The Dwellings of the Labouring Classes . . .*

18 Roberts. *Op. cit* 6

19 Fully described in Curl. *Henry Roberts . . . Op. cit* 80

20 3 (1845) 1

21 14 and 15 Victoria c. 28 and 34

22 *The Builder* 8 (1850) 369

23 The buildings are described in Curl. *Henry Roberts . . . passim*

24 All listed in the above

25 48 and 49 Victoria c. 71 (1885)

26 53 and 54 Victoria c. 70 (1890)

27 Camblin, Gilbert. *The Town in Ulster* (William Mullan, Belfast, 1951) 100

28 Curl, James Stevens. 'A Chartist Estate in Hertfordshire. Heronsgate (formerly O'Connorville)' *Country Life* (3 March 1977) See also Hadfield, Alice Mary. *The Chartist Land Company* (David & Charles, Newton Abbot, 1970) *passim*

29 Curl, James Stevens. *Victorian Architecture: its Practical Aspects* (David & Charles, Newton Abbot, 1973) Ch. 9

30 Darley, Gillian. *Villages of Vision* (The Architectural Press, London, 1975) is an excellent introduction to the subject of planned villages

31 Davidson, T. Raffles. *Port Sunlight. A Record of its Artistic & Pictorial Aspect* (Batsford, London, 1916). See also Curl, James Stevens. 'Victorian Garden Village' *Country Life* (16 December 1976)

32 Darley. *Op. cit* Many of these are cited in her useful book

33 Information on Port Sunlight in a personal communication to the author from the late Mr James Lomax-Simpson of 2 January 1977. See also the author's article in *Country Life Op. cit*

NOTES FOR CHAPTER 5: DOMESTIC ARCHITECTURE APART FROM PHILANTHROPIC AND MODEL HOUSING
PAGES 178–200

1 Suetonius, G. *Divus Augustus* 28

2 Sheppard, F. H. W. (*Ed*). *Survey of London. Northern Kensington* Vol 37 (The Athlone Press for the GLC, London, 1973) *passim*

3 Colvin, Howard. *A Biographical Dictionary of British Architects 1600–1840* (John Murray, London, 1978) 66

4 Sheppard. *Op. cit*, Colvin. *Op. cit*, and Curl, James Stevens. 'A Story of Mixed Fortunes. The Ladbroke Estate Development' *Country Life* (13 November 1975)

5 Sheppard. *Op. cit passim*. See also Curl. *Op. cit*

6 *Ibid* See also Colvin. *Op. cit* on Papworth, Nash, *et al*

7 *The Building News* (13 August 1869) 121

8 See Sheppard. *Op. cit passim*

9 Curl. *Op. cit*

10 *Ibid*

11 *Ibid*

12 *Ibid*
13 See Curl, James Stevens. 'Mixed Fortunes for a London Estate' *Country Life* (14 June 1979)
14 Sheppard. *Op. cit passim*
15 Cowie, William. *Great Western Road Glasgow* (Glasgow, 1974)
16 See 33 and 34 Victoria c. 46 (1870) and following legislation
17 This chapter derives from detailed studies made in London from 1970–72, in Glasgow from 1973–5, in Clevedon in 1974, and elsewhere in Britain during that period. Since that time Hermann Muthesius's great work has become widely available, while Stefan Muthesius's studies of English housing types have also been published. Donald J. Olsen's *The Growth of Victorian London* (Batsford, London, 1976) is an invaluable study, while H. J. Dyos's and Michael Wolff's *The Victorian City* (Routledge & Kegan Paul, London, 1973) is a useful compendium of material. For detailed studies of fabric, however, *The Survey of London* (to which the present writer was Architectural Editor in the early 1970s) is rich in material, and there have been further studies of Victorian houses in number. Mark Girouard's *The Victorian Country House* (Yale U.P., New Haven and London, 1979) is an excellent study of one very remarkable aspect of Victorian housing. Robert Kerr's *The Gentleman's House* of 1864 is a useful study of buildings as seen by a High-Victorian commentator.

NOTES FOR CHAPTER 6: NEW MATERIALS AND NEW CHALLENGES
PAGES 201–222

1 Loudon, J. C. *An Encyclopaedia of Cottage, Farm and Villa Architecture* (Longman, London, 1834) Item 1961
2 McCracken, Eileen. *The Palm House and Botanic Garden, Belfast* (Ulster Architectural Heritage Society, Belfast, 1971) 36–8. The late Dr McCracken's monograph is an important contribution to the history of conservatory design
3 Dixon, Roger and Muthesius, Stefan. *Victorian Architecture* (Thames & Hudson, London, 1985) 97. See also McCracken, *Op. cit*
4 *Minutes of the Proceedings of the Institute of Civil Engineers* 9 (1850)
5 *The Illustrated London News* (6 July 1850)
6 *Ballads.* Vol 21 of *the Works of William Makepeace Thackeray* (Smith, Elder, London, 1885) 46
7 Dixon and Muthesius. *Op. cit* 102 See also Curl, James Stevens. *Victorian Architecture: its Practical Aspects* (David & Charles, Newton Abbot, 1973) 26–7. See also Chadwick, George F. *The Works of Joseph Paxton 1803–1865* (The Architectural Press, London, 1961)
8 Elliott, Brent. *Victorian Gardens* (Batsford, London, 1986) *passim*
9 Pevsner, Nikolaus. *A History of Building Types* (Thames & Hudson, London, 1976) 235–56
10 Ferrey, Benjamin. *Recollections of A. N. Welby Pugin . . .* (E. Stanford, London, 1861) 258. See also Morris, William. *Works* Vol 22, 429
11 Loudon, J. C. *The Architectural*

Magazine Vol 4 (1837) 277 *et seq*
and *passim*
12 Loudon, J. C. *An Encyclopaedia
of Gardening . . .* (Longman,
London, 1827) 16
13 *The Ecclesiologist* 12 (1851)
269 and *passim*
14 Wihl, G. *Ruskin and the
Rhetoric of Infallibility* (Yale U.P.
New Haven, 1985) 168 *et seq*
15 Reichensperger, A. In *The
Ecclesiologist* 12 (1851) 385
16 As footnote 12
17 *Ibid* 273
18 Quoted in Pevsner *Op. cit* 228
19 Quoted in Crook, J. Mordaunt.
The Dilemma of Style (John
Murray, London, 1987) 115
20 Quoted in Pevsner, Nikolaus.
Pioneers of Modern Design
(Penguin, Harmondsworth, 1960)
133. See also Meeks, C. L. V. *The
Railroad Station* (Yale U.P., New
Haven, 1956) *passim*
21 Lee, Charles E. 'St Pancras
Station, 1868–1968' *The Railway
Magazine* (September–October
1968)
22 Sheppard, F. H. W. (*Ed*). *Survey
of London* Vol 38 (Athlone Press
and GLC, London, 1975) 98–9
23 Ecclesiological Society, The.
Instrumenta Ecclesiastica (The
Ecclesiological Society, London,
1856) 67–72
24 Hersey, George L. *High
Victorian Gothic. A Study in
Associationism* (Johns Hopkins
U.P., Baltimore and London, 1972)
182
25 *Ibid*
26 *Ibid*
27 Sheppard. *Op. cit passim*
28 See Gifford, John, McWilliam,
Colin, and Walker, David.
*Edinburgh The Buildings of
Scotland* series (Penguin,
Harmondsworth, 1984) 186–7
29 pp 195–6
30 Gomme, Andor and Walker,
David. *Architecture of Glasgow*
(Lund Humphries, London, 1968)
114
31 *Ibid passim*
32 Scott, George Gilbert. *Remarks
on Secular and Domestic
Architecture, Present and Future*
(John Murray, London, 1857) 109
et seq
33 Curl, James Stevens and
Sambrook, John J. 'E. Bassett
Keeling, Architect' *Architectural
History* 16, (1973)
34 *Buildings . . .* etc (n.p., London,
1894)
35 *Art and Life, and the Building
and Decoration of Cities* (London,
1897)
36 *Ibid* 247
37 *Ibid*
38 The Du Cane material was
kindly made available by the late
Mr A. W. Pullan, Sir Edmund's
direct descendant, to whom the
author expresses his gratitude

NOTES FOR CHAPTER 7: TRAFFIC RELIEF, REFORM AND HYGIENE,
PAGES 223–237

1 Curl, James Stevens. *Victorian
Architecture: its Practical Aspects*
(David & Charles, Newton Abbot,
1973) 62–3
2 Walford, Edward. *Old and New
London* (Cassell, Petter & Galpin,
London, Paris, and New York,
1887) V, 235

3 *Illustrated London News* (22 November 1879) 487
4 Curl. *Victorian Architecture Op. cit* 94
5 According to *The Builder. The Engineer* referred to Abbey Mills as a 'dainty palace' for machinery

6 Walford. *Op. cit* 229
7 *Ibid* 419–22
8 See *The Builder* (17 July 1879) 785, (25 June 1881) 792, and (19 March 1881) 354–5
9 (23 January 1894)

NOTES FOR CHAPTER 8: BUILDINGS FOR LEISURE
PAGES 238–257

1 Curl, James Stevens. *The Londonderry Plantation 1609–1914* (Phillimore, Chichester, 1986). Chapters on the Drapers', Fishmongers' and other Companies
2 An elevation appears in *John Tallis's London Street Views* (Nattali and Maurice, London, 1969) 3, 43
3 Reproduced in Girouard, Mark. *Victorian Pubs* (Yale U.P., New Haven and London, 1984) 22
4 Dickens, Charles. *The Works of Charles Dickens 26 Sketches by Boz* (Chapman & Hall, London, 1898) 212
5 *Ibid*
6 *Ibid* 215
7 Curl, James Stevens. 'Taking the Waters in London'. Articles in *Country Life* (2 December 1971, 9 December 1971, 11 November 1976, and 18 November 1976)
8 Curl, James Stevens. 'The

Victorian Public Houses of Belfast' *National Trust Studies 1980* (Sotheby Parke Bernet, London, 1979)
9 Curl, James Stevens and Sambrook, John. 'E. Bassett Keeling, Architect' *Architectural History* 16 (1973)
10 In his *The Growth of Victorian London* (Batsford, London, 1976) 93 *et seq*
11 *Ibid* 93
12 *Ibid* 93
13 Discussed by Olsen. *Op. cit passim*
14 Illustrated in Carrott, Richard G. *The Egyptian Revival. its Sources, Monuments, and Meaning* (University of California Press, Berkeley and London, 1978) Plate 81
15 Curl, James Stevens. 'A Victorian Coastal Arcadia' *Country Life* (2 October 1975)

NOTES FOR CHAPTER 9: THE ARCHITECTURE AND LANDSCAPES
ASSOCIATED WITH THE DISPOSAL OF THE DEAD: FUNERARY
ARCHITECTURE, DESIGN, AND THE GARDEN CEMETERY MOVEMENT
PAGES 258–285

1 Ariès, Philippe. *The Hour of Our Death* Tr. by Helen Weaver (Allen Lane, London, 1981) *passim*, xv and xvi
2 Curl, James Stevens. 'Entstehung

und Architektur der frühen britischen Friedhöfe' *O ewich is so lanck. Die Historischen Friedhöfe in Berlin-Kreuzberg*. Catalogue of Exhibition in the Landesarchiv,

Berlin, 22 April 1987 – 26 June 1987. (Landeskonservator, Berlin, and Nicolaische Verlagsbuch-handlung Beuermann GmbH, Berlin, 1987)

3 Curl, James Stevens. *Mausolea in Ulster* (Ulster Architectural Heritage Society, Belfast, 1978)

4 Curl, James Stevens *The Victorian Celebration of Death* (David & Charles, 1972) 33–53

5 *Proceedings in Reference to the Preservation of the Bunhill Fields Burial Ground* (Corporation of London, London, 1867)

6 Strain, R. W. M. *Belfast and its Charitable Society* (Oxford University Press, London, 1961)

7 Bodleian Library, University of Oxford. Bodl. MS Rawl. B, 376, ff. 351–2

8 Curl, James Stevens. *A Celebration of Death. An introduction to some of the buildings, monuments, and settings of funerary architecture in the Western European tradition* (Constable, London, 1980) 140–5

9 Chambers, William. *A Treatise on Civil Architecture* (London, 1759)

10 Curl, James Stevens. 'The Design of Early British Cemeteries' *Journal of Garden History* 4, 3 (Taylor and Francis, London, July–September 1984) 223–54

11 Miller, Thomas. *Picturesque Sketches of London Past and Present* (N.P., London, 1852)

12 Curl. *A Celebration . . . Op. cit* 212

13 Willson, Thomas. *The Pyramid. A General Metropolitan Cemetery to be Erected in the Vicinity of Primrose Hill* (London, 1842). The design dates from the 1820s

14 *The Morning Chronicle* (10 June 1830)

15 *The Gentleman's Magazine* (1830) 1, 29

16 Curl, James Stevens. 'Europe's Grandest Cemetery? The Staglieno, Genoa' *Country Life* (15 September 1977)

17 Loudon, J. C. *On the Laying Out, Planting and Managing of Cemeteries . . .* (Longman, Brown, Green and Longmans, London, 1843)

18 (14 May 1830)

19 Minutes of The General Cemetery Company *passim*

20 Curl. *A Celebration . . . Op. cit* 212

21 883 and 884, Vol 28, Westminster Sewer Plans

22 Minutes of The General Cemetery Company (1 November 1831) See also *The Gentleman's Magazine* 102 (1832)

23 Kendall, H. E. *Sketches of the Approved Designs of a Chapel and Gateway Entrances Intended to be Erected at Kensal Green for The General Cemetery Company* (London, 1832)

24 Clark, Benjamin. *Handbook for Visitors to Kensal Green Cemetery* (London, 1843)

25 Loudon. *On Cemeteries . . . Op. cit* 12–3

26 (27 December 1856) 700

27 *The Builder* (1866) 306

28 Hakewill, A. W. *Modern Tombs Gleaned from the Public Cemeteries of London* (London, 1851) Pl. 23

29 (2 September 1854) 460

30 See Curl, James Stevens. 'Neo-Classical Necropolis in Decay. York Cemetery' *Country Life* (28 January 1982) and Curl, James Stevens. 'Northern Cemetery under Threat. Jesmond, Newcastle upon Tyne' *Country Life* (2 July 1981)

31 Loudon. *On Cemeteries . . .* 25
32 *Ibid* 25
33 *Ibid* 69
34 *Ibid*
35 6 and 7 William IV, c. 136 Local
36 Curl, James Stevens. *The Egyptian Revival* (Allen & Unwin, London, London, 1982) *passim*
37 Pugin, A. W. N. *An Apology for The Revival of Christian Architecture in England* (London, 1843) 12
38 Lloyd, John H. *The History, Topography and Antiquities of Highgate, in the County of Middlesex* (Highgate, 1888) 494–5
39 Prickett, Frederick. *The History and Antiquities of Highgate, Middlesex* (Highgate, 1842) 83
40 *Ibid*
41 *Ibid*
42 Justyne, William. *Guide to Highgate Cemetery* (J. Moore, London, n.d.) 7
43 *Ibid*
44 *Ibid*
45 *Ibid* 33
46 *Ibid*
47 Meller, Hugh. *London Cemeteries. An Illustrated Guide and Gazetteer* (Avebury, Amersham, 1981) 149
48 However, Geary claimed to be the founder of the cemetery on the title-page of his *Cemetery Designs for Tombs and Cenotaphs* (Tilt and Bogue, London, 1840)
49 Loudon. *On Cemeteries . . . Op. cit* 68
50 *Ibid* See also 17
51 *Ibid* 19
52 For further information on Loudon see Curl, James Stevens.

'John Claudius Loudon and the Garden Cemetery Movement' *Garden History. The Journal of the Garden History Society* 11, 2 (Autumn 1983)
53 Minutes of the Company in the Public Records Office under 'Works'
54 Established under 1 Victoria c. 130 Local
55 Loudon. *On Cemeteries . . . Op. cit* 13 and *passim*
56 See especially Walker, George Alfred. *Gatherings from Grave-Yards . . .* etc (London, 1839)
57 13 and 14 Victoria c. 52 Public
58 15 and 16 Victoria c. 85 Public
59 (8 March 1856)
60 Curl, James Stevens. 'Architecture for a Novel Purpose. Death and the Railway Age' *Country Life* (12 June 1986)
61 47 and 48 Victoria c. 72
62 48 and 49 Victoria c. 167
63 50 and 51 Victoria c. 32
64 See *Plans and Views of the City of London Cemetery at Little Ilford in the County of Essex* (London, 1856) See also Metropolitan Burials Act 15 and 16 Victoria c. 85
65 Curl. *A Celebration . . .* 244–64
66 *Garden History* 10, 1 (Spring 1982) 93
67 Loudon. *On Cemeteries . . . Op. cit* 20–1
68 Sims, G. R. (*Ed*). *Living London* (London, 1906) 82
69 'The Wreath of Immortelles' from 'Early Sketches', in *Further Memories* (William Heinemann, Tusitala Edition, London, 1924) 166

NOTES FOR CHAPTER 10: A CONCLUSION
PAGES 286–295

1 Edited by Dyos and Wolff. See Bibliography
2 *Victorian Architecture* (Thames & Hudson, London, 1985) 144
3 *Ibid*
4 Illustrated in Pevsner, Nikolaus. *A History of Building Types* (Thames & Hudson, London, 1976) 203
5 Illustrated in Blau, Eve. *Ruskinian Gothic. The Architecture of Deane and Woodward 1845–1861* (Princeton University Press, Princeton, 1982) Plate 100
6 Gomme, Andor and Walker, David. *The Architecture of Glasgow* (Lund Humphries, London, 1968) 226
7 *Ibid* 228
8 *Ibid* 158

SELECT BIBLIOGRAPHY

The Author acknowledges the generous assistance of Mr Roger Towe in the compilation of this Bibliography.

Academy Architecture (1889–1901)
Alison, Archibald. *Essays on the Nature and Principles of Taste* (Constable, Edinburgh, 1817)
Allibone, Jill. *Anthony Salvin, 1799–1881* (University of Missouri Press, Columbia, and Lutterworth Press, Cambridge, 1988)
Architect, The (1868–1901)
Architectural History (from 1958)
Architectural Record (from 1891)
Architectural Review (from 1896)
Art Journal Illustrated Catalogue of the Great Exhibition, The (G. Virtue, London, 1851)
Aslin, Elizabeth. *The Aesthetic Movement* (Paul Elek, London, 1969)
Balgarnie, R. *Sir Titus Salt, Baronet* (Brenton Publishing, Settle, 1970)
Barnard, J. *The Decorative Tradition* (Architectural Press, London, 1973)
Beattie, Susan. *A Revolution in London Housing, LCC Housing Architects and their Work 1893–1914* (GLC and Architectural Press, London, 1980)
Beaver, Patrick. *The Crystal Palace, 1851–1936. A Portrait of Victorian Enterprise* (Hugh Evelyn, London, 1970)
Betjeman, John. *London's Historic Railway Stations* (John Murray, London, 1972)

Betjeman, John. *Victorian and Edwardian London in Old Photographs* (Batsford, London, 1969)

Biddle, G. *Victorian Stations: Railway Stations in England and Wales 1830–1913* (David & Charles, Newton Abbot, 1973)

Blau, E. *Ruskinian Gothic: The Architecture of Deane and Woodward (1845–61)* (Princeton U.P., Princeton, 1982)

Briggs, Asa. *The Age of Improvement: 1783–1867* (Longman, London, 1959)

Briggs, Asa. *Victorian Cities* (Penguin, Harmondsworth, 1968)

British Architect, The. (1874–1901)

Brockman, H. A. N. *The British Architect and Industry 1841–1940* (Allen & Unwin, London, 1974)

Builder, The (1843–1901)

Building News (1855–1901)

Burdett, H. C. *Hospitals and Asylums of the World* (J. & A. Churchill, London, 1893)

Burke, Edmund. *A Philosophical Enquiry into the Origin of Our Ideas of the Sublime and Beautiful* (N.P. London, 1757)

Cambridge Camden Society (later The Ecclesiological Society) *Church Enlargement and Church Arrangement* (Cambridge U.P., 1843)

Cambridge Camden Society. *A Hand-Book of English Ecclesiology* (J. Masters, London, 1847)

Chadwick, George F. *The Works of Sir Joseph Paxton, 1803–65* (Architectural Press, London, 1961)

Church Builder, The (1862–1901)

Civil Engineer and Architect's Journal (1837–67)

Clark, Kenneth. *The Gothic Revival: An Essay in the History of Taste* (Constable, London, 1950)

Clarke, Basil Fulford Lowther. *Anglican Cathedrals Outside the British Isles* (SPCK, London, 1958)

Clarke, Basil Fulford Lowther. *Church Builders of the Nineteenth Century: A study of the Gothic Revival in England* (David & Charles, Newton Abbot, 1969)

Clarke, Basil Fulford Lowther. *Parish Churches of London* (Batsford, London, 1966)

Clay, Felix. *Modern School Buildings* (Batsford, London, 1902)

Clegg, Samuel. *The Architecture of Machinery: An Essay on Propriety of Form and Proportion* (Architectural Library, London, 1842)

Cole, David. *The Work of Sir George Gilbert Scott* (Architectural Press, London, 1980)

Colvin, Howard. *A Biographical Dictionary of British Architects 1600–1840* (John Murray, London, 1978)

Conner, Patrick (*Ed*). *The Inspiration of Egypt. Its Influence on British Artists, Travellers and Designers*. Exhibition Catalogue (Brighton Borough Council, Brighton, 1983)

Country Life (from 1897)

Crawford, Alan and Thorne, Robert. *Birmingham Pubs 1890–1939* (A. Sutton, Gloucester, 1986)

Crook, J. Mordaunt. *The Dilemma of Style. Architectural Ideas from the Picturesque to the Post-Modern* (John Murray, London, 1987)

Crook, J. Mordaunt. *The Greek Revival: Neo-Classical Attitudes in British Architecture, 1760–1870* (John Murray, London, 1972)

Crook, J. Mordaunt. *William Burges and the High Victorian Dream* (John Murray, London, 1981)

Crook, J. Mordaunt. *Victorian Architecture: A Visual Anthology* (Johnson Reprint, New York, 1971)

Cunningham, C. *Victorian and Edwardian Town Halls* (Routledge & Kegan Paul, London, 1981)

Curl, James Stevens. *A Celebration of Death.* (Constable, London, and Scribner, New York, 1980)

Curl, James Stevens. *The Egyptian Revival.* (Allen & Unwin, London, 1982)

Curl, James Stevens. *The Life and Work of Henry Roberts, (1803–76), Architect.* (Phillimore, Chichester, 1983)

Darley, Gillian. *Villages of Vision* (Architectural Press, London, 1975)

Davison, T. Raffles. *Port Sunlight. A Record of its Artistic and Pictorial Aspect* (Batsford, London, 1916)

Dictionary of National Biography. Founded in 1882 by George Smith. Edited by Sir Leslie Stephen and Sir Sidney Lee (Oxford U.P., Oxford, and Geoffrey Cumberlege, London, 1885–1901)

Dixon, Roger and Muthesius, Stefan. *Victorian Architecture* (Thames & Hudson, London, 1985)

Donaldson, Thomas L. *A Preliminary Discourse on Architecture* (Taylor & Walton, London, 1842)

Downes, Charles and Cowper, Charles. *The Building Erected in Hyde Park for the Works of Industry of All Nations, 1851* (N.P., London, 1852)

Dyos, H. J. *Victorian Suburb: a study of the growth of Camberwell* (Leicester U.P., Leicester, 1961)

Dyos, H. J., and Wolff, Michael (*Eds*). *The Victorian City, Images and Realities* (Routledge & Kegan Paul, London, 1973)

Eastlake, Charles L. *A History of the Gothic Revival* (First published in 1872, but re-issued as part of the Victorian Library by Leicester U.P., with an Introduction by J. Mordaunt Crook, Leicester, 1970)

Ecclesiologist, The (Cambridge Camden Society, later The Ecclesiological Society, 1842–68)

Edis, R. W. *Decoration and Furniture of Town Houses* (Kegan Paul, London, 1881)

Elliott, Brent. *Victorian Gardens* (Batsford, London, 1986)

Evans, R. *The Fabrication of Virtue: English Prison Architecture, 1750–1840* (Cambridge U.P., Cambridge, 1982)

Fawcett, Jane (*Ed*). *Seven Victorian Architects* (Thames & Hudson, London, 1976)

Ferrey, Benjamin. *Recollections of A. N. Welby Pugin, and His Father Augustus Pugin* (E. Stanford, London, 1861)

Ferriday, Peter. 'The Oxford Museum'. *The Architectural Review* 132 (London, 1962) 408–416

Ferriday, Peter (*Ed*). *Victorian Architecture* (Cape, London, 1963)
Franklin, Jill. *The Gentleman's Country House and its Plan 1835–1914* (Routledge & Kegan Paul, London, 1981)
Garden History (from 1972)
Garden History, The Journal of (from 1981)
Garrigan, K. *Ruskin and Architecture: His Thought and Influence* (University of Wisconsin Press, Madison, 1973)
Gauldie, Enid. *Cruel Habitations: A History of Working-Class Housing 1780–1918* (Allen & Unwin, London, 1974)
Gentleman's Magazine, The. (1731–1868)
Germann, Georg. *Gothic Revival in Europe and Britain: Sources, Influences and Ideas* (Lund Humphries, London, 1972)
Gibbs-Smith, C. H. *The Great Exhibition of 1851. A Commemorative Album* (HMSO, London, 1950)
Girouard, Mark. *Alfred Waterhouse and the Natural History Museum* (Yale U.P., London, 1981)
Girouard, Mark. *Sweetness and Light – The 'Queen Anne' Movement, 1860–1900* (Oxford U.P., Oxford, 1977)
Girouard, Mark. *The Victorian Country House* (Yale U.P., London, 1979)
Girouard, Mark. *Victorian Pubs* (Yale U.P., London, 1984)
Glasstone, V. *Victorian and Edwardian Theatres: An Architectural and Social Survey* (Thames & Hudson, London, 1975)
Gloag, John. *Mr Loudon's England. The Life and Work of John Claudius Loudon and his Influence on Architecture and Furniture Design* (London, Oriel Press, 1970)
Gloag, John. *Victorian Comfort. A Social History of Design from 1830–1900* (Macmillan, London, 1961)
Gloag, John. *Victorian Taste. Some Social Aspects of Architecture and Industrial Design from 1820–1900* (A & C Black, London, 1962)
Godwin, G. (*Ed.* A. D. King) *Town Swamps and Social Bridges* (Leicester U.P., Leicester, 1972)
Gomme, Andor and Walker, David. *Architecture of Glasgow* (Lund Humphries, London, 1968)
Goodhart-Rendel, H. S. *English Architecture Since the Regency: An Interpretation* (Constable, London, 1953)
Goodhart-Rendel, H. S. 'Rogue Architects of the Victorian Era' *Journal of the RIBA*, Third Series, 48 (London, 1949) 251–8
Gradidge, Roderick. *Dream Houses: The Edwardian Ideal* (Constable, London, 1980)
Gray, A. Stuart. *Edwardian Architecture. A Biographical Dictionary* (Duckworth, London, 1985)
Great Exhibition, The. *Official Descriptive and Illustrated Catalogue* (Spicer, London, 1851)
Gunnis, Rupert. *Dictionary of British Sculptors 1660–1851* (Abbey Library, London, 1960)
Gwynn, Dennis R. *Lord Shrewsbury, Pugin and the Catholic Revival* (Hollins & Carter, London, 1946)

Hansen, Hans Jürgen. *Late Nineteenth Century Art* (David & Charles, Newton Abbot, 1973)

Harper, Roger H. *Victorian Architectural Competitions: an index to British and Irish Architectural Competitions in* The Builder, *1843–1900* (Mansell, London, 1983)

Harries, J. G. *Pugin: an Illustrated Life of Augustus Welby Northmore Pugin, 1812–52* (Shire Publications, Aylesbury, 1973)

Harris, Thomas. *Victorian Architecture: A Few Words to Show that a National Architecture Adapted to the Wants of the Nineteenth Century is Attainable* (N.P., London, 1860)

Hersey, George L. *High Victorian Gothic. A Study in Associationism* (The John Hopkins U.P., Baltimore & London, 1972)

Hitchcock, Henry-Russell. *Architecture: Nineteenth and Twentieth Centuries* (Penguin, Harmondsworth, 1968)

Hitchcock, Henry-Russell. *The Crystal Palace: The Structure, Its Antecedents, and Its Immediate Progeny* (Smith College Museum, Northampton, Mass., 1951)

Hitchcock, Henry-Russell. *Early Victorian Architecture in Britain* (Yale U.P., New Haven, 1954)

Hix, John R. *The Glass House* (Phaidon, London, 1974)

Hobhouse, Hermione. *Prince Albert: His Life and Work* (Hamish Hamilton, London, 1983)

Hobhouse, Hermione (*Ed*). *Survey of London, Southern Kensington 42* (Athlone Press & GLC, London, 1986)

Hobhouse, Hermione. *Thomas Cubitt, Master Builder* (Macmillan, London, 1971)

Hope, Anthony James Beresford. *The Condition and Prospects of Architectural Art* (Architectural Museum, London, 1863)

Hope, Anthony James Beresford. *The English Cathedral of the Nineteenth Century* (John Murray, London, 1861)

l'Hôpital, Winefred de. *Westminster Cathedral and its Architect* (Hutchinson, London, 1919)

Hussey, Christopher. *The Picturesque: Studies in a Point of View* (Putnam, London, 1927)

Illustrated London News, The (1843–1901)

Jackson, Basil H. (*Ed*). *Recollections of Thomas Graham Jackson, 1835–1924* (Oxford U.P., London, 1950)

Jervis, Simon. *High Victorian Design* (Boydell Press, Woodbridge, 1983)

Jervis, Simon. *The Penguin Dictionary of Design and Designers* (Allen Lane, London, 1984)

Jones, Owen. *The Grammar of Ornament* (Day & Son, London, 1856)

Kerr, Robert. *The Gentleman's House; Or, How to Plan English Residences, from the Parsonage to the Palace* (John Murray, London, 1865)

Knight, Richard Payne. *An Analytical Inquiry into the Principles of Taste* (Payne & White, London, 1805)

Kornwolf, J. D. *M. H. Baillie Scott and the Arts and Crafts Movement* (Johns Hopkins U.P., Baltimore and London, 1972)

Ladd, Henry A. *The Victorian Morality of Art: An Analysis of Ruskin's Esthetic* (Long & Smith, New York, 1932)

Larmour, Paul. *Belfast: An Illustrated Architectural Guide* (Friar's Bush Press, Belfast, 1987)

Lemere, H. Bedford and Cooper, N. *The Opulent Eye: Late Victorian and Edwardian Taste in Interior Decoration* (Architectural Press, London, 1976)

Lethaby, W. R. *Architecture: An Introduction to the History and Theory of the Art of Building* (Williams & Northgate, London, 1911)

Lethaby, W. R. *Philip Webb and His Work* (Raven Oak Press, London, 1979)

Lewis, Philippa and Darley, Gillian. *Dictionary of Ornament* (Macmillan, London, 1986)

Lindley, K. *Seaside Architecture* (Evelyn, London, 1973)

Little, Bryan. *Birmingham Buildings: the architectural story of a Midland City* (David & Charles, Newton Abbot, 1971)

Little, Bryan. *Catholic Churches since 1623* (Hale, London, 1966)

Lloyd, Nathaniel. *A History of the English House from Primitive Times to the Victorian Period* (Architectural Press, London, 1931)

Loudon, John Claudius. *The Architectural Magazine, and Journal of Improvement in Architecture, Building, and Furnishing, and in the Various Arts and Trades connected therewith* (Longman, London, 1834–8)

Loudon, John Claudius. *An Encyclopaedia of Cottage, Farm, and Villa Architecture and Furniture; containing Numerous Designs for Dwellings . . .* etc; (Longman, London, 1833, with subsequent editions of 1835, 36, 39, 41, 42, 46, 53, 57, 63, 67, and 69)

Loudon, John Claudius. *On the Laying Out, Planting, and Managing of Cemeteries . . .* etc; (Longman, London, 1843, but subsequently re-issued in a fascimile with an Introduction by James Stevens Curl published by Ivelet Books, Redhill, 1981)

Maltby, Sally (*et al*). *Alfred Waterhouse, 1830–1905* (RIBA, London, 1983)

Meeks, Carroll L. V. *The Railroad Station: An Architectural History* (Yale U.P., New Haven, 1956)

Metcalf, P. *Victorian London* (Cassell, London, 1972)

Monk, Samuel H. *The Sublime: A Study of Critical Theories in XVIII-Century England* (Ann Arbor Paperbacks, Ann Arbor, 1960)

Morley, John. *Death, Heaven and the Victorians* (Studio Vista, London, 1971)

Morris, William. *Gothic Architecture* (Kelmscott Press, London, 1893)

Muthesius, Hermann. *The English House* (BSP Professional Books, Oxford, 1987)

Muthesius, Stefan. *The English Terraced House* (Yale U.P., London, 1982)

Muthesius, Stefan. *The High Victorian Movement in Architecture, 1850–70* (Routledge & Kegan Paul, London, 1972)

Macaulay, James. *The Gothic Revival 1745–1845* (Blackie, London, 1975)

MacLeod, R. *Style and Society: architectural ideology in Britain 1840–1914* (RIBA, London, 1971)

Macready, Sarah and Thompson, F. H. (*Eds*). *Influences in Victorian Art and Architecture* (Society of Antiquaries of London, London, 1985)

McCarthy, Michael. *The Origins of the Gothic Revival* (Yale U.P., New Haven and London, 1987)

McCracken, Eileen. *The Palm House and Botanic Garden, Belfast* (Ulster Architectural Heritage Society, Belfast, 1971)

McDermot, Martin. *A Critical Dissertation on the Nature and Principles of Taste* (N.P., London, 1822)

McFadzean, Ronald. *The Life and Work of Alexander Thomson* (Routledge & Kegan Paul, London, 1979)

Newton, Ernest. *A Book of Country Houses* (Batsford, London, 1903)

Olsen, Donald. *The Growth of Victorian London* (Batsford, London, 1976)

Pearce, D. and Binney, M. *Railway Architecture* (Orbis Books, London, 1979)

Peel, Mrs C. S. *The New Home: Treating of the Arrangement, Decoration and Furnishing of a House of Medium Size, to be maintained by a Moderate Income* (Constable, London, 1903)

Pevsner, Nikolaus. *The Buildings of England* series (Penguin, Harmondsworth, various dates)

Pevsner, Nikolaus. *A History of Building Types* (Thames & Hudson, London, 1976)

Pevsner, Nikolaus. *Ruskin and Viollet-le-Duc: Englishness and Frenchness in the Appreciation of Gothic Architecture* (Thames & Hudson, London, 1969)

Pevsner, Nikolaus. *Some Architectural Writers of the Nineteenth Century* (Clarendon Press, Oxford, 1972)

Pevsner, Nikolaus. *Studies in Art, Architecture and Design* Vol II (Walker, New York, 1968)

Port, M. H. *Six Hundred New Churches: A Study of The Church Building Commission 1818–56* (SPCK, London, 1961)

Port, M. H. (*Ed*). *The Houses of Parliament* (Yale U.P., London, 1976)

Praz, Mario. *The Romantic Agony* (Meridian, New York, 1956)

Price, Uvedale. *Essays on the Picturesque, as Compared with the Sublime and the Beautiful* (Mawman, London, 1794–8)

Pugin, A. W. N. *An Apology for the Revival of Christian Architecture in England* (London, 1843)

Pugin, A. W. N. *Contrasts: Or, A Parallel between the Noble Edifices of the Middle Ages, and Corresponding Buildings of the Present Day; Shewing the Present Decay of Taste* (Dolman, London, 1841)

Pugin, A. W. N. *The Present State of Ecclesiastical Architecture in England* (Dolman, London, 1843)

Pugin, A. W. N. *A Treatise on Chancel Screens* (Dolman, London, 1851)

Pugin, A. W. N. *The True Principles of Pointed or Christian Architecture* (Weale, London, 1841)

Quarterly Review, The. (1809–1901)

Quiney, Anthony. *John Loughborough Pearson* (Yale U.P., London, 1979)

Read, Benedict. *Victorian Sculpture* (Yale U.P., London, 1982)

Richardson, Margaret. *The Architects of the Arts and Crafts Movement* (Trefoil Books, London, 1983)

311

Richardson, Ruth. *Death, Dissection, and the Destitute* (Routledge & Kegan Paul, London, 1987)

Robson, E. R. *School Architecture* (Leicester U.P., Leicester, 1972)

Royal Institute of British Architects (RIBA). *Transactions, Papers, and Journals* (1842–1901)

Royal Institute of British Architects (RIBA). *Catalogue of the Drawings Collection of the Royal Institute of British Architects in London* (Gregg, Farnborough, from 1969)

Rubens, G. *W. R. Lethaby, His Life and Work 1857–1931* (Architectural Press, London, 1986)

Royal Society of Arts, Journal of The. (1873–1901)

Ruskin, John. *Works* Edited by E. T. Cook and A. Wedderburn in 39 Vols (Longmans Green, London, 1903–12)

Ruskin, John and Acland, Henry W. *The Oxford Museum* (Smith, Elder, London, 1859)

Saint, Andrew. *Richard Norman Shaw* (Yale U.P., London, 1976)

Saturday Review, The. (1855–1901)

Saunders, Matthew. *The Churches of S.S. Teulon* (Ecclesiological Society, London, 1982)

Schimmelpenninck, Mary Anne. *A Theory of Beauty and Deformity* (Longmans, Brown, Green, Longman and Roberts, London, 1859)

Scott, George Gilbert. *Personal and Professional Recollections* (Sampson, Low, Marston, Searle and Rivington, London, 1879)

Scott, George Gilbert. *Remarks on Secular and Domestic Architecture, Present and Future* (John Murray, London, 1857)

Seddon, John P. *Progress in Art and Architecture with Precedents for Ornament* (D. Bogue, London, 1852)

Service, Alastair. *Edwardian Architecture* (Thames & Hudson, London, 1977)

Sheehy, Jeanne. *J. J. McCarthy and the Gothic Revival in Ireland* (Ulster Architectural Heritage Society, Belfast, 1977)

Sheehy, Jeanne. *The Rediscovery of Ireland's Past: The Celtic Revival, 1830–1930* (Thames & Hudson, London, 1980)

Sheppard, F. H. W. (*Ed*). *Survey of London, Northern Kensington* 37 (Athlone Press and GLC, London, 1973)

Sparrow, W. Shaw (*Ed*). *Flats, Urban Houses and Cottage Homes* (Hodder & Stoughton, London, 1907)

Sparrow, W. Shaw. *The Modern Home* (Hodder & Stoughton, London, 1905)

Stamp, Gavin. *The English House 1860–1914: The Flowering of English Domestic Architecture* (Faber & Faber, London, 1985)

Stamp, Gavin and Amery, Colin. *Victorian Buildings of London, 1837–1887: An Illustrated Guide* (Architectural Press, London, 1980)

Stanton, Phoebe B. *The Gothic Revival and American Church Architecture: An Episode in Taste, 1840–1856* (Johns Hopkins, Baltimore, 1968)

Stanton, Phoebe B. *Pugin* (Thames & Hudson, London, 1971)

Steegman, J. *Victorian Taste: A Study of the Arts and Architecture 1830–70* (Nelson, London, 1970)

Stell, Christopher. *Architects of Dissent* (Dr Williams Trust, London, 1976)

Strain, R. W. M. *Belfast and its Charitable Society* (Oxford University Press, London, 1961)

Street, A. E. *Memoir of George Edmund Street, RA, 1824–81* (John Murray, London, 1888)

Street, George Edmund. *Brick and Mortar in the Middle Ages: Notes of a Tour in the North of Italy* (John Murray, London, 1855)

Street, George Edmund. *An Urgent Plea for the Revival of the True Principles of Architecture in the Public Buildings of the University of Oxford* (J. H. Parker, Oxford and London, 1853)

Summerson, John. *The Architecture of Victorian London* (University Press of Virginia, Charlottesville, 1976)

Summerson, John. *The London Building World of the 1860s* (Thames & Hudson, London, 1973)

Summerson, John. *Victorian Architecture: Four Studies in Evaluation* (Columbia U.P., New York, 1970)

Taylor, D. and Bush, D. *The Golden Age of British Hotels* (Northwood Publications, London, 1974)

Thompson, J. D. and Goldin, G. *The Hospital: A Social and Architectural History* (Yale U.P., London, 1975)

Thompson, Paul. *William Butterfield* (Routledge & Kegan Paul, London, 1971)

Thompson, Paul. *The Work of William Morris* (Quartet Books, London, 1977)

Victoria and Albert Museum. *Marble Halls: Drawings and Models for Victorian Secular Buildings* (Victoria & Albert Museum, London, 1973)

Victoria and Albert Museum. *Victorian Church Art* (Victoria & Albert Museum, London, 1971)

Watkin, David. *English Architecture: A Concise History* (Thames & Hudson, London, 1979)

Watkin, David. *The English Vision: The Picturesque in Architecture, Landscape and Garden Design* (John Murray, London, 1982)

Watkin, David. *The Life and Work of C. R. Cockerell* (Zwemmer, London, 1974)

Watkin, David. *Morality and Architecture: Development of a Theme in Architectural History and Theory from the Gothic Revival to the Modern Movement* (Clarendon Press, Oxford, 1977)

Watkin, David. *Thomas Hope 1769–1831 and the Neoclassical Idea* (John Murray, London, 1968)

Watkin, David and Middleton, Robin. *Neoclassical and Nineteenth-century Architecture* (Abrams, New York, 1980)

Weaver, Lawrence (*Ed*). *Small Country Houses of Today* (Country Life, London, 1911)

White, James F. *The Cambridge Movement: The Ecclesiologists and the Gothic Revival* (Cambridge U.P., Cambridge, 1962)

Wightwick, George. *The Palace of Architecture: A Romance of Art and History* (Fraser, London, 1840)

INDEX

Page numbers in *italic* denote illustrations

314

124, *126*; Red House,
Bexleyheath, 116, *118*,
198; Scarisbrick Hall,
Lancs., 197; Scotney
Castle, Kent, 80, *81*;
Standen, Sussex, 116, 199;
Tigbourne Court, Surrey,
126, 129; Toft Hall,
Knutsford, 83; Tor House,
High Craigmore, 99;
Trentham Hall, Staffs., 88,
197; Waddlesdon Manor,
Bucks., 138, 198;
Wykehurst, Sussex, 138
Cheltenham, Glos., 180–1;
Collingham Gardens, 124;
Copley, 169; cottages,
159–60, *161, 162*; Domestic
Revival, 119, 177, 199, 292;
Duchy St. Est., *165*;
Glasgow, Grosvenor
Terrace, 196, Kelvinside,
195, Moray Place, *196*,
tenements, *197*; Grosvenor
Ests., 138, 198; Harrington
Gardens, 124, *127*; Holland
Park Av., 188; Kelvinside,
195, Kensington Palace
Gardens, 92, *94*; Ladbroke
Est., 180–7, *181*; Lancaster
Gate, 138, 198; Model
Dwellings, 155, *157, 158,
159*; Model Lodging Houses,
156, *157*; Model Towns,
166–77; Model Villages,
163–6; Nash, influence on
housing, 199, 282; Norton
Est., 187–92; Old English
Style, 116; Oxford Villas,
200; Picturesque, The, 19,
24, 28, 35, 56, 71, 116, 119,
130; poor, residences for,
154; Port Sunlight, 128,
171–7, 199; Queen's gate,
120, *121*; Red House,
Bayswater Rd., 124; Stanley
Cres., *186*; Stanley Gardens,
184, *185*; White House,
Chelsea, 123, 124; Windsor
Royal Society's Cottages,
160, 113

industrial: mass production of
materials, 22; Revolution, 12
institutional buildings, 231–7
Inwood, H. W. and W., 32
iron: use of, 201–19

Italianate style, 87–93, 197,
250, 292
Italian Gothic, 49, 50, 71

Jackson, Sir Thomas, G., 128
Joass, J. J., 146
John, Sir William, G., 172, 174
Jones, Sir Horace, 218, 230
Jones, O., 79, 98, 207

Keeling, E. B., 103, 182, 218,
249, 251, 254
Kemp, G. M., 72
Kendall, H. E., 264
Klenze, L. von, 99
Knight, R. P., 19, 28
Knowles, J. T., 92, 250

Lamb, E. B., 103
Lancing, College of St Nicholas,
44, *46*
Langley, B., 34
Lanyon, Lynn and Lanyon, 50,
85, 97, 292
Lanyon, Sir Charles, 87, 203
Ledoux, C. N., 32
Leeds: Corn Exchange, 289,
290; Town Hall, 74, 77, 256,
288; Temple Mills, 79
Leicester: Gaol, 25; Town Hall,
128, *129*
Lever, W. H., Viscount
Leverhulme, 171
Liddell, Hon. Thomas, 263
Little, T., 281
Liverpool: Albert Docks, *33*,
87; Anglican Cathedral, 112;
Bank of England, 73–4, 87;
cemeteries, 262; Gothic
Revival, 116; Lime Street
Station, 205; Oriel
Chambers, 215, *219*; Picton
Reading Room, 87; St
George's Hall, 74, 76, 87,
256, 288; Walker Art
Gallery, 87; Walton Gaol,
85; White Star Line offices,
136
living conditions, 13, 14
Lockwood, H. F., 167
Loddiges, G., 277, 282
Lomax-Simpson, J., 172
London: Abbey Mills Pumping
Station, 227, *228*; Abney
Park Cemetery, 277, 281,
282; Addison Ave., 189, *191*;
Albert Memorial, 71, *72*,

294; Alliance Assurance
offices, 132, *133*, 144, 147;
All Saints' Cemetery,
Nunhead, 274; All Saints'
Model Church, Margaret St,
47, 48, 56, 57, 59, 60, 214;
Angel Tavern, Crutched
Friars, *245*; Army and Navy
Club, 93; Athenaeum Club,
250; Auction Mart
Restaurant, *247, 249*;
Bagnigge Wells, 155;
Bedford Park, Chiswick,
123, 125, 178, 199;
Bishopsgate Institute, 140,
141; Blackfriars Bridge, 226,
227; Boundary St. Est., *165*;
British Museum, 75, *204*;
Brompton Boilers, S.
Kensington, 213, *214*;
Brompton Oratory, *143*;
Cadogan Est., 124; Carlton
Club, 92–3, 95; Charing
Cross Hotel, 250; Chelsea
Town Hall, 140, *142*; Christ
Church, Streatham, 98, *100*;
City of London Cemetery,
277, 280; S. Kensington,
124; Coal Exchange, 204,
206, 289; Collingham
Gardens, S. Kensington, 124;
Conservative Club, 92;
Covent Garden Market, 218;
Crystal Palace, 80, 202,
204–10, *209*; Deptford
Town Hall, 146; Duchy St.
Est., Lambeth, *165*; Eagle
Tavern, City Road, *244*;
Gaiety, The Strand, 255;
General Credit and
Discount Co. offices, 50;
Government offices, 92,
140; Great Exhibition, 215,
216, 217; Great Western
Hotel, Paddington, 250, *251*,
Grosvenor Ests., 138, 198;
Harrington Gardens, S.
Kensington, 124, *127*;
Harrod's store, 292, 294;
Highgate Cemetery, 273–4,
275, 283; Holborn Viaduct,
225–6, *227*; Holland Park
Av., 188; Holy Trinity, S.
Kensington, 112; Holy
Trinity, Sloane St., 112, *115*;
Hotel Cecil, Embankment,
253; Huxley Building,